Philosophical Aspects of Information Systems

Philosophical Aspects of Information Systems

Edited by

R.L. Winder, S.K. Probert and I.A. Beeson

Taylor & Francis

Publishers since 1798

Published in 1997 by
CRC Press
Taylor & Francis Group
6000 Broken Sound Parkway NW, Suite 300
Boca Raton, FL 33487-2742

No claim to original U.S. Government works
Printed in the United States of America on acid-free paper
10 9 8 7 6 5 4 3 2

International Standard Book Number-10: 0-7484-0758-8 (Hardcover)
International Standard Book Number-13: 978-0-7484-0758-3 (Hardcover)

Library of Congress Cataloging-in-Publication Data

Catalog record is available from the Library of Congress

Taylor & Francis Group
is the Academic Division of Informa plc.

Visit the Taylor & Francis Web site at
http://www.taylorandfrancis.com

and the CRC Press Web site at
http://www.crcpress.com

Contents

Foreword

Guy Fitzgerald

It is my perception that there is an increasing interest in the philosophical aspects of information systems. This interest is not just from academics but also from hard-nosed, real-world, practitioners. And of course the notion of the 'real-world' and whether it exists out there as an objective entity in its own right, is itself one of the key philosophical debates of concern in information systems!

The reasons for this growing interest are various but there are a number of contributory elements. Firstly, the development and implementation of information systems is not getting any easier, in fact quite the reverse. Systems are becoming more complex and the risks of failure greater. Indeed, a perusal of the popular press over the last few years would suggest that actual failure is not just a theoretical possibility but almost endemic. Failure is of course itself a complex concept but many of the failures we read about are not simply technical failures but failures of social and organizational dimensions.

Thus many people are looking to philosophy (amongst other things), not necessarily to provide answers, although that would be nice, but to provide alternative thoughts and insights on contemporary issues of information systems.

So what contribution can philosophy make to the world of information systems? There are clearly a number of areas. One of the most important is to highlight the various assumptions that underlie our actions, this is especially important as we are often unaware that we are making any such assumptions. It is all too easy to fall into the trap of thinking that there is only one approach to a solution or indeed only one solution, that all users behave in the same way, that they are motivated by the same things, or that differing views can be resolved if only we can find which of them is correct. A second contribution is the identification of the fundamental issues of concern for information systems and those that we ignore at our peril. There are clearly many but those of particular concern relate to politics, power, knowledge, cognition and concepts of rationality. Such concepts are usually conveniently ignored in most debates on information systems which may well help to explain the often surprising consequences of the systems we build. Philosophy can also point out the logic or otherwise of various arguments. It can suggest, given various assumptions about the world and various objectives, that a particular course of action is illogical or counter productive. It can highlight inconsistencies in arguments and the adoption of opposing theories of enquiry in an advocated methodology. The logical argument can be very helpful in at least cutting out various courses of action if perhaps not completely being able to define what should be undertaken. Another contribution philosophy can make is to help us focus our reflective and critical faculties, to make us think of the implications of our decisions, to recognize that the subjects of our systems are usually people rather than machines, and that systems development itself, and its results, are change processes that typically have an impact on social roles and systems rather than physical systems. A further contribution is to inform us of the philosophical 'findings' from other, related, subject areas. Information systems has a multi-disciplinary background and frequently draws on theory from other areas. We need to know what this is, what is relevant and what has been found to be useful without having to re-learn it again ourselves.

Thus, potentially, philosophy has a great deal to offer the researcher and the practitioner but unfortunately in the past this has not always been forthcoming. Few philosophers have concerned themselves with information systems, despite it being one of the major forces shaping the modern world. Perhaps it is because they do not really understand the world of information systems. But whatever the reasons in the past we are now seeing an important change.

This book pulls together a number of papers from authors who clearly understand both philosophical issues and information systems and can relate one to the other. Most of them also attempt to address the implications of what they are saying to the practising world of systems and systems developers.

Thus the book will be of particular relevance to those who wish to address the wider aspects and implications of information systems including students on the growing number of courses and modules which include an exploration of philosophical aspects and theoretical underpinnings of information systems. The book provides a good range of coverage under the following five main headings; Ethical and Political Issues, Language and Meaning, Methodology, Organizational Issues and Physical Issues. They are all well written and engaging. The editors have selected well and provided useful introductions to the sections. They are not all 'easy reads' and some require a degree of concentration and study that may tax some students. However, the effort is worthwhile and I believe the book significantly enriches the subject area. It will be a great boon to those that are teaching the subject and wish to recommend a series of thoughtful and thought provoking readings to their students.

I hope that it will also be seen as relevant not just to students but to those engaged in information systems work seeking philosophically grounded alternative thoughts and insights on current issues in information systems. And, who knows, it might just help to reduce some of the 'failures' in the future!

Preface

Stephen K. Probert, Russel Winder & Ian A. Beeson

This book represents the work of a variety of researchers in information systems whose common concern is to use philosophical approaches to help solve problems in information systems. The book is structured into five main sections. The 'Ethical and Political Issues' section includes a range of topics which have come to be seen as being of increasing importance in practical information systems development. The 'Language and Meaning' section explores some of the key difficulties in understanding the very notion of 'information' itself — a notion upon which assumptions about information systems development are implicitly based. The 'Methodology' section explores some of the theoretical underpinnings upon which information systems methodologies are based — these issues have also attracted considerable attention in the literature of late. The 'Organizational Issues' section explores some of the key philosophical assumptions upon which theories of organizations embedded in information systems methodologies — or (common) non-methodological approaches to information systems development — are based. Finally, the 'Physical Issues' section explores the (philosophical) relationship between the mind and the body — a topic which is likely to be of growing importance as computer systems move beyond text-based outputs and towards 'virtually real' interactions.

A variety of styles and topics have been included so that the full richness of the philosophical debates about issues in information systems can be holistically comprehended by the reader. The coverage of a wide spectrum of topics is further justified because it appears that a consensus about exactly how to conduct philosophically-based information systems research is unlikely to emerge. This is for two reasons. Firstly, the wide range of possible research topics within information systems requires that different approaches are taken to, for example, the conceptual foundations of Soft Systems Methodology and, for example, the implications of the use of different organizational metaphors for information systems design. Secondly, no clear consensus has emerged, within the discipline of philosophy, as to how to proceed with philosophical research *per se*. This book is testimony to the divergent traditions within both information systems and contemporary philosophy; no particular 'line' has been taken by the editors on these matters, who have chosen the contributions demonstrating both quality and diversity, rather than seeking to include contributions demonstrating conformity to some 'hidden agenda'. This is not a 'Soft Systems' book, nor is it an 'Object-oriented' book; neither is it a 'Anglo–Saxon' book or a 'European Continental' book. Rather we have chosen to include contributions from many traditions; allowing readers to decide for themselves which of these seem to be the most promising or inspiring. The references will allow the reader to follow-up their interests and preferences, and to develop an understanding of the issues at stake in a comprehensive and thorough manner.

We feel that the most likely audiences for this book are final-year undergraduate, postgraduate and research students whose studies include a significant information systems component. Though, having said this, we believe that information systems practitioners will find the material accessible and useful.

Final-year undergraduates studying an option in, say, the social aspects of information systems/information technology, or the theoretical underpinnings of information systems/information technology will find this book to be of particular interest. But this is not a 'textbook'; research students in information systems may find some of the discussions to be of particular interest in clarifying their notions of research methods, and students undertaking research in the conceptual or theoretical underpinnings of information systems will find this book to be a valuable resource. However, it would be misleading to give the impression that this book is only for those interested in the 'theory' of information systems. Information systems is a practical discipline and the editors have ensured that the contributors demonstrate their interest in solving practical problems in information systems — by the focused use of philosophical theory. In this respect, many of the chapters are concerned to provide conceptual or philosophical clarifications of the concepts used by information systems practitioners (which are often highly confusing to both practitioners and information systems students alike), whilst other chapters develop conceptual solutions to some of the central conundrums of information systems theory and practice. As you might expect, ethical issues sometimes play a prominent role in the discussions, but this is not just another 'computer ethics' book, as — in philosophy — ethical concerns have rarely been successfully isolated from epistemological and ontological (and sometimes logical) concerns, and the editors considered that such developments should be reflected herein.

There is a story behind this book. Back in 1991 a number of the authors attending the United Kingdom Systems Society conference in Paisley, Scotland, were lamenting the fact that the presentations of many of the papers which covered theoretical and conceptual issues in information systems 'clashed', or the content could not be discerned from the title — with the result that important, philosophically-based presentations were missed by many of the contributors. A consensus emerged that a symposium centrally concerned with the philosophical aspects of information systems would allow all those interested in such matters to come together, to share ideas, and to discuss (argue strongly!) those theoretical and conceptual matters with which they are concerned. This symposium duly occurred (at the University of the West of England) in April 1993. All of the contributors to this book participated in the symposium, and they have revised and improved their texts as a result of the discussions during and after the symposium. Furthermore, all the chapters have been subjected to rigorous peer review, and the reader can be assured that the review processes were both extensive and thorough. The book that has resulted is the product of much hard work by the contributors and editors. We trust that you will find this book to be both stimulating and enjoyable.

Acknowledgements

A number of people have contributed to the creation of this work and we would like to make sure their help is acknowledged since it is much appreciated by us.

The Department of Computing at the University of the West of England was where the original symposium was held and we would like to thank them for making their facilities available for the symposium to take place.

We want to thank all the participants at the symposium for making it such a successful event. Three people need particular mention: Fenton Robb for his keynote address; John Mingers for his plenary address; and Ray Billington for the entertaining after-dinner presentation on "The Philosophy of Communication".

Thanks to Guy Fitzgerald for taking time to write the foreword.

Many, many thanks must go to Tom Quick for reading a draft of the book and helping with the copy-editing and indexing.

A number of individuals from the publisher of the book need some mention: We would like to thank Andrew Carrick, Rachel Blackman, Fiona Kinghorn and Bridget Allen for: the reviews they organized which helped us improve things; the very thorough copy-edit; continuous support during the construction of this work; and limitless patience when the tome kept being late.

Ethical and Political Issues

Introduction

Stephen K. Probert

The four chapters in this section are united by concerns with the ethical and political issues inherent in the development, use and management of information systems; however, the focus in each chapter is quite different.

Fenton Robb's chapter sets the stage not only for this section, but for the book as a whole, by first of all asking why philosophy is important for information systems at all. To begin with, Robb concedes that information systems practitioners may, indeed, immediately conclude that philosophy has nothing at all to do with the practical problems of information systems development, use and management. However, Robb counters this charge by pointing out that the 'official view' of information systems development, use and management itself rests upon a number of contentious (or, at the very least, contestable) assumptions. As such, Robb employs the philosopher's classic strategy of argument for the need for philosophical analysis of the assumptions upon which other disciplines are based — from astrophysics to zoology! At a deeper level, Robb finds two (generally unstated) assumptions upon which the official — conventional — view of information systems is based. These assumptions are, firstly, that the world is sufficiently well-ordered such that the execution of (albeit carefully-made) information systems plans will yield the expected outcomes; secondly, that the past provides us with an adequate guide to the future. When he explores these two assumptions, he finds them to be highly problematic. There are ethical consequences arising from these problems, and Robb devotes the rest of his chapter to an exploration of two of these. The first he calls the 'numbers game', which arises from the 'stark fact' that information systems can only represent aspects of the world that can be realized in numbers. One consequence of this 'stark fact' is that important aspects of the world cannot be represented in this way and such aspects may be in danger of being trivialized as a result. The second ethical problem which concerns Robb is that of the growing problem of the use of information technology for the purpose of surveillance (and social control in general). Here he argues that the public interest can be put in jeopardy by such technologies. However, Robb ends on an upbeat note — and argues for the possibility that future information systems developments could have a liberating effect.

Norma Romm's chapter contains a philosophical discussion concerning how best to conceptualize 'information'. As Romm considers that there are important ethical and political consequences arising from different conceptions of information this is not an 'ivory tower' issue! Our conception of information is, she argues, connected to our understanding of how human beings relate to one another at a fundamental level. Romm's specific ethical position is concerned with the need to further debates in society, as she believes that any decision-making process in society should only take place after a number of alternatives have been considered. As alternatives are generally based on different people's viewpoints, information should be conceived as meaningful (rather than factual). Such a conception "allows us to concentrate attention on the possibility of recognizing people's right to cognitive participation in the construction of 'their world'" (p.25). Such a definition as Romm proposes requires us to "subject viewpoints to serious encounter with alternatives" (p.28). Such an approach would increase the scope for more open-ended decision-making. Romm goes on to provide two reasons why such a conceptualization of information should be adopted. Firstly, a moral argument is put forward to the effect that legitimate management is linked to "the propensity to be both critical and self-critical" (p.33). Secondly, she argues that it may, in fact, be counter-productive "for the (seemingly) powerful to ignore the quest for meaningful input on the part of those perceived to be less powerful" (p.33), and that, therefore, self-interest provides us with a motive for adopting her conceptualization of information.

Martin Spaul engages in a critical discussion concerning the usefulness of Heidegger's 'tool perspective' for information systems design. Such an approach can be contrasted with the 'representational' perspective for information systems design. Spaul argues that "any stance on information systems design is bound up, in complex ways, with presuppositions concerning the social roles of those systems" (p.36). Spaul then indicates the possible advantages of the tool perspective over the representational perspective. However, he concludes that the tool perspective is not itself without its problems, as it can appear to be "wilfully anti-intellectual, elevating the mundane and romanticizing a simpler past" (p.40). As such, the tool perspective can only have a "weakly critical force" (p.42). Spaul concludes that a new foundation for design is therefore needed. One reason for this is that information systems can be seen as aides in bureaucratic contexts (on a Weberian model), and the tool perspective is of limited utility in such contexts — as they place an emphatic emphasis on the representational nature of information. After discussing the ethical aspects of the two alternative positions he discussed earlier in the chapter, Spaul concludes that "the most that might be sought from a design philosophy is an assembly of tentative hints and models to be placed in the train of argument which is the design activity" (p.49). However, Spaul is not putting forward a negative position; rather, he is encouraging practitioners to use "the full range of our critical, social and technical awareness" (p.49) in their design activities. Underlying Spaul's argument is the firm belief that social-philosophical perspectives underlying information systems design should incorporate a critical, ethical component.

In the final chapter in this section, Anne Moggridge uses an experiential, narrative, style of presentation to draw our attention to important facets of women's experiences in male-dominated contexts. Her work is guided by considerations drawn from the critical systems and collaborative enquiry traditions of academic research, although also of key importance are the influences of several feminist writers. Moggridge highlights the importance of some crucial differences between 'women's ways of knowing' and rational-male ways of knowing, and reflects upon her own experiences of women's ways of knowing as an information systems academic. Her discussions are intended to enable (and encourage) us to "respect other people's truths and work together in a less competitive and more appreciative way" (p.57). Her chapter raises a number of difficult ethical and practical questions concerning the inclusion (or rather the exclusion) of diverse members of society in male (and male-academically) dominated forums for debate.

All four chapters in this section raise fundamental ethical questions that arise from practical ways of acting, and each chapter — in its own way — highlights the consequences of proceeding uncritically and unreflectingly in information systems practice and research. All of the authors are keen to challenge the all too often taken for granted assumptions that information systems research, development, use and management are ethically-neutral concerns, and they highlight many of the ethical consequences inherent in the practical assumptions made by information systems practitioners and academics alike. These chapters all demonstrate the need for more critically-reflective (and yet practically-committed work) to be carried out in these areas of study.

Some Philosophical and Logical Aspects of Information Systems

Fenton F. Robb

This chapter considers the world view upon which the theory and practice of information systems are presently founded. Some of the underlying assumptions and the implications of information processing are questioned from both logical and moral standpoints.

1 Introduction

I suppose that the opening chapter of a book such as this should take it for granted that the subject matter is real and important enough to give the speaker an excuse for putting forward some personal opinions and so, hopefully, encouraging the participants to voice their own views and give accounts of their own experiences. We are invited here to philosophize about information systems and, therefore, I shall say what I think that might mean and why it could be important. I propose to address some logical and moral issues. I hope this will stimulate argument, and argument is, I think, what philosophy is all about.

2 Doing Philosophy

I believe that Russell once said that philosophers were just people who preferred to know the truth. That certainly was a tall order, but it does highlight the notion that there are some beliefs that are, in some sense, 'better' than others at accounting for what exists and what is happening about us. Although I have deep-seated doubts about reaching 'the' truth in any absolute sense, I do not think that philosophers are wasting their time. What we should be trying to find is, what Feyerabend called:

"The best lousy theory there is." (Feyerabend 1975: 159)

If philosophy is about argument and about discussing the evidence we have for holding certain opinions, we should all be philosophers; particularly if we believe that 'rationality rules' and that, although we may respect irrational opinions and those who hold them, we are unlikely to gain much understanding from arguing about them.

7

To me the key philosophical question is that posed by Fisher in the form of what he calls the 'Assertibility Question' which asks:

> "What argument or evidence would justify me in asserting this conclusion to be true." (Fisher 1988)

The justification for the Assertibility Question is the assumption that if you understand something then you should be able to give an account of how you could decide whether it was true or false; what argument or evidence would show it to be so. Otherwise, it has to be said, you have little or no understanding of it at all. So, in short, can you now explain what you believe to be the case, and why you believe it? Philosophy is important because it asks critical questions about the reasons for actions and beliefs but what philosophy does not do is to curtail the kind of answer you can, or should, give to this kind of question.

Although philosophy does not provide any ready-made notion about what might constitute 'truth' or 'falsity', it does provide some hints about these things. For example, if I want to justify a belief then deduction provides me with the tools for logical argument. If I believe that my assumptions are true then the operations of deductive logic can tell me whether or not my conclusions are true or false. But of course, as we all know, deductive arguments are, like mathematical operations, really elaborate tautologies. The premises are contained in the conclusions. All that deductive logic can do is to ensure that we use our language correctly and that we can tease out the conclusions easily. Deductive argument simply rearranges what we know already and sceptical questioning shifts back to challenge the assumptions in an infinite regression. The regression has to be stopped somewhere, but where that limit is set seems determined just by the habits and conventions of the society and the institutions which influence us.

The other foundation for belief, that of direct personal experience, presents us with the opportunity of deploying inductive argument and of making general inferences from our own particular experiences and, if we believe them, from the accounts of the experiences of others. We may use those generalizations as a guide to future belief and conduct. I list some of the questions which the 'argument from experience' poses.

- How shall we know whether an experience is real or imagined? Are abnormal experiences always to be discounted? Do only common experiences, those shared by other people, count as real? If an experience seems out of the ordinary, if it seems to contradict what passes for 'common sense' or scientific truth or religious conviction (take your pick), should the person reporting it be put away to be treated by a psychoanalyst or awarded a Nobel Prize? Or should a research programme be set up to investigate the report?

- If we experience something with 'regularity and constancy' does this give us certain knowledge that the experience will recur as long as conditions remain the same? Should our belief in the truth of an experience increase with the number of occasions we experience it? Given that in our experience one event is always followed by another, can we properly say that the first is the 'cause' of the second? Can we ever be sure that a single cause is sufficient or necessary for the occurrence of a particular event? Can we ever be sure that there are no hidden causes in operation? Can we ever describe all the prior events which may be needed for something to happen? Can we countenance the possibility of spontaneous events, caused by nothing we can imagine?

- What value should we place on the accounts of others because of their supposed experiences, knowledge or expertise? Does something become more true as more people believe it? Are the opinions of majorities to be relied upon? Do democratic processes and peer reviews really 'produce truth' or do they just assign more power to the already powerful?

- Is the language we use today an highly evolved form of social communication, something that has, by trial and error, become perfected as the best medium, so far, for understanding the world? If so, does the realization of such a language in the technology of information systems open the gates for the acquisition of new knowledge and new beliefs? For example, can we compare the knowledge of specialists and experts in the various disciplines for logical coherence and consistency to find gaps where new truths may reside? Are the terms 'true' and 'false' mutually exclusive and, if not, are there degrees of truth, as distinct from the degrees of confidence that we may have that something is true?

In my view, 'doing philosophy' stands at the end of the string of answers given to the question 'why'? We resort to it to provide the last 'because' we give to ourselves and others when we question things which are ultimately inscrutable. And, at the same time, 'doing philosophy' helps us to define, and often redefine, our primary, axiomatic, beliefs. Beyond these lie our own 'just because it is so' answers to the difficult questions about existence and causality, truth and morality. These are the questions about why we exist, how we may come to think there is a world outside us, why we hold to certain beliefs about origins and ends, about creations and destinies, about efficient causes, determinism, free will, good and bad, intentionality, natural laws, social justice, fairness and the roles played by chance, serendipity, empathy, obligation and authority, and about how to distinguish axiomatic knowledge from mere superstition? So, I suggest, philosophy stands at the juncture between the 'known-to-be-certain' (or the 'taken-for-granted') and the 'totally-unknowable' in our own scheme of things.

When we can give reasons, say, for making some kind of distinction, discriminating an object from its background, isolating some feature of history for special attention, prioritizing some course of action over others, choosing some things as being the case and rejecting others, explaining some things or just taking them for granted, we are doing philosophy. I hope that this view of philosophy

9

will stimulate others to contest it. We are invited to 'do philosophy' in the field of information systems.

3 Information Systems: Theory and Practice

The title of this book presupposes that something exists that we can identify as an 'information system' and that this thing has more than one aspect. I suppose that when we speak about the 'philosophical and logical aspects of information systems' we are talking about the theoretical or abstract, as distinct from the practical, aspects of 'real world things'.

It certainly seems that the distinction between theory and practice, say in the editorials of *Systems Practice*, the division of papers at systems conferences, and that between the 'real world' and 'systems thinking' commonly employed in some systems methodologies, carries weight in systems circles. We also see around us similar distinctions between the 'pure' sciences and their associated technologies (or methodologies). Most people in the 'West' seem to have a notion implanted by their culture of two worlds, that of the contemplative academic and that of the practical worker in the field. It is commonly thought that the former offers generalized theories and principles upon which to found the practice, and that the workers in the field try them out in particular circumstances and feed back reports of successes and failures to enable the theories to be changed and improved. This mutual interaction of theory and practice leads to the progress and the refinement of both. Or so the story goes.

Is there really such interaction? Something quite different might be afoot. The two worlds might really be poles apart and rarely, if ever, have contact one with another. Perhaps most of the academics are really interested in writing clever papers and earning reputations in their peer group as wise and rigorous thinkers, paying only lip-service to the need to find new and better ways of doing things: and perhaps the practical people are mainly interested in earning their corn as best they can, just adding the gloss of the academic theory to give their practices some legitimacy, respectability or just some 'selling points'. The test of a 'good' general theory and the test of the truth of specific assertions derived from practical experience seem to be very much the same. They are both tests of utility though they are couched in somewhat different terms:

- A 'good' theory will lead to citations in the literature, research funding and more research in order to improve or refute it. Think, if you will, of Lakatos (1970), the theory of research programmes and progressive and degenerative 'problemshifts'.

- 'Good' experience is that which is specified well enough for it to be applied again in similar circumstances or, if different circumstances arise, to be modified and applied successfully once more. Do bridge builders appeal to physics or to their codes of good practice for the solution of their practical problems?

In this view of 'good' theory and 'good' practice there is no mention of any mutual interaction. The interactions between theorizing and practising do not seem to me to be the prior foundations of either activity. Contrary to received wisdom, each seems able to remain viable without the other. Because of the problems of inductive inference and incompleteness, theories cannot be either confirmed or falsified by their application in practice, nor can they be generated by inductive inference alone. The reporting of falsifying instances from practice do little to undermine theories, they simply call forward 'auxiliary statements' to 'explain' the aberration (Putman 1974).

Perhaps all the talk of the need for closer interaction between academics and practical people is simply a sign of the emergence of institutions specifically devoted to bringing these disparate interests together, regardless of the differences between the worlds they inhabit and the criteria which they adopt in judging the usefulness of work in their respective fields. The institutionalized theory and the similarly institutionalized practice of information systems may each be autonomous and owe little to the other for its continued existence.

4   Information Systems: The Official View

So what are these information systems we are going to consider? Once upon a time 'information' simply meant news, intelligence or the communication of facts. Today, a multitude of management textbooks refer to 'information' as being 'data which has been processed in order to make it useful'. To get a flavour of this we can extract from a typical text such as Reynolds (1992).

Information systems, in this view, are the means by which data are collected, typically from a transaction processing system, from surveys or data banks, reconstructed to make them useful for some explicitly expressed purpose and then transmitted to the appropriate parts of an organization where they will be used: that means to management reporting systems, and to operational and strategic decision support systems. Information has to have the same tests applied to it as are applied to data: accuracy, completeness, relevance, timeliness and auditability.

Systems philosophy, we are told, provides an overall model for thinking about something as a 'system'; as a set of interacting components working within an environment to fulfil some purpose, just like [sic] 'a living organism'. We have to understand a few key system terms such as goal seeking, boundary, interface, open systems, entropy, feedback, control, the holistic view and so on. Then we can apply 'systems philosophy' simply by defining our problem, and the scope of the system to be studied. In a very un-holistic way, we can then analyse the system into its basic components, gather data about each of them, identify and evaluate alternative solutions, choose the best one, prototype it, or test it in some other ways, then install it, train the users and monitor its performance. With 'good' data and a 'good' information system, we shall find 'good' solutions to our problems and make 'good' decisions. Though there are complicated tasks to be performed to make this all happen, in principle it is all quite simple and easy to understand.

The story does not end quite there. Information systems are said to conform to some (presumably natural) laws which govern their development. They go through six stages: initiation, contagion, control, integration, data administration and maturity. This last is achieved when the information systems people and the managers come to be:

"... jointly held accountable for identifying and capitalizing on opportunities to use information systems technology." (Reynolds 1992)

It would appear that is when the use of information systems technology becomes an end in itself.

Despite the apparent inevitability of this process of development, it is said that we can actually intervene to create and execute an information systems development strategy. This is done by defining and meeting the information requirements of the users (typically managers) through adopting the appropriate technologies. We need to understand the aims of the organization and the directions of its 'thrust'. There are five strategic 'thrust' areas for an organization: differentiation, cost control, innovation, growth and alliance. Mission statements indicate how the firm is aiming to thrust in each of these areas and these provide the foundation for assessing the efficacy of the information system.

There are, of course, specific recipes for defining the information systems plan, acquiring the resources, developing end-user computing and Information Centres, managing information systems professionals, disaster planning, and facing the critical issues of our time such as; justifying the cost of the system, ethics and the privacy of individuals. A glossary of over seven hundred commonly used information technology terms is also deemed useful. We could sensibly add a chapter or two on expert systems and computer-aided decision making under uncertainty, and maybe propose a 'war room' for the management of the inevitable crisis.

It is my belief that the majority of managers and information technology specialists would go along with much of this description of what information systems are about and how to manage them. I doubt if many would welcome any further discussion of what seems a perfectly straightforward subject. If they are so clearly defined what could possibly be the philosophical and logical aspects of information systems and why on earth should we address them?

5 Some Important Assumptions

There are quite a number of interesting assumptions in this official view of information systems that deserve closer attention than they are generally given. Let me list just a few of the more obvious:

- Objectives and problems are taken to be given or, it is thought, they can be defined by common sense. This is far from obvious.

- Mission statements and the like can be written in explicit language. But often mission statements seem little more than nicely turned rhetoric.

- All those involved are presumed to be agreed about ends and means. All contradictions can be resolved. Solutions can be (objectively) consistent with each other and with themselves over time. Managers, and users in general, can be relied upon to define the information they need and where and when they need it. But we might ask whether users really can know, before the events, what information they may need.

- If the task of defining information needs does present practical problems then there are procedures, known to knowledge engineers, for exploring the knowledge base of experts and users to determine what they are. But people are rarely agreed on means and ends, though they may capitulate to moral and social pressures.

- There are supposedly known causal relations between what the data represent and the ultimate effects which the use of the information is intended to produce. In other words, it is thought that someone really understands what is at work in the world represented by the system.

- The boundaries of the system of interest exist in the real world and can be drawn as a result of a process of discovery. However some might question whether or not the definition of system boundaries is quite as simple as the received wisdom would suggest. No suggestions are made about searching beyond the existing data sources to discover if the execution of the plans has produced unanticipated effects outside the present data capture area, and little, if any, provision seems to be made for recycling the issues over time in order to form new, possibly better, plans.

- A deeper unstated assumption which underpins the traditional approach to information systems is that the world is well-ordered and well-behaved so that the execution of the plans will produce the anticipated results. Where the world is not well-ordered then, we are told, we can safely rely on statistical inference to provide explanations and a guide for future action. Simply by using mathematical procedures we can, in effect, fill in the gaps in our knowledge, the lacunæ caused by our lack of experience.

- It is also assumed that the past provides us with some kind of guide to the future, because the same laws of natural and human behaviour persist over time; that the environment of the system remains stable: experience counts, the value of knowledge persists and understandings can be transported over time.

Let us consider further the last two assumptions; that the world is so well-ordered that information from the past can be useful in the future and that the environment of the system remains so stable that long-term planning of information systems is practical. If these assumptions are ill founded, or even slightly doubtful, then much of what is taken-for-granted in this approach to the design and use of information systems is pretty misleading to say the least.

5.1   A Well-ordered World?

To question the notion that the world is well-ordered we do not have to have resort to Heisenbergian indeterminacy. It is sufficient to observe that nothing stays still, that everything is in flux, that, for these reasons, history can never repeat itself. It is therefore irrational to expect the past to be much of a guide to the future.

The constancies and regularities which we seem to observe are not analytic, a priori and necessary. As David Hume put it:

> "... in all reasonings from experience there is a step taken by the mind which is not supported by any argument or process of understanding ... it must be induced by some other principle of equal weight or authority. ... This principle is Custom or Habit." (Hume 1777: 41)

and again:

> "All inferences from experience, therefore, are effects of custom, not of reasoning." (Hume 1777: 43)

However much evidence we gather from the past, however many stones we may observe to fall or white swans to fly by, we can never be certain that in the next moment an event will not occur that will falsify all our prior knowledge.

It is curious that, despite these clear warnings and the frequent failures of inductive inference in everyday life, we still presume that the future will be like the past, that there exist causal relations and that the world is well-ordered. It may be that the 'customs and habits' which sustain this opinion are engendered by (scientific) research methods which favour the abstraction of data from the world, which aim to discover and report simple regularities and singular causes and which cannot recognize or cope with complexity and with the discontinuities and thresholds at which state changes in systems occur.

We have glossed over the problem of induction by appealing to some ancient superstitions about chance. Statistical statements may be descriptions of a kind, but statistical correlations are not causal relations. We cannot know if there are cosmic forces acting either on Nature or on Society enforcing preordained probabilities and predetermining their behaviour to ensure that the validity of some statistical quantity is sustained. Hume remarks:

> "'Tis commonly allowed by philosophers that what the vulgar call chance is nothing but a secret and conceal'd cause." (Hume 1739: 130)

The vulgar are still with us for, as we know, many consumers of statistics, managers and accountants prominent among them, use 'cookbooks' and pocket calculators to make statistical calculations without caring very much about what they might signify.

Statistical propositions seem to me to be no more than representations of the data they address, and references to probability seem to add little or nothing to our understandings of specific things and events. Risk assessment, for example, may determine that such an event is likely to occur once in twenty years, but this assertion is of use only when making a comparison with another such event which has been assessed, using the same arithmetic, to occur more or less frequently. Risk assessment is of no value at all in any absolute sense; for, as the naïve and fearful often remark (ineptly of course), if this is the twentieth year and it has not happened yet, then the event is certain to happen! Pierce put it more exactly saying:

> "An individual inference must be either true or false, and can show no effect of probability; and, therefore, in reference to a single case, considered in itself, probability can have no meaning." (Pierce 1878)

I have serious reservations about the rationality of that cluster of assumptions which centres on inferences from reported regularities and constancies and on the notion of statistically inferred relations by means of which prediction might be made of future events from past experiences. As Hacking (1990: 7) has pointed out, this style of reasoning is of recent origin and although styles of reasoning are generally self-justifying and become embedded into our ways of thinking, this is novel enough still to deserve the casting of a sceptical eye.

Now this is not to say that all prediction is wrong or that the efforts put into gathering data, developing predictive models and so on are a waste of time. All that I claim is that we can have no reasonable grounds for having confidence in them, unless, of course, we are among Hume's 'vulgar' who think that Chance is a real world operator, a sufficient cause in itself and, even, that its operations can be predicted with certainty.

The fact that, despite their occasional failure (sometimes very spectacular), we continue to employ so-called causal, or predictive, models in singular cases suggests to me that they satisfy some deep-seated psychological needs which are surfaced under the stress of decision taking. As individuals we try to think that we are doing the 'right' thing and so we pass some of the responsibility for many decisions on to an 'expert' or 'guru' or to a body of accepted specialist professional knowledge. How often we must benefit from the 'placebo effect' of employing *argumentum ad verecundiam*.

The models and metaphors of operational research, of sociologists, of psychologists and of systems methodologies may provide, not so much well-founded reasons for action, as just the kind of gospels, myths, legends and apocryphal anecdotes needed in contemporary society to legitimize decisions and provide the excuses which will be required when things turn out differently, particularly when the unintended consequences turn out to be adverse. Their possible relationships to any real world seem to be much less important than the conviction about their truths which arises from mastering their complexities.

After all this is said, some of these methods do work much of the time and, applying the test of utility, I think, inconsistently, that we should continue to try to refine them and to adjust them as we learn from the mistakes we make when using them. Yet we should always be alert to their fragile a-rational foundations and anticipate that they are about to fail us: but with what probability we cannot possibly know!

5.2 A Stable Environment?

The assumption that a given information system will have a lifetime determined mainly by technological change rather than by changes in its environment also seems to deserve examination. To illustrate this point, and to demonstrate how it is that the represented world surrounding information systems is in such flux that it would be folly to discount it, I want speak briefly about the nature of conversations and the consequences of their continuation over time in social contexts.

My argument runs as follows: Conversations with other people, with ourselves and with the 'world outside', so far as we can encounter it, are part of the circular processes of production of new distinctions and new definitions which create and sustain 'institutions' (Robb 1992). These are: 'supra-human real world entities of a natural kind', autonomous, autopoietic and, being of an order higher than that of the conversations which beget and sustain them, are, a fortiori, beyond our control. Information systems are embroiled in these processes in ways which I shall not consider here because to do this would be to abuse the privilege offered to the author of an opening chapter.

Whether or not you share this understanding of social processes, you may agree that the processes of dividing and subdividing the world are continuous and self-exciting. New categories of people, things and events are thus being invented, and each new category has its own unique set of 'problems', its own newly created properties and interconnections with other categories. Many of these new categories and altered relationships require new definitions in information systems. Some entail the addition or subtraction of different classes of stakeholders and information users. Some require novel methods of data capture, and all entail that there be reconsideration of the significance of the data that can be captured and the information that can be generated.

So even if we set aside the problems of induction, causation and chance, there simply cannot be continuity between the representations of the past and of the present unless the categories of the world of interest in the two periods are unchanged. And in these days that is a most unusual condition. Information systems may take many years to develop and it is not surprising if, by the time they are up and running, they turn out much less useful than was expected.

These trends are realized in the business world in the following main areas:

- The commodification of public sector, commercial and industrial organizations which can now be bought and sold, in whole or in part as if they were on offer on supermarket shelves.

- The merging of firms and the divestment of their parts in a continuing and ever accelerating process of 'short-termism', such as the creaming-off of profitable activities and asset-stripping, invades both the private and the public sectors.

- The flattening of organizational hierarchies as power and authority are concentrated at the top and as the responsibility, which was formerly that of a class of managers, is diffused throughout the organization making every individual personally accountable for a specified contribution to the organization (all in the name of 'emancipation' and 'empowerment' of course!).

Because of these tendencies, incompatible information systems are thrown together and highly integrated systems have to be partitioned. Somehow reporting, accountability and performance monitoring have to be sustained and realigned to these new situations. Higher management, often unwilling to understand the intricacies of information systems, prone to the blandishments of computer and systems salesmen and consultants, rarely seem to get involved in what, to them, is simply a technical matter best left to experts. But often the experts are too narrowly experienced to cope with the scale and speed of change required, and so they often defend the status quo for their own jobs' sake. Sometimes a manager without particular information systems expertise is then put in charge of the experts to 'knock their heads together'. The results are around us in the form of half-baked systems cobbled together to cope with change, up and running just in time to be revised, and grandiose plans for integrated corporate systems which never leave the planning stage.

Perhaps even more disturbing is the concealment of knowledge about the fragility and vulnerability of the information systems themselves. Some information and control systems are very central now to the working of society. Those of potentially dangerous plant, of aircraft, power stations, energy distribution networks, of banking and financial organizations, of police and emergency services and of communications channels upon which much of modern life depends are now long past their maturity and may be prohibitively expensive and technically very difficult to replace. Because of the rate of change of information technology there is be a natural reluctance to address these problems lest a decision is taken to invest in an out-dated system. We may expect that decisions will be delayed until the systems are driven to the limits of their capabilities and many will be addressed after it is too late. A society trained to depend on these systems may well be undermined by their catastrophic failure.

All this adds up to a view of information systems designers trapped between rapid technical changes on one hand and the urgent need to make rapid changes to accommodate their changing environments on the other. There may be no time for the leisurely construction of root definitions or of total corporate information systems. Long-term strategies, which may have taken years to develop may be destroyed overnight at the stroke of an accountant's pen.

Information systems themselves are among the engines of change and if they are to remain viable in the future they will probably have to have the capability to change themselves. Little attention has been paid to the need for this recursion in the received view of information systems.

6 Moral Philosophy and Information Systems

Let's look now at just a few of the many ethical problems which the use of information systems generates such as the problems of playing numbers games and of surveillance.

6.1 The Numbers Game

The most obvious, and, possibly the most intractable problem with information systems that demands philosophical attention is the stark fact that information systems represent some kind of world which is realized only in number. Although some 'user-friendly' systems seem to deal in non-numerical language this is simply an illusion. The utterances in apparently natural language are being generated by a calculating engine churning numbers about and attributing words to the results. The use of information systems forces on us an appreciation of the world through accountant's or statistician's eyes. But the things in the world which are or can be measured by such numbers are a minute proportion of the things which we could perceive to exist and which affect us all.

The criteria which are used to assess what constitutes real knowledge in the social world are now almost all related to numerical representations, to accounting or statistical norms and to deviance from such norms. The natural sciences devote most of their vast resources to measurement, and the social sciences aspire to achieve the same level of (mis)understanding of their respective domains. Important aspects of people and societies cannot be captured adequately in number alone, that much must be obvious.

I would argue further, that people and societies can be changed and their properties can be reduced almost to number alone by the schemes of representation which are applied to them. If such schemes of representation are applied with adequate force, they shape the things observed to the point that all but the observed numbers are what matter, not only to the observers but also to the observed as well. The patient in the waiting room, and the hospital administrator alike, sensitized by some 'Charter of Customer Care', become more concerned about the time spent waiting for treatment than about the efficacy of the treatment when it is delivered. Indeed surprisingly little is known about the latter topic.

Numbers are open to manipulation as changes are so easily made to the data definitions that are in use. For instance, there have been twenty or so changes in the definition of 'unemployed' in the last decade, all favouring the impression of the efficacy of the then Government's actions. Notice too that many grossly misleading correlations have been published and represented as causal connections, for example, between unemployment, poverty and crime; all of which conveniently serve to cloak the obvious issues: that the 'problem' of the unemployed is lack of work, and that of the poor is (as Shaw remarked in 'Major Barbara') poverty.

The simplified, but highly specific, definitions of people which information systems are forming can lead to us to adopting these as guidelines for our own behaviour and as definitions of our own identity. We, the measured, are very adaptable. Typically we respond to being measured by playing along with the numbers games and in so doing we abandon belief in our own judgement and surrender to the operational and moral standards of the organizations and institutions which initiate the measurements.

Managers and academics alike are often applying as much, if not more, effort to getting the numbers to 'look right' than they are to doing what they thought they were employed to do. Scoring an high research rating becomes much more important to an academic department than assessing the originality of the contributions made to new knowledge by its individual members.

At the heart of all this lie information systems with their monocular view of the world. The fact, well known to the natural scientist, that observation changes things, is all but totally ignored in the social sciences but, as the practice of ever more detailed surveillance extends, so too will changes occur in social behaviour; in what ways we can only speculate.

6.2 Surveillance

There is a trend which Foucault (1977) and many others have discerned. It is the increasing use of information for the purposes of surveillance and social control, the tendency for the ever more fine definition of the individual being observed and the increasingly remote and more anonymous identity of those in control.

Bentham's 'Panopticon' was an architectural design for an ordered society, specifically a prison, in which the members of the society, the prisoners, could be identified and observed at will, individually, at any time: but the regulators of the society, the warders, could not be observed by those being regulated. Thus control could be maintained without the constant presence of the warders. The design of the system, its largely passive technology, enabled effortless representation and hence easy regulation of the many by the very few. Above all, the presence of the mechanisms of surveillance was ambiguous. There need be no warders, only the perception that warders might be there. By this simple means the 'requisite variety' (Ashby 1952: 229) needed to control a system with very great variety was provided. For Bentham this provided a model for the regulation of a Utopian state. An obvious modern example of ambiguous surveillance is the regulation of many potentially errant motorists by the 'speed camera' which may or may not occupy the boxes prominently situated by our roadsides. And, of course, it was the mere presence of the technology in *Nineteen Eighty-Four* which empowered the Thought Police and enforced belief in the cardinal precepts of Newspeak:

"War is peace, ignorance is strength, freedom is slavery." (Orwell 1949: 7)

But there was no Big Brother.

Marketing research and investigative journalism have shown what is possible in today's world. The technology to meet the needs of the state, the corporations and of the individuals in power is developing fast. The hidden cameras, the tapped phone lines, the hidden agendas in questionnaires, the concealed microphones, the long focus lenses of prying cameras are now commonplace. Artificial memories, providing continuous recordings of all activities in controlled spaces, in banks, shops, streets, factory floors and places of recreation are in widespread use. Shortly, it is anticipated, that workplaces and classrooms will also be similarly observed, and audio visual monitors will record every conversation and every iota of gossip. Conversations will be shaped accordingly; they may even stop altogether. In time, data from these and more conventional sources will tend to become more coherent and more easily available to selected groups.

Given a positivistic milieu in an organization for example, and a description of what is needed to make the organization work correctly, the information systems can ensure that correct behaviour is constantly maintained in the interest of productive efficiency, effectiveness and economy. These systems do not need to exercise total surveillance, they can perform their tasks simply by their mere presence, and by their known potential to recall everything. So when things go wrong, the recorded history, what someone considers to have been the precursing events, is there for inspection (or destruction) and for the assignation of blame.

The technology of surveillance is neither neutral nor reliable. Cameras do lie; tapes can be doctored and great, but unacknowledged power, resides in the hands of those who determine what aspects of the world are to be surveyed, when and how. If the effectiveness of the organization is the overarching criterion for measuring behaviour, what objections could any reasonably loyal member have to being so monitored? What an host of philosophical questions such systems raise.

Until recently accounting information was almost the sole means of representing corporations and corporate activities, and money numbers were the purveyors of corporate truths. Now information technology is coming to provide alternative ways of viewing these entities, and activity measurements and other non-money numbers are coming to replace accounting (Robb 1994a). Like accounting itself, information systems have escaped surveillance by accountancy. They are now largely beyond the reach of critical accounting practice and it seems to be now taken for granted that expenditure on them is an unavoidable overhead.

Because accounting defines its domain to be confined to that of the business entity and its role as that of safeguarding only the interests of shareholders, it will not shift its attention to wider issues, to the interests of other stakeholders, the workers, the communities, society, nation states and the environment. Few attempts have been made to count the social and the environmental costs of the information revolution, but they must be enormous as machines replace people and as capital replaces labour as the main cost to business, to production and to administration. No one knows the extent of the social costs being carried by the state, the communities, the unemployed and the taxpayers.

Information systems are not cheap and there have been dramatic cases in which some very shady deals have been made to install vastly expensive and over-ambitious schemes. Many useless systems have given rise to enormous bills for taxpayers, consumers and corporations. Few people have been held to account for these penalties of incompetence. There are no generally recognized codes of conduct governing the behaviour of information systems professionals; and there are no explicit sanctions to be levied against those who misrepresent their own expertise, who abuse commercial confidences or misuse their specialized knowledge. Although there are certain minimal qualifications for some kinds of technical experts, the field is wide open to anyone to put him/herself forward as a specialist, consultant or guru to advise on the specification, design and installation of information systems. This has been such a growth area that there has been a chronic shortage of adequately experienced people and the gaps have been filled from such unlikely sources as academe and the large accountancy firms. The public interest, if not the interests of the corporations and governments, is put in jeopardy by the ways in which information systems are installed and their powers deployed. As to the formation of ethical codes of conduct, policing and disciplining of information systems specialists little has been said.

The arcane technologies of information systems have placed their internal workings quite beyond the reach of most auditors. In consequence, there are horrendous cases of fraud, sabotage and data and program corruption on such a scale as to require the cloak of secrecy to be drawn over them lest their publication shakes all confidence in the organizations involved.

The obverse side of surveillance by information systems has yet to be revealed. The rapid growth of networked personal computers, information highways, bulletin boards and what almost passes for conversation conducted electronically may herald the emergence of new kinds of institutions realized in world-wide information networks. We can only speculate what influence these may have but maybe in Paine (1994) we can have a foretaste. Sylvia Paine describes HURIDOCS [HUman RIghts Information and DOcumentation Systems network] which collects information about abuse of human rights. Reports are made and posted to bulletin boards almost instantly, patterns of abuse can be detected and the culpable individuals tracked world-wide.

As to the future development of information technologies, it seems to me that the creation of public artificial memories could have a liberating effect. 'Memory lapses', such as those which seem to afflict cabinet ministers and others in high office and positions of power might be overcome. Such information systems could be used to promote open government and increase public accountability where this is notably absent at present. The information technologies of the future might enable the prisoners to see what the warders are up to. And that, I think, might be a 'good thing'.

7   Conclusion

I hope that I have exposed some of the more pressing issues about information systems which deserve attention from various branches of philosophy. I have tried to speak about the metaphysical, logical and moral aspects of these systems and to promote some reflection. Thank you for the privilege of offering my notions to you.

Implications of Regarding Information as Meaningful Rather Than Factual

Norma Romm

This chapter explores the implications of offering a definition of information as meaningful, that is, as produced through the participation of people in constructing and reconstructing their world. The importance of regarding information as a locus of meaning is explored in the light of the problem that information which passes as neutral and impersonal may serve to repress alternative accounts of 'the world', and thereby to buttress specific power relationships. It is shown how cultural forms of information processing could be re-framed to enable practices more conducive to the shifting and tempering of power relations. It is argued that such forms themselves rest upon a definition of information as meaningful (human productions) rather than factual (or impersonal). The chapter's plea to define information as meaningful rests on an ethical position — and uses ethical argumentation to support the suggestions offered.

1 Introduction

This chapter offers a definition of information which concentrates on the cultural and political implications of regarding information as meaningful rather than factual. Its focus is on the construction and use of information in contexts of organizational interaction, where human activities are organized and coordinated. It is argued that the way in which we regard information is connected to our way of human relating. The possibility of engendering more dialogical relationships requires a consideration of information as constructed and reconstructed in processes of social conversations — conversations whose character can be more or less coercive.

The reference to information in a way which precludes public discussion and discursive accountability can be seen as related to the very definition of information itself. To the extent that information is seen or presented and legitimated in terms of its supposed factual content, it authorizes a picture of the world — rather than inviting debate on the construction and relevance of the picture. Conversely, insofar as information is treated as a product of specific world-construction activities, it invites discursive inquiry as to its ongoing meaning and relevance. The treatment of information as a locus of meaning is able more fully (than other approaches to information) to recognize the right of all people in society to a viewpoint on meaningful reality.

This chapter argues that struggles to shift power relations in society (and in specific organizations and enterprises) involve struggles over, as Wexler (1987: xiv) puts it: "the means of producing discourse, over language and the practice of forming discourse". Blockages of discourse or narratives of repression ensue when attempts are made to block people's capacity to participate in recoding the meaning productions which are produced.

A specific ethical position is advanced in this chapter by proposing a view of human relations in which it is incumbent upon people to be aware of the partiality of their 'position' — as a basis for ongoing confrontation between opposing positions. The suggestion is that it is possible to facilitate debates in society in which people's positions can shift as they encounter challenges levelled by others and, indeed, as they reflect back on the 'bad news' connected with their adoption of a particular position. The phrase 'bad news' is derived from Gouldner (1980: 18). It refers to any 'information' which is hostile to one's initial position and which hence represents 'hostile information' for that position.

This means that any decision-making in society should take place after a process of discourse, which includes the opening up to alternatives, as well as the conscious recognition of the bad news connected with the adoption of any viewpoint. It does not mean that decision-making becomes impossible. Rather, as McKay & Romm (1992: 124) argue it has the following implications for decision-making. It implies:

- that individuals recognize that decisions are made on the basis of a viewpoint which is always contestable;

- that decisions result from an effort to take account of alternative interpretations of meanings; and

- that decisions become as 'open-ended' as possible, allowing for the adopted 'plan' to be improved by those executing it.

The conception of information as meaningful may be seen as one of the ways of contributing to an ethic of discursive accountability. Hence it is preferable to emphasize that the information to which humans have access is humanly constructed (in terms of meaning-making enterprises).* In this regard, it is

---

*In defining information as meaningful, the argument draws on Checkland & Scholes' (1990: 303) suggestion that information embodies the process of attributing meaning to 'data'. However, this

noteworthy that authors who argue for information-content as, in principle, separable from meaning-content often recognize that information thus defined is *inaccessible to us*. Mingers (in this volume, concluding comments p.83) argues that once we recognize this, "our focus should be on meaning and meaning systems". Although Mingers adheres to a definition of information as referring to propositional content of signals (received from 'the world'), his conception of this content as being inaccessible to us, and his suggestion that we *focus on meaning and meaning systems*, is compatible with the argument in this chapter. It highlights that the 'information' *to which we have access* is not neutral, standardized or impersonal, but reflects the meaningful input of those who confront it. The suggestion in this chapter is that we emphasize the impossibility of separating out information from meaning. This allows us to concentrate attention on the possibility of recognizing people's right to cognitive participation in the construction of 'their world'. McKay & Romm (1992: 56–62) discuss the significance of cognitive participation — which points to the (ethical) requirement for social participation, not only in responding to 'information' but, indeed, in contributing to its construction.

2 Information as a Vehicle of Power

Several authors have commented on the way in which information systems, devised to systematize and structure the input of 'data' in order to render it usable in human life, may become enclaves of power. The link between information and power is summarized by Porter (1994: 228) as follows: "In a world that respects information, information becomes powerful". In similar vein, Robb (1994b: 13) (drawing on Foucault's argument concerning the link between power and the construction of 'knowledge') argues that: "Information systems are vehicles of power and where power lies so do a large number of ethical issues".

Robb (Robb 1994b: 9, in this volume p.16) points to the way in which information is structured through the making of distinctions and forming definitions. Information is created through processes of dividing and subdividing the world, thus constructing the images that 'those involved' form of the world. The focus of this chapter (implicit in that of Robb) is the question of how 'those involved' are able to present their accounts (distinctions, definitions and subdivisions) as containing 'knowledge', in a way that precludes a dialogical process of (re)assessing the relevance of the constructions. Robb highlights the ethical issues as follows:

> "There are problems about who defines the systems, what kinds of information are retrieved and to what uses the [information] systems are put. These issues have received little attention commensurate with the powers, real and potential, which information systems confer on those who control them." (Robb 1994b: 13)

chapter stresses that 'information' may embody struggles over processes of coding and recoding the world, and it offers a conception of discursive accountability which is rooted in a specific ethic.

Robb (1994b: 15) concludes his paper by proposing that: "Information systems could be used to put power in the hands of the presently powerless, if we had but the imagination to discover how." He argues that information could then become a vehicle to "... promote open government and increase public accountability where this is notably absent at present." (in this volume p.21). His views on the potential for shifting power seem to be related to his suggestion that it is possible to criticize "some important assumptions" in the "official view of information systems" (in this volume p.12). For instance, he proposes a critique of the assumption that the task of defining information needs ultimately can be referred to 'knowledge engineers' and of the assumption that the relevance, and attendant use, of information is knowable by someone who "understands what is at work". But he does not concentrate, in his paper, on exploring the question of how the very construction and production of information, can exercise constraints on debate about its relevance.

Porter (1994: 217) casts light on the issue by noting that the respect for information is linked to the notion that information represents, as far as possible, neutral and well standardized knowledge. He indicates that:

"The usual strategy for inspiring trust in science, as in business and government, is to cultivate the appearance of impersonality, or objectivity. This can be done by writing in the impersonal passive voice, by loading a text down with factual material and references, or by explicating choices using the language of statistical inference and decision theory rather than personal judgement." (Porter 1994: 221)

Porter is concerned about the way in which information is presented as standardized and universal: he argues that the appearance of impersonality serves to buttress the positions of the powerful who benefit from the constructions which pass as neutral. But Porter also seems to suggest that some form of 'standardization' may be necessary in a world which demands public accountability of 'the powerful'. Insofar as decision-power is legitimated via 'information', it is necessary that the information is not merely a product of whimsical construction — but does have some claim to testability. Public accountability requires that the information used to write reports, to account for decisions, to take further actions, etc. does have some credibility. Wherein may this credibility lie — once we have asserted that the 'information' is always an human construction?

We can address this question by turning to a consideration of some of the ethical questions arising from the power of information and by asking whether it is possible to define the notion of information itself so that it can become a vehicle for power-shifting, rather than for the concentration of power. As Foucault has been one of the inspirations for many of those questioning the link between knowledge and power, it is relevant to consider his conception of ethical action and thereafter to derive a notion of information which encourages a concentration on ethical issues.

3 Ethical Considerations in the Definition of Information

Foucault's considerations on thought and thinking, are tied directly to his definition of the notion of people as ethical subjects. He argues that: "It [thought] is what establishes the relation with oneself and with others, and constitutes the human being as an ethical subject." (Foucault 1986: 334). He goes on to suggest that: "... it [thought] is what allows one to step back from this way of acting or reacting, to present it to oneself as an object of thought and question it as to its meaning, its conditions, its goals." (Foucault 1986: 388). Foucault's conception of (ethical) thought is linked to his critique of an alternative approach — wherein we approach 'the world' by defining truth outside of the moment of critical encounter between persons, and in which we fail to allow 'the other' a right to an independent view. He contrasts an (ethical) attitude with what he calls 'polemics' in which we "define alliances, recruit partisans, unite interests ... and establish the other as an enemy" (Foucault 1986: 383). In criticizing the polemic attitude, Foucault concurs with much of Habermas' critique of the way in which domination may enter discourse. Foucault, however, is wary of Habermas' requirement for consensus as a regulative principle of argument. According to Foucault we have to admit tension, while admitting the right of the other to continued opposition — cf. Foucault (1986: 378). It may be suggested that Habermas' (1982: 223) admission of the fundamentally hypothetical character of all propositions, makes provision for a similar ethic; one in which people are required to take responsibility for actions taken, having subjected these to the 'test' of discursive engagement — cf. Romm's (1991: 152) discussion. To some extent Habermas' call for self-reflection and for the taking of responsibility in the light of a recognition of fallibility, may be seen to concur with the Foucauvian ethic. A detailed debate between Foucault's and Habermas' positions is outside of the scope of this chapter. What is relevant, though, is that both call for knowledge/truth presented as neutral 'information' to become subjected to criticism; and both conceptualize that this criticism can contribute to, and will be tied up with, the possibility of tempering the repression which denounces people's right to cognitive participation. Both plead, on moral grounds, for not suppressing alternative ways of conceiving and seeing 'the world'. They plead for a critique of practices which ground themselves in authoritative visions of the world or in authoritative visions of the 'correct' method of striving to attain (representative) knowledge.*

If we bear in mind aspects of Foucault's position as outlined above, we see that Gouldner's (1980) injunction for people to engage in serious confrontation with others who may point out 'bad news' for their stance, again points to a similar ethical requirement. In terms of this requirement, if one defends one's position

---

*Romm (1991) outlines a 'non-realist' critique of the Popperian as well as so-called 'realist' conceptions of the empirical basis of science (as constituting the route to representative knowledge) by referring largely to Habermas' alternative account. Probert (in this volume p.131) for his part indicates that Quine's thesis of epistemological holism can be used to subvert the notion that we can test ideas logically with reference to 'experience'.

on the grounds that it is the only rational or viable way to proceed, i.e. to think, as well as to intervene in the world of 'action', then one is acting unethically. The requirement is that one converses with alternatives and uses this conversation as the basis for how one acts. It does not imply a consensual account of 'best' action to be undertaken in 'the circumstances', but rather that actors are prepared to subject their vision to argument, even though they recognize the fragility of all argument. It requires, as McKay & Romm point out, that decision-making takes into account: the contestable character of its underlying viewpoint; the requirement to subject viewpoints to serious encounter with alternatives; and the requirement to allow for the open-endedness of decisions, including their flexibility upon 'implementation'. Romm (1994a: 25–7) further explores this argument in the context of examining Ulrich's critical systemic approach to planning, drawing out possible implications for the notion, and practice, of accountable action.

4 Modes of Information Processing: Implications for the Definition of Information

The discussion above suggests that "... transactions of meaning and power among individuals in real situations ..." — see Beeson (in this volume p.217) — may be shifted and that shifts towards less coercive forms of meaning-construction are directly linked to shifts in our approach to 'information'. But how may we enable the possibility of these shifts? Quinn & McGrath's categorization, of the way in which cultural settings enable ways of relating to 'information', serves as a starting point to consider this question. Quinn & McGrath (1985) argue that we can categorize information processing styles into four types, all of which may gain some credibility in organizational culture. Their argument concurs with Spaul's (in this volume) indication of 'cultural strands' embodying different approaches to information.

Quinn & McGrath (ibid.: 319–20) define the four types of information processing styles as follows:

1. *Rational* information processing: a process of analysing patterns and using this as a basis for developing known means-ends chains, which are used to clarify goals.

2. *Adaptive* information processing: information is generated via intuition and hunches about possibilities, with stimuli being used to make quick decisions, which, however, are easily adaptable.

3. *Consensual* or *Group* information processing: time is taken to "seek out diverse opinions and search for solutions that integrate the various positions". Information is constructed and developed through a process aimed at generating consensus in decision-making.

4. *Hierarchical* information processing: treats messages from a static view, with the subject being seen "as if in a photograph". The orientation is towards security in the long term and on attaining the single best answer to optimize activity in terms of a perpetuation of the status quo.

Quinn & McGrath (ibid.: 325) argue that all of these styles of information processing may become legitimated in organizational settings. They become embodied in 'culture' in the sense that they become recognized as patterns of response to 'the world'. This is not to say that any one type of approach ever reaches full ascendancy (to the total exclusion of other types) in any real organization — indeed we might be able to categorize processes "by descriptions from all four quadrants" (ibid.: 331). They go on to say:

"The most buffered hierarchy [characterized largely by hierarchical information processing] has some aspects of the adhocracy [with attendant adaptive information processing], and the most existential clan [with an orientation to consensual information processing] has within it some aspects of the instrumental market [with an attendant utility of a rational information processing style]." (ibid.: 331)

They then argue that their preferred response to considering the relationship between these forms of information processing, is one of 'transcendence' — where the contradictions between them can become 're-framed'. The transcendence that they endorse is one in which we do not attempt to "reject any of the quadrants", but rather where we consider all four types in terms of their "congruence with situational demands" (in the cycle of human organization).

They do not elucidate further their position in this respect. However, in terms of the discussion in this chapter, what is of particular relevance is the way that they show that:

"... reflected in the four cultures ... are some implicit beliefs about desirable end states. These are embedded theories of effectiveness that not only offer different definitions of effectiveness but also specify the mode of information processing that will result in the desired outcome. When made explicit all four reflect easily recognized schools of organizational thought." (ibid.: 325)

The modes of information processing are not neutral in regard to the collection and systematizing of usable material, but already in their very style of approach to 'the world' they contain a conception of 'the desirable' way to organize. Now Quinn & McGrath resolve the issue of the seeming contradiction between the variety of styles by suggesting that each is appropriate at different points in the cycle of organization. The thought processes of all four types thus all 'have a place' in human organization. Of course, they do point out that they need not all be pursued in the form in which they have been presented in their categorization

— and that 'transcendence' may require us to reformulate/reconsider the styles. As indicated above, they offer not specific suggestions in this regard.

What this chapter suggests, in terms of Quinn & McGrath's categories, is the following:

- Styles one and four (*rational* and *hierarchical*), when utilized, have to be placed in a context which allows for discussion on the meaning and relevance of the patterns and pictures 'detected' in the information-processing process. The means-ends schema and patterns of predictability have to be recognized to be rooted in the creation of variables *whose relevance themselves require discussion/argument.* Once this is recognized, the way is opened for (dialogical) confrontation with alternative accounts of relevant variables and indeed alternative ways of approaching 'the world'; for example, ways offered by the other categories.

- As regards the second (*adaptive*) style, here again it is incumbent on those relying on hunches and intuitions to invite responses from others and to use these as part of the stimuli that inform decision-making. Even if the need for quick responses and risk-taking is endorsed, this does not, and should not, preclude an openness to learning — defined as *confrontation with challenges and bad news presented by others* — on an ongoing basis to be used for continued adaptations.

- Finally, as regards the third (*consensual* or *group*) style, the impetus towards 'harmony' should be recognized as itself containing a 'dark' side — cf. Gouldner (1975) — which needs to be tempered by a culture of respect for difference. The quest for a consensual response to the construction and interpretation of 'information' on the grounds that effective action requires a shared viewpoint, may serve unnecessarily to discount continued tension. As, for instance, McKay & Romm (1992) and Romm (1994a; 1994b) have indicated, shared viewpoints are not required for negotiated 'ways forward' to be generated. What is required is that the various parties become committed to *reflect on their initial frames of meaning* — this reflection in turn may "yield a sensitivity" to what Brown (1989: 158) calls "an alternative range of considerations". Romm (1994b: 334) argues that in processes of 'group' negotiation, "none of the participants may be entirely satisfied with the outcome, but for the time being, it may be seen as a workable arrangement". The quest for negotiation, thus defined, may be preferable, as a mode of human relationship, to the group endorsements implied in Quinn & McGrath's third category.

The above re-framing of Quinn & McGrath's categories is consistent with the ethical requirements for confrontation with 'the world' discussed above. It should be emphasized that, in terms of these requirements, one cannot leave untouched the types of processing style that their categories have drawn out (for consideration). One has to re-frame them in terms of their implications for human relating. Jackson & Carter (1991: 120) have argued that, in the midst of the variety of patterns of organizational approach that can be located, the most tolerant solution may not be simply to grant all equal credence. For such a solution does not take into account the *constraint towards repression* that some styles are more likely to foster. Hence Jackson & Carter plead for moral choices to be made. It could be argued, in terms of their moral plea, that types *one* and *four* of the styles categorized by Quinn & McGrath, in the form there categorized, seem specifically to forbid further recoding and reworking of the 'information' constructed. On these grounds, we may be required to make a moral choice to destabilize these patterns of information processing; for instance, in the way suggested in the outline above, by recasting the patterns as meaningful, rather than as disembodied patterns. The information gathering of types *two* and *three*, being less grounded in a quest for 'impersonality', would seem more conducive to an openness to reconstruction; for example, of the kind outlined above.

5   Possibilities for Shifts through Redefining Information

The discussion above has concentrated on indicating ways in which we can envisage information as meaningful and hence enable less repressive forms of human relationship (than if information is treated as de-personalized). What is implied in the discussion is that, if information is viewed as potentially containing cognitive participation in defining meaningful reality, then the question of whose participation has been invited and whose excluded comes to the fore (a question which, as noted above, Robb has highlighted as an ethical one).

Deetz (1985: 265), like many before him, points out that ethical concerns in human organization can be seen as linked to the question of the power of 'management' to preclude "voices that are essential for the human dialogue". His concern is that if "managerial logic has been internalized by other potential participants, [then] contrary conceptions are rarely thought and less often spoken". Deetz contends that "under current conditions" this kind of:

> "... ideological domination is largely built into the structure of organizations and protected from ... assessment. Hence we have ideologically based organizational decision-making and one-sided effects on the development of the human community." (Deetz 1985: 265)

Deetz argues that although one may speak of ideological domination — defined as the exclusion of the variety of voices 'essential for the human dialogue' — this does not necessarily imply that a one-sided managerial logic is seen as intentionally imposed. As he puts it: "The ethical concern advanced here is not that managers as a group make decisions that are intentionally or carelessly detrimental to the development of the human community" (Deetz 1985: 265). Deetz argues that much of the ideological domination consists more in a 'managerial logic' becoming internalized, as a recognized mode of thought and practice, and hence left largely unchallenged.

Deetz sees domination as being perpetuated because managerial logic is largely 'protected from assessment'. Ethical considerations, he hopes, can contribute to opening up this logic for debate, by raising questions concerning 'the kind of people' that we wish to foster. The ethical question for Deetz is: "If we ... manage in this way ... what kind of people will we become?" (Deetz 1985: 257).

Deetz suggests that, for ethical reasons, we need to open up to debate the 'current' modes of thought, which themselves often exclude the variety which dialogue implies. His suggestion concurs with the discussion above, where it was shown how information processing styles may be re-framed to invite debate and argument in processes of cognition. But this still leaves unaddressed the issue as to whether one can, as an intervenor in social organization, draw on ethical concerns to shift the logic that dominates the information processing style, and that often seems to forbid reworking or re-framing. On what grounds does Deetz believe that ideological domination (for example through styles of information processing) can be averted by raising ethical considerations? Deetz's 'answer' to this question can be gleaned from his suggestion that often the domination of a logic that seems to forbid re-assessment, is unintentional, and is simply written into cultural patterns. This being so, the intentional raising (by some intervenor) of the potential for repression in the logic, and the appeal for reconsideration on ethical grounds, may indeed serve to open up to discussion the information processing style(s), and hence to temper the repression which consists precisely on their failure to be assessed. In other words, Deetz believes that one can invoke the language of ethics to raise questions which will gain an hearing and serious consideration by management (those whose logic dominates), as well as by other interested participants (including those working within organizations and the community served by the organizations). Hence, for him, the raising of ethical questions, in the way that he does, may in itself serve to shift and temper current, largely un-assessed, patterns.

This chapter argues, with Deetz, that it may be possible to address 'management' and others alike, by introducing the question of 'the kind of people' we wish to become. This means that it may be possible to introduce into 'managerial logic' (and 'recognized' cultural patterns) a re-framing of information processing styles; 'information' may be used to invite discursive assessment and re-assessment of our responses to 'the world'. Public accountability of the kind called for by Deetz, Porter, Robb, etc., then becomes linked to the opportunity for people to assess the relevance and construction of the knowledge guiding decision-making: the ability to renegotiate decisions on the basis of a discursive consideration of meaning productions, then becomes central. As pointed out above, this is not identical with the quest for consensus, but rather the quest for decision-making to take place in the light of, and in serious encounter with, opposing viewpoints.

But will a definition of information as meaningful help to foster the above practices? And why may we believe so? This question can be approached on two levels:

1. One can invoke the moral level of human encounter and argue that people may become sensitized to what McKay & Romm (1992: 61) call a 'norm of discourse'. Sensitivity to this norm would mean that it becomes culturally 'accepted' that the legitimacy of information processing lies in its ability to embrace continuing and serious encounter with 'bad news' as presented in dialogical confrontation with alternatives. This in turn means that legitimate management becomes linked to the propensity to be both critical and self-critical — cf. McKay & Romm (1992: 149) and Schön (1983: 320–5).

2. There is another dimension on which one may be able, as an intervenor, to shift potentially repressive social relationships in which the variety of voices is silenced or not given serious attention. And this is by appealing to 'management' on grounds that refer to the threat of their own self-destruction, or the destruction of their would-be plans.* Romm (1994b: 332) has shown, with reference to various sociological arguments, that it may become counterproductive for the seemingly powerful to ignore the quest for meaningful input on the part of those perceived to be less powerful. She suggests that those wishing to 'play the power game' in society by attempting to force their conceptions of 'realistic' action on others, often find that such practices are self-destructive. The argument is that:

   "People who believe that they have the power to force their vision and their attendant plans on others need to realize that their attempts to do so are often likely to be unsuccessful. This is especially so in a world where people are becoming increasingly aware of their 'right' to participate in the formation of an independent viewpoint." (Romm 1994b: 333)

   The second sentence of the above quotation is especially significant in terms of the argument in this chapter. It highlights the idea that it may become less possible for 'management' to proceed in terms of an information processing style that forbids the recoding of meaning, to the extent that people express their 'right' to cognitive participation. To this extent an information processing style that forbids repackaging, may become self-destructive.

To·summarize: Whether one addresses 'the powerful', in positions of official power, on ethical grounds, or, alternatively, on more strategic grounds (appealing to the likely lack of 'success' of their management logic in the face of possible resistance that may ensue), the space for such addressing is enabled through the cultural recognition of information as meaningful. A definition of 'information' as meaningful, creates the space to shift the (potentially repressive) power relation. It is for this reason that this chapter calls for such a definition of information.

---

*This does not imply that one regards 'management' as being one's sole client — but rather that one recognizes them as a client whom one has to take into account if one is attempting to shift power relations. It does not preclude working with and supporting other clients.

6 Conclusion

In this chapter, it has been asserted that when dealing with information systems, the information-content should be treated as open to ongoing 'discursive repackaging'. This definition of information has been proposed by exploring the cultural and political implications of regarding information as meaningful rather than factual. It has been argued that shifts of potentially repressive human relationships are enabled via a widespread treatment of information as rooted in discursive accountability. The ethical stance adopted has been developed by drawing on the work of various authors who have raised the problem of the 'power of information' as causing moral concern.

The Tool Perspective on Information Systems Design: What Heidegger's Philosophy Can't Do

Martin W.J. Spaul

This chapter examines the opposition between the tool perspective on information systems design, rooted in the philosophy of Heidegger, with traditional design approaches rooted in Cartesian philosophy. It is argued that it is unproductive to view this as a purely philosophical conflict, and that the political and moral dimensions of each philosophy must be explored to develop a balanced perspective on information systems design. It is concluded that a balanced design approach must operate in a more flexible framework than that offered by any distinctive school of philosophy.

1 Introduction

This chapter is concerned with the 'tool perspective' on information systems design, a convenient label for a set of challenges to traditional design practice mounted by Winograd & Flores (1986) and Ehn (1988), and prompted by the early philosophy of Heidegger (1962: Division I). The tool perspective (a phrase due to Ehn) focuses on computer support for embodied action and unreflective skills, and is presented in deliberate opposition to the commonly-adopted 'Cartesian' design philosophy which regards information systems fundamentally as representations of an objective world — a stance epitomized by information systems practitioners as diverse as database designers (Date 1990), theorists of artificial intelligence (McCarthy & Hayes 1969) and modellers of organizational decision making (Simon 1976, Simon 1981). The tool perspective has been influential in Computer Supported Cooperative Work (CSCW), the design of direct manipulation interfaces and the development of digital technology for embodied settings (e.g. the Apple Newton); it is also closely related to well-known critiques of artificial intelligence and expert systems (Dreyfus 1991, Dreyfus & Dreyfus 1986).

The purpose of this chapter is to caution against the crusading tone of the principal formulations of the tool perspective and its portrayal as a replacement for, or improvement on, the Cartesian approach. It will be argued that this tone is the result of an inadequate characterization of the issues involved. Although Winograd & Flores (1986: ch.12) and Ehn (1988: Part IV) deploy Heidegger's philosophy in a critically reflective spirit, there is much in their work to suggest that they regard Cartesian and Heideggerian philosophies purely as opposing epistemologies, internally devoid of political and moral content. This reading is reinforced by Dreyfus' polemics against artificial intelligence, which are largely conducted within an apolitical and ahistorical framework — cf. Weizenbaum (1976). This chapter will attempt to show that this portrayal of a purely philosophical, epistemological conflict is misleading; and also to show that carrying on this debate from within the Cartesian and Heideggerian self-understandings suppresses the important political and moral choices which are expressed in an epistemology. This chapter shows that, under a critical re-description, the opposition between the two design approaches may be seen as less stark, and that the 'ideological' (in the broadest sense) connections of any design philosophy should be interrogated closely. The suggestion is made that any stance on information systems design is bound up, in complex ways, with presuppositions concerning the social role of those systems.

This investigation is carried out from an approximately 'post-modern' position, principally defined by the pragmatism of Rorty (1989) and non-foundational versions of critical theory (Adorno & Horkheimer 1973). From such a position, any attempt to find a 'foundation for design', the subtitle of Winograd & Flores (1986), looks reductive and limiting. The search for a 'sound foundation', a consistent, unitary set of principles from which all practice may be derived, while it may be the reflex reaction of the scientist or mathematician, has the potential to stifle the continuing dialogue which constitutes the pursuit of knowledge in the human sphere (including the activity of information systems design).

2   Representation vs. Absorbed Coping

In this section, the conflict between Cartesian and Heideggerian foundations for design is described in terms of the self-understandings of both positions. The result of a conflict pursued in this vein is a stand-off: both approaches have particular defects which compromise practical design methodologies. As long as historically-entrenched philosophical positions are reproduced in this conflict no enlarged perspective on design practice seems to be possible.

2.1   *Cartesian Representationalism*

Insofar as mainstream work in information systems design has been founded on an explicit philosophy (and the lack of such a philosophy need not be a criticism) it has been founded on naïve realism. Symbols within an information system are taken to be representations of a 'real world' of individuated objects. Such an assumption is to be found in most mainstream texts on information systems; two random examples taken from recent database texts provide an illustration:

"Projects, parts, suppliers, etc., thus constitute the basic entities about which the company needs to record information (the term 'entity' is widely used in database circles to mean any distinguishable object that is to be represented in the database) ... we regard an entity as any object about which we wish to record information." (Date 1990)

"The central notion present in any semantic data model is that of a (data) object ...Concrete objects can be collected to form sets of objects, and objects are always of a predefined (object) type. What is essential is that a set of objects can be directly represented and manipulated ..." (Vossen 1991)

This conception is reasonably characterized as 'Cartesian representationalism' since it adopts a Cartesian view of knowledge: the inner mind mirroring the outer world in representations, with the exercise of the mind being the manipulation of such representations (Rorty 1980). The form which underlies modern work in databases may be traced back to Frege's (1893) semantic account of formal and natural languages, through a line of inheritance which includes model theory and the relational calculus. For Frege, the fundamental elements of the language in question (basic symbols in the case of a formal language, words in the case of a natural language) are assigned a sense and a reference, and the formation rules of the language (its grammar) provide a systematic mechanism by which senses and references may be compounded to give the meaning and truth conditions of, finally, sentences. This model has been pursued enthusiastically for most of this century; for an historical survey see Coffa (1991), and for a developed exposition see Davidson & Harman (1972).

An influential formulation, and practical application, of Cartesian representationalism is that made by Simon in his unified theory of human intelligence and organizational decision making. For Simon, both the human mind and the organization may be profitably viewed as a 'physical symbol system':

"A physical symbol system is a machine that, as it moves through time, produces an evolving collection of symbol structures. Symbol structures can, and commonly do, serve as internal representations ... of the environments to which the symbol system is seeking to adapt. They allow it to model that environment with greater or less veridicality and in greater or less detail, and consequently to reason about it. Of course, for this capability to be of any use to the symbol system, it must have windows on the world and hands too. It must have a means for acquiring information from the external environment that can be encoded into internal symbols, as well as means for producing symbols that initiate action upon the environment. Thus it must use symbols to designate objects and relations and actions in the world external to the system." (Simon 1981: 27)

This unified theory motivates a set of related research programmes: 'classical' artificial intelligence (based on representation, heuristic search and deduction), the study of heuristic decision making in humans (particularly business executives and political/military strategists), and, as an hybrid of the other two, the production of computer based support for the decision making process.

As a theory of knowledge, and as a design foundation for information systems, the Fregean model is based upon a strong, and debatable, set of assumptions: it must regard as (relatively) unproblematic the idea of an objective world of individuated objects to which human beings have access; the central function of language, the centrally important activity in human communication, must be that of fact-stating; also, it should be possible to carry through the reduction of all that we intuitively are pleased to call 'human knowledge' to this form — the classic expression of these assumptions is by Wittgenstein (1961). In information systems, these assumptions surface as a faith in the objectivity and universal applicability of data analysis techniques and a marginalizing of the organizational pragmatics of data use. In artificial intelligence and decision theory these assumptions surface in a focus on attempting to formulate ever more encompassing 'knowledge representation' formalisms; and as the belief that all human action is, at root, 'rule-guided' and best described as the application of 'tacit knowledge'. The pathologies of Cartesian design seem to grow from these assumptions: systems which fail to formalize organizational reality from the perspective of naïve users (Lewis 1993), systems which do not fit into natural patterns of work (Lyytinen et al. 1991), and accounts of intelligence and decision making which have little room for intuition and experience (Dreyfus & Dreyfus 1986).

2.2 Heideggerian Hermeneutics

The philosophy of Martin Heidegger, especially its early formulation in 'Being and Time' (Heidegger 1962), provides a perspective radically different from that of the Cartesian 'mirror of nature'. Heidegger starts from a position of trying to show that the entire Western philosophical tradition, from the time of Plato, has misrepresented and distorted the nature of human being in the world. His theory constructs a sustained alternative to the idea that the world, and people's place in it, can be understood on the basis of detached theory, and that all knowledge can be represented in some neutral linguistic medium. Properly speaking, Heidegger undercuts classical epistemological problems with a strongly-hermeneutic ontology which ensures that such problems cannot arise. The outline of Heidegger's position elaborated below is based on Dreyfus (1991), a work circulated in notes and manuscripts from the late 1960's onwards and the main source of awareness of Heidegger for Winograd, Flores and the artificial intelligence community.

Heidegger's philosophy has many facets but, for the purposes of understanding the tool perspective on information systems design, this section will concentrate on Heidegger's account of concerned engagement in practical activity and the use of equipment (tools). This account also provides an implicit critique, and explanation, of the Cartesian position. The status of this critique is not that of conclusive proof, but a rhetorical strategy designed to show that Cartesianism is implausible and that its endemic defects can be explained and resolved within the more embracing Heideggerian scheme.

For Heidegger, the most fundamental form of engagement with the world is that of coping with everyday activities, activities in which we encounter 'equipment' (material, tools, furniture, etc.). Equipment is encountered not as detached objects for theoretical contemplation, but as something which we use in connection with our activities — it has a role (an 'in-order-to'), which defines it. The way of being of such equipment is that it is encountered as available ('ready-to-hand'), and disappears from conscious contemplation when in use. This transparency of equipment in use also applies to the user; in absorbed coping with the world the self-aware Cartesian ego is nowhere in evidence (extreme cases of which are the sportspeople in performance, or the soldier in combat). Absorbed coping, the fusing of self and world in action, is treated as a basic entity: Dasein ('being-there'). The Cartesian ego and the objects of theoretical contemplation are regarded as less basic than absorbed coping, arising when the unreflective flow of activity breaks down for some reason (a tool fails to do a job, a door jams, etc.). When breakdown occurs, equipment becomes conspicuous and mental activity (deliberation) becomes apparent. The move to detached theorizing and the appearance of the objects of theoretical reflection (individuated objects with abstract properties, see Section 2.1 above) accompanies a complete withholding of the practical attitude; such objects are occurrent (or 'present-at-hand').

This reorientation is accompanied by an account of the structure of the world in which practical roles are fulfilled; a structure which is key to the tool perspective. Equipment is said to fit into an holistic context of meaningful activity — any item of equipment has a point only because of the existence of other equipment and projects which involve that equipmental whole. These contexts have a general structure: equipment is used 'in-order-to' carry out some task, to reach a goal 'towards-which' we work, 'for-the-sake-of' some general project. The structure of the equipmental whole is invisible during 'absorbed-coping', but is revealed at points of breakdown.

Within Heidegger's scheme, the Cartesian account of knowledge and action appears as a reversal of the true priorities in our experience of the world. A Cartesian attempt to account for our intellectual functioning beginning with occurrent objects and their properties is an attempt which, in Heidegger's terms, is doomed to failure since there is no means by which the available can be explained in terms of the occurrent; the meaningful world of human experience must always elude such a programme. Heidegger's work generates explicit difficulties for classical artificial intelligence, since the procedural representation of human abilities in computer systems is a direct operational expression of the Cartesian reduction of embodied skill to the tacit possession of detached theory. The difficulties faced by the organizational use of information systems

39

designed on Cartesian lines are more subtle, but no less real. The 'information' which circulates in an organization is embedded within a complex context of concerned activity; and the abstraction of 'data objects' into a detached theory is, for Heidegger, to lose the important element of human concern.

The status of these conclusions will be pursued further in Section 3. However, at this point it is worth noting that Heidegger's account, while it undercuts Cartesian foundationalism (a building-block theory of knowledge), is offering a foundational narrative of a different sort — a revelation of the truth which the Western philosophical tradition has obscured. It is also worth noting, in preparation for a consideration of a Heideggerian philosophy of information systems design, that Heidegger's privileging of everyday unreflective activity has its own pathologies. From a Cartesian standpoint he appears wilfully anti-intellectual, elevating the mundane and romanticizing a simpler past; the stance, as has been immoderately remarked, of a stupefied peasant — an attitude which breeds as many dangers as that of excessive intellectual detachment.

2.3   A New Foundation for Design

From the standpoint of Heidegger's hermeneutics, traditional representationalist information systems developments appear radically misconceived; an attempt to force computer support for human activities into a mould which distorts human experience. It is no surprise, from this perspective, that information systems, as a discipline, has an history of user alienation, expensive failures and unfulfilled promises to reproduce and augment human intelligence. Also, it is no surprise that a philosophical reorientation should seem to promise the transformation of, and advances in, information systems design:

> "All new technologies develop within the background of a tacit understanding of human nature and human work ... We encounter the deep questions of design when we recognize that in designing tools we are designing ways of being. By confronting these questions directly, we can develop a new background for understanding computer technology — one that can lead to important advances in the design and use of computer systems." (Winograd & Flores 1986: xi)

Winograd & Flores put the Heideggerian 'new background' to work in CSCW, producing a system (The Coordinator) to mediate human communication with information technology. The focus for design is on the pattern of communication between participants in recurrent situations rather than any canonical reduction and representation of what is being communicated. The specific 'conversational structure' supported by their system is inspired by Searle's (1969) speech act theory (somewhat strangely, since Searle's position on intentionality is the antithesis of Heidegger's). Their overall approach is broadly that of ethnomethodology — see, for example, Heritage (1984), investigating the conversational structures and information flows which mediate the construction and maintenance of organizational reality. Winograd & Flores use the notion of recurrent patterns of communication to subsume traditional Cartesian applications under their scheme as examples of 'systematic domains', in which human communication has been sedimented into precise forms (such as account sheets and formatted records).

Ehn (1988: Part IV) treats the 'toolness' of computer artefacts more literally. In one of a series of experiments in the democratic design of computer systems to support working life, he adapted Heidegger's philosophy and Winograd & Flores' outline design approach into a practical method for preserving craft skills in a computerized context. The motivations for preserving a craft ideal were diverse, ranging from a concern for democracy and individuality to an æsthetic attachment to craft activity (a trait also found in Heidegger). A key requirement of his methodology was that it ensured that the computer-based systems produced should be under the control of the skilled worker, who could continue to work within a tradition, preserving the master–apprentice system. The strong Heideggerian link emerges in Ehn's view of the priority of practical engagement:

> "... there are two aspects of craftsmanship that I think should remain as cornerstones to our design ideal. The first one is the priority of practical understanding in design and use of computer artefacts, as opposed to just relying on detached theoretical reflection. No matter how technically complex a computer artefact is, it is possible and desirable to anchor design and use in practical understanding ... The second cornerstone I want to maintain is the design ideal of computer artefacts as tools augmenting skills rather than replacing them." (Ehn 1988: 373)

Ehn is committed to a strong position on the nature of, and possibilities for, information technology even within an Heideggerian framework. The principal opportunity for the exploitation of information technology is seen as in a support role for 'practical understanding', as part of the flow of unreflective activity. However, this neglects the kind of support which an information system might provide in the state of detached reflection which accompanies the breakdown of unreflective activity; support for which a Cartesian model might, in the absence of further argument, seem appropriate.

Ehn's position is not simply Heideggerian, he works within a strong political tradition which brings a blend of Western Marxism and Scandinavian democratic socialism to the workplace. From such a political position, it is obvious that Heideggerian nostalgia is not an adequate motivation for a position on design:

> "... a simple return to traditional values is no solution to the problems of modern purposive rational society, and that only approaches that explicitly deal with their own values, and use them as a basis for change of technology and organizations, can be a challenge to modern society. My point is that the tool perspective is such a humanistic value rational design principle." (Ehn 1988: 407)

The problem for Ehn is that he seems to accept Heidegger's phenomenology in its own terms and use it as a key element in the politics of design. The tool perspective is only persuasive as a 'humanistic value rational design principle' (Weber's concept of the 'wertrational') if one has a prior commitment to Heidegger's outlook on technology and modernity. To make it generally persuasive one would have to examine the full range of political influences on, and consequences of Heideggerian philosophy. Ehn's reliance on the critical force of the tool perspective sits uncomfortably with his enthusiasm for Habermas (Ehn 1988: Part I), who regards Heidegger's thought as antithetical to an emancipatory politics (see Section 3.2 below).

These problems are multiplied when it is seen that the tool perspective, like any other design approach, has its own pathological defects. These are apt to be overlooked in the current climate of enthusiasm for user friendliness and intuitively accessible systems. Whilst these are important design aims, a concentrated focus on the ease with which computer systems support everyday activities can lead to an unquestioning attitude towards the wider social and political structures which surround these activities — the tool perspective, like Heidegger's general philosophical position, has only weakly critical force. An interesting case study is provided by Laurel (1990). In a large, and admirably creative, work on computer interface design, the deeper social purposes and needs which drive the production of computer packages get scant mention. It is no defence to characterize such work as 'purely' concerned with matters of low-level ease of use, one cannot disengage a study from its social setting so easily. An enthusiastic pursuit of novel approaches to accommodating user psychology, the analysis of task structures, etc. leads to a form of temporary blindness: one forgets that these smoothly-designed packages will be used by real people, doing real jobs against a social and political background which embodies an unequal distribution of power and influence. From a Cartesian standpoint, in which knowledge is the key to empowerment and progress, a limited concern with supporting unreflective activity is apt to appear trivial; and the suspicion grows that the tool perspective, unless balanced by a strong political awareness, plays into the hands of consumerism.

3 Essentialism vs. Critical Encounter

The conflict between Cartesian and Heideggerian design philosophies cannot profitably be pursued for long from within the self-understandings of the two positions. This section attempts to enlarge the context in which this conflict is conducted by viewing both positions in their historical, cultural context and emphasizing the value of a pluralistic framework for discussion. Putting aside the urge to find a fixed foundation for design yields a different conception of a design framework, one in which a broad argumentative process allows different valuations to play their part in design.

3.1 Representation and Bureaucratized Knowledge

The self-understanding of Cartesian representationalism has achieved a notoriety in recent years as the 'grand narrative of the enlightenment' (Lyotard 1984): a conception of enquiry in which man, by exercising the faculty of reason, progressively attains truth about an objective, independent world. Once this grand narrative is dislodged from its central position as the touchstone of all enquiry, and can be seen as simply a local narrative which legitimates one part of Western culture, it is possible to portray it in quite different terms. One portrayal, of considerable interest when considering the design of information systems, is as the culture of organized bureaucracy elaborated by Weber — see Weber (1948), especially Chapter 7, also Brubaker (1984); for a perspective from historical anthropology see Goody (1986). The intimate connections between bureaucracy and technology are examined by Gouldner (1976).

For Weber, 'bureaucracy' is a general term used to cover a variety of the rationalized processes which have come to govern the Western way of life; and the characteristics of bureaucracy are general and abstract, applicable not only to organized administration, but also — in varying degrees, and amongst others — to science, education and scholarship. Central to Weber's analysis of bureaucracy is the distribution of regularized tasks amongst officials deemed competent, on the basis of qualification, to discharge those tasks. Officials are ranked in an hierarchical structure of authority, occupying and discharging their roles as a vocation for which they have undergone lengthy training, ensuring an impersonal and objective stance. A bureaucracy is based upon the maintenance and management of a corpus of documents (files) by trained officials obeying exhaustive rules; all matters and persons dealt with by the bureaucracy are recorded and treated regularly. A key part of Weber's analysis is the promotion of a culture of objectivity reinforced by education:

> "... bureaucracy promotes a 'rationalist' way of life ... the bureaucratization of all domination very strongly furthers the development of 'rational matter-of-factness' and the personality type of the professional expert ... institutions of higher learning are dominated and influenced by the need for the kind of 'education' that produces a system of special examinations and the trained expertness that is increasingly indispensable for modern bureaucracy." (Weber 1948: 240)

This perspective enables us to make headway with certain aspects of the clash between the Cartesian and Heideggerian world-views. The pathological failings of Cartesianism (as a philosophy or foundation for design) occur at the points where an account of everyday experience is required; which is precisely what the 'culture of bureaucracy' view would predict, since the intuitive, the personal and the domestic are strictly segregated from the discharge of an official role. The structure of the knowledge required to discharge an official role (which includes that of the disciplined scientist or engineer) need have little in common with the structure of knowledge required for everyday reasoning or personal interaction.

Winograd & Flores highlight four characteristics of human experience which are the core of the opposition between Cartesianism and their Heideggerian stance:

> "Our implicit beliefs and assumptions cannot all be made explicit ... Practical understanding is more fundamental than detached theoretical understanding ... We do not relate to things primarily through having representations of them ... Meaning is fundamentally social and cannot be reduced to the meaning-giving activity of individual subjects." (Winograd & Flores 1986: 32–3)

All of these principles apply plausibly to everyday activity; Dreyfus (1993) patiently collects specific instances which reinforce this view. However, bureaucratic contexts are structured precisely to invert these principles, and to provide a cultural goal — the achievement of 'the view from nowhere' (Nagel 1986) — for doing so. The learning of explicit codes and rules constitutes one way of ensuring that officials have explicit belief systems; detached theoretical understanding is a means of nullifying the effects of individual emotion and instinct; explicit representation in 'the files' is the only means by which matters and persons can be addressed; and the disciplined standardization of meaning (through dictionaries, etc.) ensures that meaning-giving can be an isolated, individual activity (with uniform results). It may still be argued that everyday activity and its characteristics are 'more fundamental'; but the question remains whether an Heideggerian approach can provide comprehensive means of theorizing the activities which are performed in organized bureaucracies.

A more comprehensive theoretical approach to this question is provided by Habermas' (1987b) opposition between 'system' and 'lifeworld'. Habermas suggests a means of diagnosing the social condition of modernity based on a balance between a systemic 'sphere' (concerned with the production of the material conditions of life) and a symbolic 'sphere' (concerned with the reproduction of culture, values and beliefs). Both contexts undeniably have important roles, but they have different imperatives and logics. This tension between imperatives generates one of the major dilemmas of modernity: what balance between system and life-world should we choose? A systemic, controlled way of life brings material benefit and control over nature; but at the cost of eroding traditional values and personal relationships. What logic we choose to apply and what values we choose to affirm in any particular social venture, say in the design of a computerized system of working, is a moral and political question.

The dispute over the 'foundations for design' now takes on a far more problematic character; since an attack on Cartesianism cannot be sustained by appeals to phenomenological accounts of the structure of everyday experience. The dispute is transformed into a broader one about the moral and political probity of a disciplinary culture. Specifically, for information systems design the issue is that what looked like a debate about the most promising way to construct usable information systems may be seen to depend on the outcome of a debate about the social role played by formalized information systems, and which of those roles are, morally, worth pursuing. A Weberian analysis highlights their role in promoting and maintaining a culture of objectivity and discipline in organizations and society, a culture for which Cartesianism is the official philosophy. At best, this philosophy should only be abandoned selectively in the light of our best judgement about the moral and political results of basing our designs on it. As Habermas — no ally of Cartesianism — shows, the systemic imperatives of production and control cannot simply be ignored; rather, they should be understood and controlled.

3.2 Heidegger's Essentialism

Heidegger's self-understanding is more difficult to analyse than that of the Cartesian, since there are deep contradictions within his work — see Rorty (1991: 27). In some respects his work may be seen as thoroughly anti-foundational, one of the precursors of post-modernism; in others he may be seen as an arch essentialist, offering a meta-narrative of all human understanding. For the purposes of this chapter, what is required is some insight into the extent to which Heidegger's essentialism has affected the debate on the foundations of information systems design, and the distortions to which this has given rise.

The anti-foundational aspect of Heidegger's thought, a key factor in dislodging the grand narrative of the enlightenment from its central position in the intellectual life of the West, is the demonstration that we need not see experience as divided, inevitably, into knowing subject and known object. By constructing a consistent terminology for discussing experience which avoided traditional distinctions, he was able to show that much of what had passed as the necessary conditions of knowledge could be seen as simply a cultural feature, an historical accident. From this demonstration a more general lesson about plurality could be learned:

> "... he would like to recapture a sense of contingency, of the fragility and riskiness of any human project — a sense which the onto-theological tradition has made it hard to attain. For that tradition tends to identify the contingent with the merely apparent." (Rorty 1991: 34)

When this aspect of Heidegger's thought is brought to the fore, it seems difficult to speak of having reached 'the truth of being' or a 'new foundation for design', since any candidate to receive such an accolade may be seen as just one more historical accident, another way of speaking. However, Heidegger can also support a radically different reading, one which assures us that we have reached some sort of essence or foundation from which we can work safely.

Heidegger's work is characterized by a nostalgia for a lost time before the philosophical tradition covered up the truth of being; a lost time which he identified with pre-Socratic Greece, and one which he thought he could be instrumental in recovering. When this aspect of his work is attended to, we can easily be seduced into thinking that he can lead us to an authentic understanding which will shake off the problems associated with traditional ways of thought. This is largely the basis of the trope used by Winograd & Flores (see Section 2.3

45

above) in announcing their reorientation in design. Rorty trenchantly points out what is wrong with a nostalgic belief in a redemptive force which will undercut the errors of accepted wisdom:

> "... is it in fact the case that we in the twentieth century are less able to question common sense than the Greeks were? Offhand, one can think of a lot of reasons why we might be more able to do so: we are constantly reminded of cultural diversity, constantly witnessing attempts at novelty in the arts, more and more aware of the possibility of scientific and political revolutions ..." (Rorty 1991: 47)

From the enlarged perspective of modernity, progress is not a matter of insights into universal, underlying simplicities; it is a more complex matter of attending to the babble of conflicting voices which make up our culture and adding another in the best way we can. In this light, a sedimented 'design philosophy' will be at best a temporary reflection of an historically-specific cultural moment, and not a permanent achievement.

A further dimension may be added to this discussion by the current controversy over Heidegger's political associations — see, for example, Ott (1994) — and their relationship to his philosophical position. Habermas (1987a: ch.6) and Bernstein (1991: ch.4) have both argued that Heidegger's drift into Nazism was facilitated by a persistent characteristic of his philosophical thought: that of 'abstraction by essentialization'. Heidegger's attachment to true, meditative thinking involved a mode of reasoning in which the history of being was seen as an essence underlying the mere accidents of historical events. This devaluation of real, present suffering in favour of contemplating the underlying movement of history represents a dangerous simplification of political and moral problems. The search for underlying simplicity — and worse, the conviction that one has found it — distracts from the world of everyday events where moral and political conflicts are enacted. A search for the essence of computer artefacts is also perilously close to Heidegger's later search for the 'essence of technology', and an abstracted, simplified moral stance on the place of technology in the life of the West. Heidegger's infamous elision of mechanized agriculture and death camps (Bernstein 1991: 130) might, with some justice, be paralleled by the observation that, considered from a tool perspective, head-up displays for military aircraft are 'equivalent' to digital prosthetics for the disabled. There is no single framework within which a technology may adequately be judged; the fit of a technology with some pre-defined context of action is only a fragment of an highly contingent context of judgement. Who uses a technology, and with what particular results, is at least as important as any remote theoretical perspective.

3.3 The Morality and Politics of Design

The history of computer science has been marked by many 'landmark' designs which have engaged the imagination of those working in the field and have set research agendas: this has occurred in the field of hardware (e.g. the architecture of the Atlas computer), programming languages (e.g. the specification of Algol60) and software packages (e.g. Sketchpad, Visicalc). Two prophetic designs which helped set the agenda for modern workstation technology were Bush's (1945) 'Memex' blueprint and Engelbart's (1963) early oN-Line System (NLS) experiment. It is instructive to pursue the basis of the appeal which these designs had, because it reveals the way in which a single design idea can manifest Cartesian and Heideggerian components; and the way in which their persuasiveness is based on a broader cultural appeal.

Bush's 'Memex' was a purely conceptual design which pre-figured many later developments: desktop computing, databases and hypermedia. It was driven by the idea of gathering up all human knowledge and making it available on a desktop to anyone with a use for it; Bush envisaged that the work of historical research, for example, would be transformed:

> "The historian, with a vast chronological account of people, parallels it with a skip trail which stops only at the salient items, and can follow at any time, contemporary trails which lead him all over civilization at a particular epoch. There is a new profession of trail blazers, those who find delight in the task of establishing useful trails through the enormous mass of the common record." As cited by Kling & Dunlop (1991)

This dream is at once Cartesian and Heideggerian: it embodies a representationalist view of accumulated knowledge (only in a rationalist framework does it make sense to speak of the gathering up of all knowledge); and a set of ready-to-hand tools for surveying that mass, supporting the concerned activity of the user. It must also be said that it reads rather oddly, to a contemporary eye, as a description of the activity of an historian. More pertinently, the dream is infected with the scientism endemic to Western culture in the early post-war years, and with a similarly dated form of pioneering individualism. Its ultimate appeal is not that of the intuitive truth of any particular design philosophy, but that it taps a complex set of cultural currents. In a different cultural milieu the entire project would make no sense. The post-modern mistrust of the idea of the unambiguous text has eroded interest in the 'common record' in intellectual circles, although the success of multimedia encyclopedias testifies to its survival in popular culture. Similarly, Bush's dream is untroubled by a point which the Frankfurt School and Foucault have, in their different ways, made a commonplace: that the supposedly neutral 'common record' is the product of an exercise of power which marks it indelibly.

Engelbart's design, inspired by Bush, was the practical precursor of the modern workstation; his emphasis was on the production of a system to augment the human intellect:

> "By 'augmenting the human intellect' we mean increasing the capability of a man to approach a complex problem situation, gain comprehension to suit his particular needs, and to derive solutions to his problems ... We

refer to a way of life in an integrated domain where hunches, cut-and-try, intangibles, and 'human feel for the situation' usefully coexist with powerful concepts, streamlined terminology and notation, sophisticated methods and high-powered electronic aids." As cited by Kling & Dunlop (1991)

The remarks made above concerning Bush's blueprint still apply in this case; but novel issues emerge from considering Engelbart's practical programme and its more recent outcomes. Bush and Engelbart both describe their systems as aids for a range of 'professional experts': lawyers, scientists, diplomats, historians. However, as Kling & Dunlop (1991: 19) point out, neither Engelbart's system, nor recent workstations have fulfilled this promise; their primary use remains the support of prosaic tasks such as editing memos or preparing accounts. Kling & Dunlop diagnose this failure as resulting from a lack of appreciation of the social setting of the tasks in question. In an under-socialized frame of reference it might appear that information systems might radically transform the performance of key social roles; amidst a complex social reality, the outcome is somewhat different. The vision which inspires a designer need not be the determinant of the final use of the artefact designed.

Bush and Engelbart were motivated by a central tenet of the Enlightenment dream: that knowledge empowers. Knowledge was conceived as an almost palpable social good which could be distributed by computer systems, thus making information technology an agent of social progress. As Winograd & Flores (1986: 136) argue, to adopt the tool perspective means giving up these rationalist pretensions for information systems; but they have another vision of empowerment to replace the one which has been lost. Information systems designed from the tool perspective will work with people rather than against them, and a more humane working life will result. However, the discussion above places into question whether this constitutes a convincing route to social progress. Securing the social benefits which might accrue from a technology is unlikely to be the result of applying a simple formula.

4 Conclusion

The argument of this chapter has circled around a single, central question: what should we expect a design philosophy to be and do? The answer that is given to this question depends crucially on the status which is accorded to philosophy. On the one hand philosophy might be given its traditional high valuation as an analytic and investigative activity which yields fundamental insights into the structure of the world and the nature of human existence. In this case it will appear reasonable to use a philosophy as a central pillar in the design of information systems, deriving methodologies and system paradigms. This chapter has argued that, at least in the case of the two prime candidates for a 'first philosophy' of information systems, this attitude has led to unacceptable anomalies and omissions. An alternative attitude, which recognizes that philosophy is not a pre-eminently active force in the practical world (Williams 1985: 93–5) values philosophy as a discursive activity; one which gives us reflections of related sets of beliefs and attitudes from practical life, but does not govern them. Seen in this light, the most that might be sought from a design philosophy is an assembly of tentative hints and models to be placed in the train of argument which is the design activity (Rittel 1984); a train of argument which demands the full range of our critical, social and technical awareness.

Thoughts Towards a Framework for Critical Practice

Anne Moggridge

This chapter explores an alternative understanding of the nature and generation of knowledge which draws upon research in the areas of collaborative inquiry and women's experience of knowing. It includes an account of the author's experience of participating in the Philosophical and Logical Aspects of Information Systems symposium and suggests links with current work in human-centred systems development and critical systems thinking.

1 Introduction

In developing my contribution to the symposium for this book, I have chosen a form and style which reflects my concerns more personally than the original position paper. I have considered and discarded the 'obvious' approach of expanding upon the academic content of the paper and chosen instead to include the story of my preparing for, participating in and reflecting upon the symposium. In this way I hope to present an account which is faithful both to my intellectual understanding and also to my personal experience.

I approached the symposium with some trepidation for two reasons. Firstly, I am concerned, both intellectually and personally, that information systems research and practice undervalues people's experience and subjective knowledge in its preoccupations with philosophy, technology and logic. Secondly, I believe that my position reflects values which are often perceived as 'female' and inferior. The prospects of raising these issues in a predominantly male arena was decidedly daunting. I experience most conferences as revolving around a defined and dominant framework of ideas within which people position themselves and argue. I am aware that my own ideas do not fit easily into the established information systems discourse and I did not expect my paper to sit comfortably with others presented at the symposium. My task was not to criticize the stance of others but to attempt to find a way of bringing my own ideas in.

My intellectual stance draws upon work in the areas of information systems, critical systems and collaborative inquiry. In recent years it has also been shaped by the work of a number of feminist academics. My personal commitment is to ground this understanding by developing and practising ways of working with people which value personal and experiential forms of learning and knowledge. I see some prospects of these different forms of knowledge being applied together in collaborative approaches to systems work that closely match the principles of human-centred systems development suggested by Pain et al. (1993). I believe that they are also important to our understanding of critical practice generally. Jackson (1991) describes critical systems thinking in terms of its commitment to demonstrating critical and social awareness, and to human emancipation in both theory and practice. It is my interest in understanding how the key ideas of critical systems could be applied in practice, that inspired the title chosen and used for the first time at the Philosophical and Logical Aspects of Information Systems symposium.

The paper produced for the symposium itself was a short position paper which outlined three strands considered relevant to the development of a framework to guide critical and aware practice. The paper is reproduced in its original form below. Rather than expand upon the content of the paper by giving each strand equal time in the supporting talk, I chose to concentrate on the strand which I perceive to be most lacking in the current debate in general and specifically in discussion of the gap between critical systems theory and practice. I wanted to try and make some of my concerns and experiences as a woman accessible to a wider group of symposium participants than the one other female present. I attempted to do this by talking on the theme of 'women's ways of knowing'. The content of my symposium talk is covered in the section following the paper. To illustrate my concern to share, reflect upon and learn from personal experience, I then describe and try to make sense of my experience of preparing the paper, presenting the talk and reflecting upon the outcomes. Finally, I conclude with some personal observations and thoughts for the future.

2   The Position Paper

This section contains the position paper I produced for the symposium; it is unchanged except that detailed references now appear later.

THOUGHTS TOWARDS A FRAMEWORK FOR CRITICAL PRACTICE
Introduction
This paper outlines some important themes that I believe should be given more prominence in debate within the systems community. The themes I refer to are all 'people-centred' and reflect my own preference for reading about, writing about and discussing issues that can readily be connected to people's experience of life. Three main sources of ideas, rarely included on the systems agenda, inform my position. These are outlined below and representative references are cited. No attempt is made to associate any of the themes with established philosophical traditions.

1. Collaborative Inquiry

    I use the term collaborative inquiry here to refer to a collection of approaches to understanding and improving our ways of working with others; they are characterized by a commitment to undertake research *with* and *for*, rather than *on* people. Much has been written about action research in relation to the development and use of systems methodologies yet accounts of this research often imply that ultimately it is primarily the methodology that is being researched; the problem situations encountered are merely useful vehicles for furthering this research. More collaborative approaches to research in action should result in richer descriptions of the conduct and outcomes of research from the perspectives of others involved who do not have a vested interest in the methodology. Approaches to collaborative inquiry and examples of their use are well documented by Reason & Rowan (1981), Reason (1988) and most recently Denzin & Lincoln (1994).

2. Feminism

    The writings and experiences of women are too often excluded from the debate. Women's ways of knowing, communicating, researching and working with others are explored by, for example, Goldberger et al. (1987), Marshall (1993) and Reinharz (1992) respectively. I believe that both soft systems and critical systems thinking and practice will continue to be impoverished (and, to me, oppressive) if they remain reluctant to explore the male dominance of their broader academic community. The gendered nature of academic debate in general is discussed at length by Collinson & Hearn (1994); the work of Taket & White (1993) highlights the gendered nature of much of the systems discourse.

3. Human-centred systems development

    Recent publications in the sociology of science and the area of human-centred systems development re-examine political aspects of the systems development process. Bloomfield & Best (1992), for example, shows how Information Technology consultants exercise and maintain power in systems development through the process of problem definition. Green et al. (1993) explores the impact of gender relations on computer systems design from a variety of perspectives. In particular both these sources challenge the received wisdom of the straightforward division between 'the social' and 'the technical', whether as requirements or as aspects of the development process. It is argued that these divisions can and should be negotiated yet all too often they are taken as given, given as defined by the dominant community in general and systems developers in particular.

Summary

Hence I would like to see more concern in our discussions and writing for ways in which we can work with other people to respect and value difference, yet reduce inequality. Revisioning definitions of skill is one important aspect: the division between social and technical concerns can be negotiated; so-called 'social' skills can be valued at least as highly as technical skills; the view of 'communication' skills which places most emphasis on those skills that enable individuals to persuade others to share their views can be broadened to one which encompasses other attention skills necessary to facilitate mutual learning. In theories too we can move from the established view of the isolated individual seeking to understand and control his world and work to encompass a more feminine understanding of sense-making as a less competitive and more collaborative endeavour. The picture is incomplete but I believe all these ideas have potential as important components of a developing framework to guide critical practice.

3   The Talk

This section covers my symposium talk. The description of the talk is taken from the notes I had prepared beforehand and is, as far as possible, a faithful account of what was said.

The position paper I have produced for this symposium outlines three intertwined strands which I believe are important in life and work in information systems. It is not possible to do justice to each strand in the time available so I have chosen to expand upon one and raise some issues relevant to knowing and information systems which are otherwise unlikely to find space on the agenda for debate at this symposium. I have, perhaps unwisely, entitled this strand 'Feminism' and I recognize that this may already have sounded alarm bells for some participants. How to say what I want to say has been the subject of considerable thought and some agonizing on my part. I have chosen to expand upon the work of Nancy Goldberger et al. for two reasons: firstly because its subject matter concerns perspectives on reality and processes of acquiring knowledge and hence is appropriate for a symposium with a particular concern for philosophy and secondly because it is grounded in women's experiences of coming to know and contains little reference to the stereotypical male/female differences that are often perceived as anti-men when presented by a woman. I am not convinced that polarized debates about the generality or form of differences between men and women do anything more than reinforce established positions. Nevertheless, I speak as a woman who identifies strongly and personally with this work.

The work of Goldberger et al. is based on interview data gained from women of a variety of ages, from a variety of ethnic backgrounds and with a range of experience of education. It is argued that in cultures such as our own where rationality and objectivity are highly valued relative to the emotional, the intuitive and the personally felt, it is difficult for many women to develop the sense of worth and confidence necessary to make a contribution. When women spoke of their own epistemologies they made frequent references to the metaphor of 'gaining a voice', of speaking and listening rather than seeing and believing. Drawing on Perry's framework for charting people's epistemological development, Goldberger et al. identify five epistemological positions which were represented by varying proportions of the women they interviewed. Like Perry's stages, each one in some ways 'includes and transcends' earlier ones but there is neither a one way track nor a prescribed route through the positions; rather they are positions into which women can grow or retreat at various stages of their lives. I shall describe each of the five positions then I shall explain what sense they make to me.

Unspeakable knowledge: Silence. *Women in this category adopted silence as a survival strategy perceiving themselves as passive, reactive to and dependent upon external figures and authority. Their sense of self is grounded in everyday action and not expressible in words. Knowledge is something created and owned by others which they feel incapable of connecting with.*

Received knowledge: Learning through listening to others. *Here women find them-selves capable of receiving but not creating knowledge. They believe knowledge has some tangible existence which they may be able to access by listening carefully. In this way their listening skills may become highly developed but the sources of the knowledge they acquire are always external, their own experiences have no comparable value.*

Subjective knowledge: The inner voice. *By contrast, women in this position value inner knowing most highly, trusting what 'feels right' and becoming increasingly suspicious of external authorities. Logic and detached analysis may endanger the capacity for feeling and may be avoided altogether. Women experience themselves not as "constructors of knowledge but as conduits through which truth emerges" (Goldberger et al. 1987: 212). Goldberger et al. believe that this experience is important for women's development of a sense of identity. They come to rely on their personal and intuitive knowing as an open yet strong basis for authentic interaction with others.*

Procedural knowledge: The voice of reason. *Only women who had recently studied at or worked in Higher Education were identified with this position. Here concern is with developing and being able to evaluate and articulate justifications for what is known. The methods and techniques of science and frameworks for critical thinking attain high status as mechanisms for challenging and validating what is thought to be true. It is rare for such women to lose all sense of the subjective however, rather their sense of interpretations is relative, some are more justifiable than others. The value attached to the different criteria for trusting claims to know can shift with time. Hence some women in this category had become increasingly uneasy with institutionally defined 'right' ways to learn and think and begun to listen again to their inner voice.*

Constructed knowledge: Integrating the voices. *Transition to this stage involves redeveloping the more personal sense of self and beginning to integrate inner and external voices to give importance again to what is intuitively felt as well as what is authoritatively defined in formal education. Integration and balance become key themes in women's thoughts, feelings and actions as they seek to remain sensitive and open to the voices of others yet be true to themselves.*

From their research, Goldberger et al. conclude that most women are drawn towards the kind of knowledge that is connected to their own experience and are less attracted by abstract concepts which have no bearing on their being in the world. They go on to discuss the broader implications of their work for human development, growth and change. Rather than summarize the authors' conclusions, I will now say a little about the sense this model makes to me and how it is connected to my own experience before returning to the conclusion of my paper.

Coming to know: A personal view. *Having spent most of my life engaged in formal education it is perhaps unsurprising that I have been most preoccupied with acquiring and disseminating that form of knowing which Goldberger et al. name procedural knowledge. I do not recall prolonged periods of silence yet this is a position into which I still occasionally retreat when the voice of authority is feeling too overbearing. Like most of us I did my share of learning through listening to others at school in particular and thought little about my own experience. Continuing in education meant an almost seamless transition from learning by listening to learning to reason, analyse,* *evaluate and justify. Since joining a research group at Bath University whose focus is approaches to collaborative inquiry I have learnt to understand, develop and value that part of knowing that is grounded rather than abstract, felt rather than taught and to listen carefully to that inner voice that I suspect I paid scant regard to in my earlier years. The need to integrate the voices in my work was somehow felt but unarticulated and unaddressable. Now I seek to balance the two and through that find ways of working and researching which are consistent with my values as a woman and an academic. As Goldberger et al. (1987: 218) observe this is often a difficult place to be and it is with a balance of determination and trepidation that I have spoken from this place today.*

In future work I hope to make further progress in demonstrating the importance of valuing both intellectual and personal understandings of the nature and origins of knowledge for developing more human-centred approaches to research and practice in information systems. In my paper I conclude that such development will need to embrace further insights into the nature of authentic participation, currently being explored through collaborative inquiry in other fields, if we are to achieve the aims of critical systems thinking in practice.

4 Preparing, Speaking and Reflecting

This section describes my experience of preparing for, participating in and reflecting upon my symposium session.

4.1 Preparing the Paper

This phase covered several months and should perhaps more representatively have been entitled 'contemplating the symposium'. The symposium title had been fixed, it was to be Philosophical and Logical Aspects of Information Systems. That part of me that lets the extremes of the inner voice dominate made it quite clear that here was an arena for competitive intellectual debate in which I could not engage and in which my ideas would, at best, be seen as lacking the necessary logic or rigour or possibly slightly frivolous, at worst they would be shouted down. In their analysis of men and masculinities Collinson & Hearn (1994: 3) add weight to this view that "conferences are all the more likely to become the site for the creation and elaboration of masculine intellectual pecking orders and adversarial discourses where the majority of participants are men."

I had the choice between falling back on the voice of reason and living with a sense of fraudulence, as Goldberger et al. observed in some women who now felt that the voice of reason that they had acquired was not necessarily their own, or finding a way of getting over the barrier that was stopping me from knowing what I needed to write. I discussed my dilemma with fellow researchers and made progress by adopting the suggestion that I engage in a free fall writing exercise triggered by the title "All systems conferences are a waste of time because ..." and quickly reminded myself that this was not always the case. I decided that, logical or not, I would write what I thought was important and keep open the possibility that I might enjoy myself at the symposium. Needless to say, I still left writing the paper until the last minute.* Even having committed to paper, I delayed the decision on what to say on the day until a couple of days before the symposium, by which time I could confirm that one other woman would be attending and that the symposium streams were organized in such a way that I could count on one or two friends in the audience. I reread Goldberger et al. and it 'felt right'.

4.2   My Symposium Session

My talk was received in silence but encouraged by occasional nods of understanding or agreement which I took comfort and maybe strength from. I finished in time to allow the full ten minutes of questions. Regrettably the session was not taped, there is no external record of the dialogue that followed so the detail and interpretations will remain distributed across the memories of those present. My own recollections and interpretations are summarized below.

Despite my attempts to frame the talk in a manner which would discourage discussion along these lines, the first 'question' from the audience was a strongly expressed opinion about the futility of attempting to make general statements about differences between men and women. I offered a brief 'defence' along the lines that I had been talking about some women's experience of knowledge with which I identified strongly, but the battle lines were drawn and exceptional women were being cited as examples. The other participants took over at this point, explaining to each other what I was getting at, demonstrating how well each understood the issues and cutting me out of the discussion altogether — male academics in action, intending perhaps to help the weaker sex and speaking for her to each other. I seemed to be watching. Familiar patterns of speaking and silence were back and as the session broke for coffee it began to dawn on many of us that we had each played a decidedly gendered role in the debate.

The debate continued in corners of the symposium for the rest of the day and included a peace-making session between myself and the first questioner, not a meeting of the minds exactly but a better understanding of each other's history and respect for each other's concerns. I seemed to have generated more interest than I had expected, I am less confident that this was matched by understanding.

5   Conclusion

Reflecting on this whole episode now, I offer some brief, personal conclusions and leave readers to draw others for themselves.

My intention in writing and speaking as I did was to create a space to explore an alternative understanding of the nature and generation of knowledge. Such an understanding might enable us to respect other people's truths and work together in a less competitive and more appreciative way. However, it is difficult to raise new questions that are relevant to life as well as intellectual exercise without forcing or making it easy for people to retreat to entrenched positions. I hope that each of us learnt a little from the experience, nevertheless.

---

*The author commented that "The editors may wish to observe at this point that I have done the same with this chapter!" at this point.

In participating in the symposium I also set out to challenge my own assumptions and patterns. Yet there is a sense in which the way I describe and interpret the preparation and presentation of my ideas to the symposium participants comes full circle leaving me more experienced but little wiser about how to frame my concerns so that they can be integrated with other (dominant) frameworks already well established in our area.

I have chosen the form of this chapter to reflect my intent and my values: it is both personal and academic, felt and thought, acted out and reflected upon. It is an attempt to recover the space to speak that I lost for a while at the symposium and to restate my sense of some important issues for us all.

Acknowledgements

I would like to thank friends and colleagues at Bristol and Bath for encouraging me to participate in the symposium and for commenting on this chapter and Norma Romm for being there.

Language and Meaning

Introduction

Stephen K. Probert

The four chapters in this section are united by concerns with the problems of the concepts of data, information and meaning. Gilligan, Mingers and Gregory attempt to provide greater conceptual clarification of these concepts and some of their surrounding issues, whilst Kamm prefers to explore the implications of viewing information (and information systems) through a particular (and indeed a pervasive) socio-philosophical perspective — that of the 'organicist' view of information.

Gilligan's initial considerations concerning the concepts of data and information lead him to uncover two different (and contradictory) accounts — based on two different traditions in information systems thinking. He goes on to briefly explore a further three accounts (again from different traditions). Following Wittgenstein, he argues that the proponents of the accounts are in fact operating within different 'language games'. He then poses a number of probing questions concerning how it is that we are ordinarily able to operate with the concepts of data and information in the world. After some discussion, he concludes that: "Unless we can distinguish in the world data and information then the way in which we use these words is appropriate only to their use in our language games and not to our understanding of what is in the world." (p.68). He traces the connection between information and change, and argues that the informational outputs of information systems inform and (consequently) change the activities of their recipients. If, as Gilligan argues, the concept of change is central to developing an understanding of the concept of information, then one would think that it might be central to current debates in information systems — at a conceptual level at any rate. However, Gilligan concludes that: "Despite emerging new technologies, we do not yet have a systems view which accommodates and understands change as the essential activity of information systems." (p.71). Thus, Gilligan opens up an issue which has practical implications for information systems designers, i.e. the need to better understand the nature of the link between information and action if better information systems are to be created.

Mingers notes that three concepts are often discussed in a confused manner: data, information and meaning. His aim is: "… to develop theories concerning the nature of information and meaning, and the relations between the two." (p.74). He then explores a number of theories of information — particularly those that attempt to explain the apparent semantic concept of information (rather than those which focus attention on the relevant syntactic structures). However, he finds that the (extant) theories he explores are wanting — for a variety of reasons. As a result, he is drawn to Dretske's theory (of knowledge based on information). To support his case he outlines what he considers to be the inter-subjective nature of language; in his view language is: "... neither independent of the mind (objective) nor dependent purely on an individual (subjective), but based on prior consensus and agreement." (p.77). If this is so, then (Mingers argues) information will be that which makes a difference to its recipients — where those recipients share a 'consensual domain' of a (common) language. To buttress these arguments, inspiration is sought from Habermas's arguments concerning 'communicative theory and social action', which is primarily used to support the view that: "Linguistic acts are therefore, at base, always practical actions concerned to bring about particular effects." (p.78). Mingers argues that such linguistic acts must conform to certain pre-requisite conditions under which successful communication can take place. Such a view allows Mingers to 'drive a wedge' between information and meaning such that: "Information, carried by signs, is an objective feature of the world... Meaning, however, is generated from information by receivers and can be either inter-subjective or subjective." (p.80) This means that information is essentially 'out there' whilst meaning is essentially 'in us', and as such it precise content depends on our beliefs, understandings, and so forth. From this position, Mingers draws a number of conclusions concerning the nature of information and meaning; finally arguing that we can distinguish between three different 'levels' of meaning (understanding, connotation and intention). Concerning the nature of information systems, and based on his previous arguments, Mingers concludes that: "Information systems is, therefore, a misnomer. We should really be concerned with the much larger domain of meaning systems or sense systems, seeing information as but a part of this." (p.84). Again, Mingers raises issues which have practical implications for information systems designers, as meaning systems (or sense systems) would surely require the use of different modelling techniques to be employed, if they are to be adequately understood, than most of those currently 'in vogue'.

Whilst in Gilligan and Mingers philosophical analysis is used essentially to clarify concepts, Gregory employs philosophical arguments to (firstly) dimensionalize and clarify a problem concerned with the references of statements generated by computer-based information systems (he calls this "the real world mapping problem"). Having clarified the nature of this problem, he goes on to use philosophical analysis to develop a solution. He begins by clarifying the nature of "real world mapping problem" — which essentially concerns how it comes about that statements generated by a computer refer to states (events, actions, etc.) in the real world. A number of important philosophical distinctions are explored before Gregory attempts a solution to this problem. The discussions include issues concerning the relationship 'universal' statements and 'particulars', and between 'logical' and 'factual' truths. Having conducted this philosophical 'under-labouring', Gregory constructs his arguments to show that computer-based information systems: "... do not function in isolation but in the context of a wider system of belief ... beliefs encompass a plethora of universal factual truths and it is these that complement the logical truths returned by the machine in such a way that they can be mapped on to the real world and produce genuine information." (p.93). He argues that such beliefs determine the nature of the informational outputs from computer systems. He therefore concludes, as far as the problem of information systems design is concerned: "... that while the logical elements of the machine can be created by the system designers, the users' systems of beliefs, which are essential for reference to the real world, cannot." (p.94). Gregory finally concludes that, without logico-philosophical input, models of information systems currently in widespread usage, are too limited in scope to provide a satisfactory basis for information system design. Gregory's work, too, has practical consequences for information systems designers, as systems of belief, which Gregory argues must be properly understood, are not often discussed in the standard literature on information systems design. This could prove to be a serious omission.

Kamm's study is concerned with understanding the implications of the (ubiquitous) organic metaphor, as applied to organizations, for the concepts of information and information systems. His study is to a large extent based on an analysis of the works of Talcott Parsons. Initially, Kamm finds that, in the writings of those in the 'organicist' tradition of organization theory, the problems of the coordination and integration of organizational actors is of paramount importance. Whilst 'motivational' factors play a part in ensuring effective integration: "Since coordination involves the use of information the implication would be that an organismic view of the development of information systems would see the important questions as those relating to the meaning conveyed by information within the accepted culture of the workplace." (p.98). He contrasts this view with one which he considers might be applicable in the (also ubiquitous) 'mechanicist' views of organizations, which: "... tend to treat information as 'data plus meaning', with the greatest attention given to establishing the integrity and security of data." (p.98). Kamm goes on to argue that, within the tradition of the organic metaphor, the concept of information is inherently connected with the concept of trust: "An organismic approach ... will regard trust as involving an understanding that information is used in a way which does not undermine a sense of shared interest." (p.102). At this stage of his argument, Kamm is able to draw the interesting conclusion that trust (how it is handled, given, etc.) is central to understanding the role of (and the design of) information systems within organizations. He links these concerns with the wider problems of integration in 'networked' organizations — in which many academics and practitioners give information technology a leading (usually an 'enabling') role to play. Information systems can play a role here because: "The integrative role of information can therefore be seen as a means of giving the organization a shape which is particularly appropriate as the more formal structures decline." (p.103). However, Kamm argues that whilst information may play an integrating role (as a 'symbolic medium', in Kamm's terms) its limitations in this respect can: "... point to criticisms that can be made of the whole approach to organizational development." (p.104). Kamm indicates his unease with some of the arguments that an 'organicist' view of information (and information systems) entail by referring to some of Habermas's arguments. He concludes that, whilst there are definitely attractive features of the 'organicist' view of information, both the 'organicist' and the mechanistic views of information: "... define the role of information as an organizational resource for particular purposes, and therefore raise significant issues concerning its nature and management." (p.106). No doubt, Kamm will continue to explore the implications of other metaphors for the concept of information in the future, but his discussions herein are surely both apposite and timely.

All four authors share a common concern to clarify our understanding of the concept of 'information' (and thereby the concept of 'information systems'), albeit that they employ differing methods and strategies to do so. As there can be little doubt that the concepts of 'information' and 'information systems' are used in many different ways (and for many different purposes) by writers in the information systems discipline, the need for conceptual clarification of these concepts could hardly be clearer — or more pressing. Whether one agrees with the authors of the works that follow (and one probably cannot agree with all of them without contradiction!), it appears to be safe to conclude that the authors will force many people to re-think their ideas on these important topics. It can only be hoped that those of a resolutely practical orientation will take note.

Patterns on Glass: The Language Games of Information

Jim Gilligan

Using Wittgenstein's theory of language games from the Philosophical Investigations and a liberal application of Ockham's Razor, the use of the words data, information and the relationship between them is considered, and the consequences of current use evaluated in the context of emerging technologies for computer based information systems.

1

The literature of information systems contains many texts which preface a detailed study by asking what we mean by information, declaring the nature of information to be uncertain: or by giving an often unsupported definition for the sake of argument, teaching or the text.

So commonplace is this condition that it appears to be no longer discomforting. Here are two examples from many:

Checkland & Scholes state that:

"Information equals data plus meaning." Checkland & Scholes (1990)

Checkland expands on this by saying that:

"Human beings appear to be uniquely capable of attributing meaning to what they perceive ... This transformation of data into information by the attribution of meaning makes the study of information a very broad and hybrid field ..." Checkland (1992a)

Clearly Checkland sees the distinction between data and information and the relationship between them as not only useful, but fundamental.

If Checkland may be taken to represent the 'soft' side of systems, Date may represent the 'hard' side. In *An Introduction to Database Systems*, Date says that:

"The terms data and information are treated as synonymous in this book. Some writers distinguish between the two ... The distinction is clearly important — so important that it seems preferable to make it explicit, where relevant, instead of relying on a somewhat arbitrary differentiation between two essentially similar terms." Date (1986)

Date is unconcerned that for his general purpose any difference between data and information does not matter. He has no use for the distinction.

Wittgenstein states in *Philosophical Investigations*:

"... for a large class of cases ... the meaning of a word is its use in the language." (Wittgenstein 1958: para.43, p.20e–21e)

As it is an assertion of this chapter that information and data belong to such a class, we can accept that there may be a use, as Date suggests, in which these words are indeed synonymous, for example, data modelling.

Is it then possible to find a use for these words and their relationship where they are necessarily different? Clearly this is so for Checkland where the subjective attribution of meaning to transform data into information is fundamental. This transformation demands that data and information are not synonymous.

This indicates, as Wittgenstein suggests, many possible different uses for words like data and information and the relationship between them. That is, many possible language games in which the words data and information are used in a particular way with a particular relationship between them.

Note that these uses are not definitions, one against the other, but linguistic 'pieces' used to play a particular language game. Their relationship to the real world is quite another thing ...

2

Five uses which follow are given as examples:

1. *Data and information as synonymous.*

   This use, suggested by Date, is useful for data-centred activities and to systems methodologies which are data driven.

   Its application outside such activities is limited, not least because we do distinguish data and information in many common language games. A common meaning of information is 'useful' data. By ignoring this 'usefulness', whatever the reality, we deny a common use, and so one of the significant meanings of the word.

2. *Information = Data + Meaning.*

   Suggested in many information systems texts, for example (Checkland & Scholes 1990). It implies that information exists as a form of data, but only in the presence of the attributed meaning given by a subject.

If we are to use the word information in this sense, it arrives and departs with the subject while being bound to the data. Taken literally (and how else are we take it?) this also appears to deny our common use of the word, for we commonly speak of information as being different from data in itself.

3. *Information as data which brings about a change in the subject.*

The level of information is determined by the probability of change to the subject's actions, for example Ackoff & Emery (1972).

Here again information is a product of the contact between subject and data. Data will only become information by the fact of change in the subject. A railway timetable is only information to a traveller when it is read. Again, the abstraction of information from the physical data appears contrary to common use, and yet, in some sense, this level of description appears to convey what we mean when we say that information is useful.

4. *Autopoiesis as a biological metaphor for systems thinking.*

Suggesting information as a trigger to action in the subject. Data is of no information value until it triggers, through consensual meaning, a change in the subject which is characteristic of having received information (Maturana & Varela 1980).

Again, information is not embedded in the data in any physical sense, but the data somehow becomes recognized as information through its triggering of a response in the subject. This touches on some common understanding that information is recognized rather than created by the subject.

5. *Meaning as created from information.*

The act of the subject is first to recognize information, then process that information to produce meaning.

The information existing in data or signs is not recognized by all subjects equally, but where the subject recognizes information the attribution of meaning is an act on the part of the subject.

This language game creates many questions when contrasted with common use: How does one recognize information before knowing what it means? What is the different state in the world between information and data? Is information that which it is possible to deduce or induce from data? In which case does it not exist in the object, but in the potential for deduction/induction in the subject? Does an object gain or lose information with the coming and going of subjects? In what sense does an object which has never been seen by a subject capable of attributing meaning to it contain information rather than data?

These several cases show the range of language games in which the words data, information and the relationship between them can exist. The first shows how such a use provides for a practical activity in the world, while the last shows how far a language game can move from common use while remaining internally consistent.

It is not the purpose of this chapter to question the validity of any of these various language games, but to highlight the need to question which game is being played in any particular situation, and how useful it is to our purpose. These uses are not definitions. A language game does not touch reality, it has only an internal consistency which may or may not be coincident with reality.

3

Let us, for example, consider the argument that information exists objectively in data but that it may not be touched by us for we perceive the world only through our senses and such information is not directly available to our senses.

This may prove to be a useful language game, but derived from traditional metaphysics it has many weaknesses as a picture of the world. One might argue, for example, that as our senses are part of the world how else should we expect to touch the world? That our senses and experience may be limited or differ does not change the world, only our trust in their touch. It may be argued that that it is language such as this we should distrust and not our senses.

Yet we need not even begin this metaphysical argument. The significant fact is that for a large class of cases within the study of information systems there is no use for the belief that data contains information which cannot be contacted by the senses.

For Wittgenstein (1958: 95e, para.270), a system which provides a result with no external verification cannot speak of that result as true or false. Searle says simply:

> "If there is no distinction between getting it right, and believing we have got it right, then we can't talk about right at all." (Magee 1987: 338)

It follows, how are we to say that there is a difference between data and information if there is no way to perceive that difference in the world?

The riddle "What is information?" returns to this point: If there is no distinction between the existence of information and believing in the existence of information, then we cannot talk about information at all.

Unless we can distinguish in the world between data and information then the way in which we use these words is appropriate only to their use in our language games and not to our understanding of what is in the world.

There may be language games in which the word for some thing or quality called information is necessary. However, unless it can be shown to be necessary, it should be avoided if we wish to prevent conceptual confusion.

For a large class of cases within language games used for the study of information systems, it will suffice (and therefore it should be the requirement) to use the word information in its original sense, that is, as a verb. There is no information: we are 'in formed'.

This is not to say that we cannot use the word information in the ordinary sense of the word, in other language games, where this type of abstraction is shared by many other words. For example, we can go for a walk. Or rather, we can go walking. We can have a conversation. Or rather, we can converse. The use of the noun 'a walk' suggests the verb 'go walking'. As such these are harmless. If, however 'We can go for a walk' were taken to mean that the walk already exists as a separate physical presence, or that we create it as an action as we go, leaving it behind as we travel, or that there are an infinite number of physical walks in the world from which we choose one, then we have lost touch with the reality of the world through a conceptual confusion of language. We have been 'nouning the verb'.

Indeed, the term 'Information-as-Action' (Kampis 1993) has been coined from this tendency. Failing to remove information as a thing and replace it as an activity, the hybrid term 'Information-as-Action' attempts to combine the two. This may be useful to a particular language game, but only to a particular language game.

> "... the riddle does not exist." (Wittgenstein 1961: 6.44–6.5)

4

Is there then value in a language game which does not use the word information other than as a verb? Such a use would retain the term 'information system', for the meaning is intact, indeed improved. These are systems intended to do something, they are intended to inform.

It would lose the difficulty of abstraction, the sense of information as a somehow intangible 'thing' or quality of things. This both simplifies and is compatible with points 3, 4 and 5 on page 67, for it frees us from the metaphysical and leaves us with subject based disposition, intention, and action.

Once we accept information only as a verb in this language game there are further significant consequences for systems thinking and systems practice.

The underlying systems force, confirmed by a new understanding of the word information as an activity, is the system dynamic — that is, change.

The response of systems thinking and practise in the past has been to minimize or ignore change. In hard systems to create supposedly definitive solutions. In soft systems to create no 'solutions' at all, believing them to be unsound by definition. Of course, in some cases Soft Systems Methodology (SSM) sets out to create 'feasible, desirable change'. However change in this sense is intended to bring about a new position which is considered both feasible and desirable. A move from one systems position to another, even if we allow for embedded, recursive or cyclic patterns.

The belief of the pre-Socratic Heraclitus in an 'Eternal Fire', that is, change as the underlying force of the world, has a parallel here and indeed with modern physics. Russell states that in modern physics:

> "... energy has had to replace matter as what is permanent. But energy, unlike matter, is not a refinement of the commonplace notion of a 'thing', it is merely a characteristic of a physical process ... it the the burning,

not 'what burns'. 'What burns' has disappeared from modern physics."
(Russell 1961)

Information is an activity of change. Seen as the underlying force of all
information systems, change is not the means to systems solutions — it is the
essence of the system. Management of change, management of information is the
task.

5

In this new language game, the activity of change is the natural condition of
systems. Information systems inform and change, feeding the disposition,
intentions, and acts of participants.

While we currently lack the systems thinking to support this view, within
the field of computer-based information systems, we do have some emerging
technology:

1. Client–server systems for example. The user, through the client, can
   increasingly determine the physical presentation of the data which comes
   to inform them.

2. Object-oriented techniques provide a means to accommodate client-server
   developments.

3. Temporal databases afford a much deeper and wider vision of data and
   process.

4. The increase in processing power available from computer systems —
   massively parallel systems, and at a personal level, the recent Power PC,
   Pentium, and Arm7 processors.

5. Most significant of all, the creation of global networks, such as the Internet,
   mean that an information system need know only where data is, rather than be
   required to process and store it: thus the world data systems become a global
   'server' to each individual system 'client'.

The power and flexibility afforded by these emerging technologies suggest we
may be moving towards a situation which is capable of supporting more complex
information systems dynamics that we have so far attempted. These may create
a new generation of computer-based information system: allowing for change,
encouraging change, generating new modes of informing, and so allowing for and
demanding better management of change.

We lack the systems view to take us to these things.

6

Much of the philosophy of the twentieth century has been concerned with
language. Plato's Cave, we might say, has no entrance but a window — the
window of language. In this window the glass is not clear.

The manipulation of language into forms which no longer correspond to our sensory experience of the world is accepted. Patterns on the glass may distract our attention from the world as we experience it to a study of the patterns themselves.

The patterns of language, not being of the world, do not have to correspond to the world. If our vision of the world is distorted by the pattern and we recognize that distortion, it is harmless. Where we take the distortion to be reality and reify the glance of light on the pane, it may cause confusion.

Using words to declare the limitation of words is a measure of the problem. In the use of signs we have recourse to the signs themselves. Wittgenstein wrote:

> "But if you say: How am I to know what he means when I see nothing but the signs he gives. Then I say: How is HE to know what he means when he has nothing but the signs either?" (Wittgenstein 1958: para.504)

The study of information systems has extended far beyond the exclusive study of computer-based information systems. However many conceptual errors in the latter field have become established in the language employed by the former. It is suggested here that the words which underpin our present enterprise require careful reconsideration.

In particular, when we speak of information we may become so enthralled by the language game, by the patterns on the glass, that the world behind becomes obscured.

The consequences of this for information systems thinking and for the methodologies which we apply to those systems in practise are fundamental. Despite emerging new technologies, we do not yet have a systems view which accommodates and understands change as the essential activity of information systems.

If we turn away from attempting to define and produce the substance of information, we may discover new benefits and new opportunities in providing for the activity of information.

My own research is currently engaged in identifying a systems view which recognizes the nature and importance of change, accepts information as an activity rather than a resource, and incorporates emerging technologies in support of the requirement for the management of change within information systems dynamics.

The Nature of Information and its Relationship to Meaning

John Mingers

This chapter concerns one of the fundamental aspects of information systems — the nature of information itself. It argues that there is little agreement or even debate about this elementary concept, particularly with regard to its semantic and pragmatic aspects. After critically evaluating several theories claiming to deal with semantic information, it suggests that Dretske's theory of information and knowledge is most suitable as a basis for information systems. It goes on to develop the relationship between information and meaning, drawing on Maturana's theory of autopoiesis, and to consider pragmatic aspects via Habermas' theory of communicative action. It concludes with an analysis of different levels of meaning interpretation and generation.

This is a revised version of the paper "Information and Meaning", Systemist 15(1) 1993.

1 Introduction

Information systems could not exist without information and yet there is no secure agreement over what information actually is. As Lewis (1991) and Dretske (1981) point out, few books concerning information actually define it clearly. The most common assertion is that information is data that has been processed in some way to make it useful.

Traditional information systems approaches have said little explicitly about their underlying philosophy, but in practice they have assumed an *objectivist* position. That is, that data and information are independent of their producers neutrally reflecting real world structures (Lewis 1993). An alternative view argues that information is essentially *subjectivist*, created by people and reflecting their particular expectations, values and beliefs. Checkland formulates this view as "information equals data plus meaning" (Checkland & Scholes 1990: 303). That is, by attributing meaning to data we create information. The problem with this latter formulation is that the terms and their relations are not precisely and clearly defined. Thus what is *data, meaning and information*, and how exactly do meaning and data interact to produce information?

The main aim of this research is to develop theories concerning the nature of information and meaning, and the relations between the two. That is, to conceptualize information at the levels of semantics (meaning) and pragmatics (use).

2   Terms to be Used

Following Stamper (1973; 1985; 1987), we take *signs* as the most primitive elements which may convey information, thus including *data* as a particular type, and use his semiotic framework to provide structure:

empirics — the study of sign transmission and the statistical properties of the repeated use of signs;

syntactics — the study of the relations between signs and their properties without regard to their meaning or use;

semantics — the study of the relations between signs and that which they signify or represent, the *meaning* of signs;

pragmatics — the study of the relations between signs and their *users*, and their *uses* in practical human activity.

Practical information systems encompass all these aspects and we are primarily concerned with developing semantic and pragmatic theories of information.

We shall also use the term *intersubjective* in contrast to subjective. This reflects the view that language and meaning are not *individually* subjective, but based on common experience and agreements between groups of subjects.

3   Existing Theories of (Semantic) Information

The most well-known theory of information is that of Shannon & Weaver (1949). Their theory — based on earlier work by Hartley (1928) — has become known as information theory but in fact has nothing to say about the semantic and pragmatic aspects of information. It is purely concerned with measuring the amount of information that a particular code or channel could transmit. Indeed, it would be better called a "theory of signal transmission" (Bar-Hillel 1955) as this is its subject matter. There are a number of more recent theories, all based on Shannon's work, which claim in various way to deal with information *content* — its meaning.

Bar-Hillel & Carnap (1952; Bar-Hillel 1952b; 1955; 1964) claim that they can define and measure *semantic* information. Very briefly, they consider propositions in some restrictive descriptive language. Any particular proposition will rule out or be contradictory to a number of others. The more propositions it rules out, the greater its information content. So a tautology which is compatible with anything has zero information; a contradiction which is compatible with nothing has maximum information. This has a number of limitations as a theory of *semantic* information:

- The theory does not deal with the real world, only with the properties of formal systems. The probabilities, and therefore amount of information, are defined purely in terms of the number of possible state descriptions. It ignores the relative likelihood of these in the real world.

- The theory does not deal with information for a particular person, given what they already know or what they intended, nor communication of meaning between people.

- The approach is hopelessly unrealistic and impractical for real-world languages and domains.

- The theory assumes that propositions are meaningful in themselves, in some absolute sense, independently of an interpreter.

The last of these is the most serious difficulty from the point of view of this chapter.

Jumarie (1990) has proposed an extension to Shannon's mathematical theory to bring in the observer and measure 'relative information'. The information content of a message now depends on both the *syntactic* structure of the symbols and the *semantic* structure of the observer. The syntactic information depends on the number of possible symbols (e.g. words) and their probabilities of occurrence as usual. But now, each word may have a number of different meanings and each will have a conditional probability dependent on the particular observer. There is thus an additional uncertainty term in the Shannon formulæ. Whilst this does get away from the idea of objective information, it is really simply an extension to the mathematical measurement of the amount of information (or rather uncertainty). It does not say anything about how or why particular meanings are generated or selected, and information remains simply a metric.

MacKay (1956) has made a genuine attempt to link information and meaning. For MacKay, information theory concerns processes which form representations, and the relationship between representation and represented (or signifier and signified). Information is that which justifies the representation and it can be measured in terms of the complexity of, or number of steps in generating, the representation (traditional information theory can be interpreted as the number of binary decisions needed to identify a message). Language and gestures have meaning(s), and this meaning has an effect on the receiver. The effect is to *select* a particular state in the receiver. Meaning is thus a selective function, its actual result being dependent on the various states of the receiver. Thus two messages may be different but mean the same thing to an individual, and the same message may mean different things to different people. The *information content* of a message is the amount of change brought about. Thus a message that is repeated

75

has the same meaning (it leaves the system in the state it is already in) but has no information since it produces no change.

MacKay's work has been further developed by the sociologist Luhmann (1990: original in German, 1971). For Luhmann, meaning is the central concept of sociology and, put briefly, it is what allows us to process our over-burdening, instant to instant, experiences. Meaning is 'experience-processing'. *Meaning* both selects what will become our experience, but also fills this out with reference to what we are not directly experiencing. Meaning functions both at the level of society and of the individual, and in both situations meaning is the presupposition and the product of its particular selections. For an individual, meaning frames our experiences — it selects from our perceptions and through its structure of possibilities presents us with experiences. These, in turn, restructure our expectations, our readinesses for meaning. *Information* is that which is surprising, that which is unexpected and alters our structure of expectations. So events and messages that are repeated can still have meaning but will carry no information as the expectations will have already changed.

This is an interesting and sophisticated theory which appears to be quite compatible with, and could provide an underpinning for, Checkland's formulation mentioned in Section 1. However, it does leave information with a rather subsidiary role, and does not accord well with some of our common intuitions. For instance, we normally hold that books, papers, timetables etc. contain information, yet by this theory they do not if we do not read them, or if we have read them already. It is therefore worth investigating another theory of semantic information (Dretske 1981), one which deals with both information and meaning in a more naturalistic way. Kary (1990) has a theory of information flow which is quite compatible with Dretske's, but which is by no means as comprehensive.

4 Foundations for Information and Meaning

In order to develop a theory of information/meaning at the level of semantics and pragmatics a number of foundation theories will be utilized. In particular, Maturana & Varela's cognitive theories developed from their theory of autopoiesis; Habermas' theory of communicative action, and specifically his development of 'universal pragmatics'; and Dretske's theory of knowledge based on information. Until these foundations have been laid, information and meaning cannot be distinguished and so we will refer to information/meaning to indicate the general effect of a sign on a receiver.

5 Maturana & Varela's Cognitive Theories

Maturana & Varela (Maturana 1975; 1978; Maturana & Varela 1980) have developed radical theories, from a biological perspective, concerning the nature of living organisms, their nervous systems, cognitive capacities and language. These ideas have been explored in the context of information systems by Winograd & Flores (1986), Winograd (1987), Harnden & Mullery (1991), Stephens & Wood (1991) and Kensing & Winograd (1991).

Autopoietic systems are *organizationally closed* although interactively open. Being organizationally closed means that the changes of state which the system undergoes are determined by its own structure at a particular point in time, rather than being determined by the environment, so long as it continues its autopoiesis. It is *structure-determined*. Its interactions with its environment can only perturb it, or trigger particular changes of state, and, indeed, its structure determines what can and cannot be a trigger for it.

Humans are primarily differentiated from other organisms by the development of their nervous system and their use of language. Maturana & Varela show that the nervous system, although not autopoietic, is also structurally-determined. Successful behaviour comes about because of *structural coupling*. The structure of a system will change and develop in such a way as to be suitable for the environment or autopoiesis will be unable to be maintained. The matter, however, is always contingent and the resulting structure is never *determined* by the environment. Systems may become structurally coupled to each other — mutually triggering behaviours may develop — and this is the basis of language.

This leads to the main critique of the idea of objective or absolute information/meaning. It is quite simply this. No sign or symbol or sentence determines its own effect on a receiver — it can never do more than trigger (or not trigger) particular structural change. Thus nothing is intrinsically informative, no interaction inherently instructive. The apparent meaning inherent in signs, and the successful communication using such signs, actually reflect the similarity of cognitive structure of the people involved.

6   Intersubjective Information/Meaning

It might appear that this line of argument will lead to information/meaning becoming individually subjective. Whilst it is possible that particular signs or sign systems could be so, it will be argued that language, and other signs used in communication, are *intersubjective*. That is, neither independent of the mind (objective) nor dependent purely on an individual (subjective), but based on prior consensus and agreement.

The essential characteristic of any sign or symbol is that it stands for or points to *something other than itself* (for whomever it is a sign). Moreover, all signs must ultimately be manifest or embodied in a physical medium since they can only affect people through the senses — sight, sound, touch etc. Following Bateson (1970; 1973), that which is most elementary are *differences*. If some area of the world were completely uniform then it could have no effects at all. It is actually differences which are endlessly transmitted around the physical medium.

Information is based in *differences that make a difference*. That is, differences which *do* trigger changes in the nervous structure of an observer. Organisms without nervous systems react to differences, e.g. in chemical concentrations, but the nervous system generates a new domain of interactions, that is *relations between differences or events* which occur simultaneously or over time. It is this which allows interactions with the general as well as the particular and makes possible the development of abstract thought, descriptions and language. In the struggle for survival, interactions developed between people which were not direct but indirect. They served to 'orient' or direct attention to other common interactions in order to coordinate the cooperative actions of groups of people. Such symbolic gestures were the basis of language and can be seen as elementary descriptions of the environment. Always, however, they are based on shared experiences and structural coupling. In language or 'languaging' the linguistic behaviours themselves become the subject for coordination. At this level of abstraction, the whole domain of language becomes available including the possibility of self-description and self-consciousness.

Language is essentially a consensual domain. This means that it is inevitably intersubjective. It is a domain of interactions under structural coupling — the particular behaviours, gestures and signs are essentially arbitrary and only succeed because of the structural similarities of those involved. There can be no communication unless both sender and receiver have essentially the same structure already. Language, and thus information/meaning, is primarily connotative not denotative. It references shared experiences, activities and understandings, not objective entities.

7 Habermas, Communicative Action and Universal Pragmatics

The work of Habermas (1979; 1984; 1989) on critical theory and a communicative theory of social action has already provided a number of ideas for conceptualizing information systems — for example, language as action, speech acts, and intersubjectivity (Goldkuhl & Lyytinen 1982); rational reconstruction, language games, and conversation (Goldkuhl & Lyytinen 1984); typology of social action, and knowledge-constitutive interests (Lyytinen & Klein 1985); Lehtinen & Lyytinen (1986); critical social theory, knowledge-constitutive interests (Ngwenyama 1991); typology of social action (Lyytinen et al. 1991).

As argued above, language and communication come about because of the need to coordinate action effectively. Linguistic acts are therefore, at base, always practical actions concerned to bring about particular effects. The aim of universal pragmatics is to produce a *rational reconstruction* of the grounds or conditions necessarily implied by human communication. What is it that we *always* take for granted in linguistic action?

Habermas limits the domain of actions that he analyses to those intended to reach understanding or bring about an agreement (*communicative action*), as opposed to *strategic action* where an individual wishes to succeed personally in spite of or against another. In communicative action between people (i.e. aiming to reach an agreement or understanding) the utterance, or speech acts, imply certain presuppositions or assumptions. One of these is simply *effectiveness*. The act is *comprehensible* — the hearer understands what is said. This essentially concerns the level of semantics already discussed. However, from a pragmatic point of view, there are three wider *validity claims* which are raised by a speech act and which an hearer implicitly accepts. These are *truth*, *truthfulness* (sincerity), and *rightness* (legitimacy).

A validity claim simply means that a particular aspect of a speech act is in fact correct. It may not be — it is up to the hearer to accept the claims, or to dispute one or more of them. The claim to truth means that the states of affairs implied by the utterance are, in fact, correct; that its propositional content, or existential presuppositions are true — what it assumes is actually possible or feasible. The claim to truthfulness or sincerity refers to the motivation of the speaker and the assumption that he/she genuinely and sincerely intends what they say. Finally, the claim to rightness or legitimacy concerns accepted social norms within a particular group and assumes that the actions or practices implied by the speech act are consensually valid.

These three validity claims actually refer to three different 'worlds' to which any utterance is related:

- the *objective world* of external nature which obtains or can be brought about;

- the *subjective world* of internal nature, constituted by people's private experiences; and

- the *social world* of society consisting of consensual, intersubjective practices and norms.

The world, *my* world, and *our* world.

Each validity claim relates primarily to a specific purpose or function of communication — truth with the presentation and representation of knowledge, rightness with the establishment of social contacts and relations, and truthfulness with the expression of self. These functions can be equated to particular types of speech acts as developed by Austin (1962) and Searle (1969).

Finally, the validity claims imply different forms of rational argument when they are called into question (Habermas 1979: 19–20). If the problem concerns the initial meaning or understanding of an utterance, then an *explicative discourse* is necessary. This could be linguistic (examining the syntax) or hermeneutic (exploring the semantics). Problems of truth, that is concerning states of affairs or feasible possibilities, require a *theoretical discourse*. This involves some form of empirical-analytic approach to observing the world and discovering effective instrumental action. Questions of normative rightness call for *practical discourse* in which moral, ethical and social claims are debated and argued. Finally, a person's sincerity may be questioned. If the person is being deliberately and knowingly untruthful to achieve certain ends then it is not a case of communicative but strategic action. However, if the person is unknowingly insincere because of illusion or self-deception then rationality requires that they be willing to undergo *therapeutic critique* in order to develop through self-reflection and enlightenment.

8 Dretske's Account of Information

We now reach a point where we can distinguish between *information* and *meaning* and theorize the relationship between the two. It will be argued, following Dretske (1981), that meaning develops from information. Information, carried by signs, is an objective feature of the world in the same way as are physical objects and their properties. Meaning, however, is generated from information by receivers and can be either intersubjective or subjective. Information does not depend on people's knowledge, beliefs or understandings, whilst meaning does.

Any event in the world carries information — information about its own origins. How likely or unlikely is this event? That depends on what other events could have happened and their relative probabilities. We cannot say a priori *what* the information is, but we can measure it. The amount of information reflects the reduction in possibilities brought about by the event. Note that this information is independent of any observer.

We can next consider how this information is transmitted. How, for example, a sign can carry information about something other than itself. We must assume that there is some causal link between the source and the receiver or else no information can be transmitted. The degree of correspondence may vary from complete to zero. In general, the sign or receiver will have a number of possible states as will the source or signifier. These states will have differing probabilities of occurrence. The amount of information that can be carried is calculated for both source and receiver. If there is complete transmission it means that every state of the source is linked with every state of the receiver and vice versa. In practice this is unlikely. The receiver will be affected by things other than the source (noise), and information from the source will not affect the receiver (equivocation).

It is important to see that we may not know about the possible states of the situation and their probabilities but *they still exist independently of our knowledge*. However, the amount of information available to someone does depend on their prior knowledge. In particular, their prior knowledge of the possible states of the source.

The next important step is seeing that if a sign carries the information that a particular state of affairs obtains, then it also carries all the information that follows from that state of affairs (Dretske uses the term 'nested in'). These consequences or necessary conditions could be analytic, nomic (based on general empirical laws), or follow from the logic of the situation. Clearly, signs potentially carry an enormous amount of information.

9 Information and Meaning

The aim now is to clarify that relationship by showing how objective information makes possible non-objective meaning. This is done using two related distinctions — analogue and digital, and difference and distinction.

The physical world (in which all signs and signals are ultimately embodied) is essentially analogue — a continuum of differences rich in information. The digital is discrete — it is yes/no, on/off, a distinction rather than a difference. The analogue is full of information and yet is ambiguous and imprecise. The digital is very precise and well-bounded but carries only limited amounts of information.

The argument here is that the transformation of information into meaning involves a digitalization of the analogue. Given analogue information, e.g. a picture, a linguistic description carries only *some* of the information in *digital form*. Much of the information in the picture is not conveyed. That which is conveyed is that which is stated plus the information nested in this — i.e. what follows analytically, nomically or situationally from this. When analogue information is digitalized there is inevitably a loss of information. The digital signal carries less information than the analogue.

The importance of this for information and meaning is the argument that our perception and experiences are analogue while cognition and meaning are progressive digitalizations of this experience. This explanation shows how the objective information is converted into (inter) subjective meaning. At every stage it is the knowledge, intentions, context of the receiver that is determining what counts as information and what particular aspects of the available analogue information are being digitalized into meaning. To be precise, meaning, or the semantic content of an information source is that information *and only that information*, which is held in digital form.

Note that we can *never* consciously interact with pure information — we are always already immersed in meaning. Just as we can never interact *in an unmediated way* with the physical world, the nervous system digitalizes information into meaning automatically. Also, meaning always leads on to some form of activity. This may be manifest, or just internal.

It is this aspect of intentionality, of bringing forward only specific semantic content, which distinguishes humans from information processing machines. Some machines transmit all the information that they receive, e.g. a television. Some digitalize it to a greater or lesser extent, e.g. a sensor in the road converts pressure differences into a count of cars passing which is fed to a computer. But in all cases they transmit the information that they carry and all its consequences — they are not able to impose an higher order intentional structure on it and lose some of the information. They have not been able to discriminate between the relevance of different aspects of the information.

10 The Link to Semantics and Pragmatics

We have so far only considered the precise mechanism by which information triggers meaning — how meaning is generated, not what meaning is generated. We need now to relate this to the semantic and pragmatic aspects of communication, the theories of Maturana and Habermas.

A direct physical sign only carries information about that which caused it. However a linguistic sign carries information both about what it describes — its *propositional* content — and about its production by a particular speaker — its

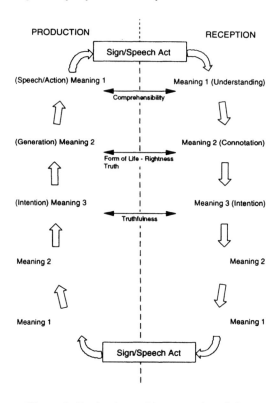

Figure 1: Production and interpretation of signs.

---

illocutionary content, or what it is supposed to achieve. Thus information is also available about the pragmatic intentions of the speaker and the validity claims underlying the utterance — is the speaker mistaken (truth)? Have we understood correctly (comprehensibility)? Is the speaker sincere (truthfulness)? Are they assuming different social rules (rightness)?

11   Levels of Meaning

In considering how information is converted to meaning, I suggest that it is useful to consider three different steps in this process, or three different levels of meaning. They apply to the *production* of signs as well as their interpretation and are illustrated in Figure 1.

11.1   Converting Information to Meaning

- *Meaning 1 — Understanding.* This is the first level of meaning in which the receiver comes to understand the primary meaning of a sign or linguistic message. This is the level of understanding that can be expected from all competent speakers of a language, all those who share a particular form of life (Wittgenstein 1958). It corresponds to the semantic content outlined above — that is, the digitalized information without its analogue nesting. The main validity claim it involves is that of comprehensibility although others may be involved.

- *Meaning 2 — Connotation.* This level brings in the complex of other meanings, beliefs and implications which are associated with the primary meaning. For example, the knowledge and experience that the receiver has about bears. This meaning will not primarily be individual but will be differentiated between groups who have different forms of life. This extends the digitalized meaning to include nested consequences known and available to the receiver.

  This level is mainly concerned with the validity claims of truth and rightness. Is the propositional content of the sign actually correct? Does the state of affairs actually exist? And are its claims about social rules and roles acceptable?

- *Meaning 3 — Intention.* Meaning 3 is finally the individual meaning for a particular person and the implications of that meaning for action; the intentions it will lead them to have. This will add in their own personal experiences, feelings and intentions at a particular time and result in a particular activity, which may of course be simply remembering it for future use. This level of meaning is subjective rather than intersubjective.

  At this level sincerity will be a primary validity claim. Is the source truthful? Did the speakers mean what they said? Are they reliable? Questioning this may lead to the conclusion that the speaker is acting strategically rather than communicatively, and thereby to appropriate action.

11.2 Producing Signs from Meaning

Here we are concerned with the obverse of meaning generation, that is sign production. This is of much greater importance in the non-direct signs such as human language where questions of truth and truthfulness arise. We can trace three similar stages from the intention of the speaker through the actual enactment of the sign/utterance — *intention, generation, action.*

12 Conclusions

Information and meaning must be distinguished, but rather than meaning creating information, meaning *is generated from* information.

Signs carry objective information but humans cannot access this — we are always already existing within a domain of meaning. Meaning is expressed in and conditioned by language, which is intersubjective — that is, based on agreement and consensus.

The meaning that is generated from information, and that which generates further information, depends both on our linguistic forms of life and on our individual circumstances and intentions at the time.

Information systems is, therefore, a misnomer. We should really be concerned with the much larger domain of *meaning systems* or *sense systems*, seeing information as but a part of this.

This would lead us to consider the semantic and pragmatics aspects of the production of signs and the generation of meaning and their relationship to the social context in which they occur.

Mapping Information Systems on to the Real World

Frank H. Gregory

There is a problem about explaining how systems that are true by definition can be informative about a world that is not. This problem is particularly relevant to the design of computerized information systems. A solution is offered based on the distinction between logical and factual truth.

1 Introduction

The real world mapping problem is the problem of explaining how a system that is an invention of the human mind helps us to understand a world that is not. It is self evident that some systems of rules and definitions, such as those that constitute the game of chess, do not help us to understand anything beyond themselves. Others, such as mathematics, do. The real world mapping problem is the problem of understanding which systems will help us understand the real world and which will not.

This chapter will show that real world mapping is a particular problem for information systems. It will present a logical analysis of the problem and suggest a solution. The solution is in the form of a logical template to which all information systems should conform.

Section 2 looks at the background of the mapping problem. Section 2.1 explains how an adequate solution has escaped both the philosophy of mathematics and the philosophy of logic. Section 2.2 uses the example of Britain's 'Poll Tax' to show how real world mapping is a problem in current information system design. In Section 2.3, the bizarre results of an information systems mapping failure are emphasized by a comparison with the fiction of Franz Kafka. Section 2.4 explains why systems maintenance is not usually a solution to the mapping problem.

Section 3 seeks to explain, in terms of philosophical logic, how languages can have reference to real world objects and events. The difference between universals and particulars and between logical and factual truth is described in Section 3.1. Section 3.2 presents the arguments that both logical and factual truth are required in a system that maps on to the real world. The first part of the argument is that factual truth cannot be derived from logical truth; this argument comes from David Hume and is well known. The second part of the argument is that a system which includes factual truth also needs to include logical truth; this argument is, to the best of the author's knowledge, original. Section 3.3 explains the way in which logical truth is determined. Most existing computerized information systems have a logical form that comprises only logical universals and factual particulars; Section 3.4 explains why these cannot be informative about the real world.

Section 4 gives a logical template for an information system. This comprises three elements: logical universals, factual universals and factual particulars.

2 Background

2.1 Mapping and Mathematics

Einstein posed the mapping problem for mathematics: "How can it be that mathematics, being after all a product of human thought independent of existence, is so admirably adapted to the objects of reality?" An answer to this has not emerged and currently pure mathematicians, for example, often seem to be perplexed about why their subject is useful (Barrow 1992: ch.1).

The term 'the real world mapping problem' is a term of the present author's invention. There is no universally recognized name for the problem, instead the problem pops up in various places under various names and in various guises. In Hofstadter's *Gödel, Escher, Bach* (1980) the term 'isomorphism' is used to describe the situation when a system of rules and definitions corresponds to the real world. But Hofstadter's popular book does not explain how, why and when an isomorphism occurs. When one looks for the academic literature giving an account of this notion one finds that it does not exist. Hofstadter poses puzzles but does not provide the solutions.

One would expect that the subject would be addressed in the philosophy of mathematics. While much of this work bears upon the issue, a straightforward solution is rarely offered. Indeed, there are hardly any works that confront the problem directly. The absence of adequate coverage in the philosophy of mathematics might be explained by the problem being shunted sideways into the philosophy of logic. This move might be legitimate because there are a number of arguments to the effect that mathematics can be reduced to logic (Haack 1978). Given this, the question now becomes "How does logic map on to the real world?". The problem here is that some authors would argue that logic does not map on to the real world, nor is it intended to. The later sections of this chapter will argue that the solution does lie in the area of logic but that logic does not map on to the real world itself, rather it is the role of logic to describe the mapping process.

There is an initial plausibility, and one that will be substantiated in a later section, that computerized information systems are, like mathematics, systems of rules and definition. As such they are an invention of the human mind and it needs to be explained how these systems, such as stock control systems, can help us to deal with real world objects and events such as the movement of stock in a warehouse.

The lack of an adequate theory is a more pressing problem for information system design than it is for mathematics. The early systems of arithmetic existed in 9000BC (Barrow 1992). Over millennia people have had the time to learn how to use mathematics even though this process of learning may have been driven by trial and error rather than theory. People have built up a tacit understanding of how, when and where mathematics is useful. Computerized information systems are simply too important in our daily lives, and the time frame for their development too short, to allow a tacit understanding to be built up by trial and error. Another problem is that information systems tend to define their own terms of success, their measures of performance tend to be internal rather than external. The result of this is that they can create their own surrogate reality in which the need for real world mapping is not even perceived.

2.2 The Poll Tax

That something very strange is happening with information systems is evident from cases that arose with the introduction of Britain's Poll Tax.* Local government had previously been financed by rates, a tax levied by local government on the 'real estate' in their area. Under the Thatcher administration this was changed to a tax on people living in the local area. Local governments brought in computer systems companies of their own choice to change their systems. Many of these companies based the new system on the old system of rates and seem to have overlooked, or at least failed to accommodate, the fact that people, unlike buildings, have a tendency to move.

The local authorities sent some Poll Tax bills, for the forthcoming year, to people who had recently moved from their area and who were not liable to pay. These bills were sent to their old address and in cases where there was no subsequent occupier, these bills were not forwarded. When these people failed to pay, the local authorities placed the matter before the court. The courts sent a summons to the old address. When there was no response to the summons the court tried the people *in absentia*, found them guilty, and ordered a fine to be paid. When the fine was not paid a bailiff was called. Bailiffs were quite capable of locating most of the people who had moved because they were registered in the area they had moved to and were paying Poll Tax to the local authorities of that area. The result was that some people, who had moved from an address that was not subsequently occupied and who were paying Poll Tax to their new local

---

Editors note: Formally this was called the 'Community Charge' but it was commonly known as the 'Poll Tax' since it was a tax levied on those entered on the electoral register. The 'Poll Tax' was introduced in April 1990 and withdrawn, to be replaced by 'Council Tax', in March 1993.

authorities, first discovered that they had been tried, found guilty of an offence they had not committed, and fined when a bailiff arrived at their doorstep threatening to seize their furniture and household goods. (This actually happened to the author.)

This case is interesting not because it shows how incompetent information system design leads to a travesty of justice but because it shows how extensive the real world mapping problem has become and how readily people accept a situation that belongs in the sort of fiction written by Franz Kafka.

2.3 The Trial and the Castle

Kafka's novel *The Trial* (Kafka 1983) tells a story about Joseph K. who is arrested for a crime that is never specified. During the course of the book it becomes doubtful that he has even been accused of anything. The purpose of a trial is normally to determine whether the accused committed the crime referred to. In Kafka's story the trial has no reference. This is strikingly similar to the Poll Tax case where people were penalized for a crime that was never committed.

In spite of the lack of reference Kafka's story seems to make sense. It has an internal coherence despite the near paradox of some of the situations. The characters are not concerned with how the system maps on to the real world, it is as though the real world has ceased to matter. When K. considers the legitimacy of the proceedings in which he is involved he says "They are in fact only legal proceedings if I choose to recognize them as such". What we have here is a system in which belief alone is a sufficient justification of the system. In the Poll Tax cases it seems that the court determined that a crime had been committed just because the local authorities believed that a crime had been committed.

The reader might think that the Poll Tax problem would not have arisen if people leaving an area had notified the local authorities that they were leaving. However, this presumes that there was a mechanism to do so and that this information could be accommodated in the system. Problems in this area are the subject of another of Kafka's works. *The Castle* (Kafka 1983) is a full length novel that describes how K., who has been hired as a land surveyor by the authorities of a principality, arrives and tries, unsuccessfully, to register his presence in the principality with authorities that called for his services.

Kafka's works are classics of twentieth-century literature. They can be contrasted with George Orwell's (1949) *Nineteen Eighty-Four* or *Animal Farm* (Orwell 1971). Orwell's vision of was of a evil dictatorship working through a centralized and efficient bureaucracy. Kafka's world is of nebulous systems populated by hapless individuals; a system which everyone assents to but which nobody, including the officials, can seem to understand. Kafka's works are generally considered to be a disturbing view of life and society. They are not, like Orwell's *Nineteen Eighty-Four*, considered to be prophetic. Yet it is Kafka that seems to be becoming an appropriate model for modern information systems. The connection between Kafka and work in the area of information systems has already been noted by Probert (1991) who argues that some aspects of Soft Systems Methodology are Kafkaesque.

2.4   The Maintenance Argument

There is an argument to the effect that if an information system suffers from a lack of reference and fails to map on to the real world then this can be rectified by systems maintenance. It is the argument that the problems with systems like the Poll Tax would have been sorted out given enough time (the Poll Tax system never got the time because the scheme was abandoned).* The fact that the Poll Tax system was trying to bill non-existent residents would have been noticed and the system modified to overcome the problem. With successive modifications the system would come in to line with reality and system requirements. Space constraints prevent a detailed discussion of this argument. However, there are a number of a priori reasons why this is inadequate and these will be briefly described.

1. The viability of the maintenance argument assumes that either a mistake does not matter much or that there is a manual check on the system. In many systems, such as safety critical systems, a mistake is just not acceptable. One might argue that mistakes in official systems such as the Poll Tax are not acceptable either. If a manual check on the system is anything other than fortuitous, then the fact that the system might make an error in a certain area will have been anticipated. This will not help to deal with problem that have not been anticipated.

2. A maintenance solution assumes that the rate of change in the environment is slower than the rate of maintenance. Maintenance backlogs are a practical problem because manual maintenance is labour intensive and time consuming. For many systems the rate of environmental change will be faster than the rate of maintenance.

3. Alterations made to correct a lack of reference in one part of the system can have a knock-on effect that causes a lack of reference to develop in another parts of the system.

4. People who use an information system have a tendency to believe the system. Like the characters in a Kafka novel if the system indicates that something does not exist they will tend to act as though it does not exist despite physical evidence to the contrary. In these circumstances the need to correct the system is never officially recognized.

3   Logic and Language

3.1   The Difference between Logical and Factual Truth

Unlike robots, information systems produce 'statements' and many of these are putative descriptions of objects or events outside the information system itself.

Editors note: The Poll Tax system was replaced due to popular demand: the protest riots, reminiscent of the Peasant's Rebellion of 1381 consequent on the Poll Taxes of 1377, 1380 and 1381, in a number of cities led to a change of policy.

As such, they are tractable to analysis in terms of logic and the philosophy of language.

In order to understand how an information system that fails in reference can continue to operate it is necessary to make a number of logical distinctions. A distinction needs to be made between universals and particulars and between logical and factual truth. Universals are statements that refer to all members of a class and have the form: "All cats are animals", "No cat is a dog" etc. Particulars are statements that refer to particular members of a class and have the form: "Tiddles is a cat", "Some cats like milk", "That is a cat", etc.

The term 'logically true' is used to describe what is inevitably true in a contrived system. In formal systems there are axioms and rules of production; applying the rules of production to the axioms results in theorems all of which are logically true. Behind human conversation there are definitions and statements that follow from definitions by the law of non-self-contradiction, all of these are logically true. Language is, as Wittgenstein taught, a game; logically true statements are the rules of the game. The contradictory of a logically true statement is meaningless.

The term 'factually true' is used to describe what is contingently true; that is, what is true but not logically true. It is used to describe true statements about objects and events in the real world. One could equate the real world with the physical world, however, this might involve an unwarranted assumption that the laws of physics govern everything that is not a contrived system. All factually true statements are contingent, this means that they are always open to falsification and that the contradictory of a factual statement is not meaningless.

An example might help to illustrate this distinction.

i. All panthers are black.

ii. All crows are black.

Statement i is, in standard English, a logical truth. Standard English is what lexicographers try to capture with their dictionary definitions. English speakers play a language game and have agreed that one of the rules of this game is that 'panther' is the word for a black leopard. Therefore, the statement "Some panthers are yellow" is self contradictory and meaningless. There are, of course, variants on standard English. Among a group of regular interlocutors the word 'panthers' might stand for the members of a political movement and the word 'yellow' might for stand for 'cowardly'. In this language game "Some panthers are yellow" might be true. What counts as a logical truth depends upon the language game that is being played.

Statement ii is, in standard English, a factual statement. Although "Some crows are yellow" is false, it is not self contradictory and it is meaningful.

3.2 The Need for Both Factual and Logical Truth

Logical truths are true because of the way we have set up our language or system. Factual truths are true because of the way the world, the world which is not entirely an invention of the human mind, is. Two important points must be recognized about the relations between logical and factual truth. The first comes from David Hume and states that a factual truth cannot be derived from a logical truth. One cannot infer a factual statement from a set of statements all of which are logically true. This is a well known principle that underlies all of modern physical science. When some people first become acquainted with these ideas they are apt to think that it is only factual truth that is important. This is a mistake.

The second important point is that any system that contains factual truth must also contain logical truth. A more formal way of expressing this is that any factually true statement implies some logically true statements. This is because if we say that "All crows are black" is factual then we must have criteria for identifying crows that are independent of their colour. Those criteria must be logically true. If they were not then it would always be possible to say of any yellow crow-like thing that it was not a crow. That is, if we come across a thing that is just like a crow except that it is yellow we could say on the basis of this experience "It is not true that all crows are black" or we could say "This yellow thing is not a crow". If it is always possible to say that things that are not black are not crows then "All crows are black" could not be falsified and, therefore, could not be factual. Logical truths form an indispensable glue that binds factual statements together.

Some people have found this argument rather hard to follow so it is worth making the point in greater detail. When we say a statement is falsifiable we mean that it can be shown to be false by a counter example. If every crow we have come across has been black then we will be justified in believing that all crows are black. We will be justified in believing this until we come across a crow that is not black. This might be 'Edgar' a crow that is white. But there is a problem here. How do we know that Edgar is a crow? There must be certain attributes that Edgar has which will allow us to recognize him as a crow and obviously being black is not one of these attributes. Another way of putting this is that there are certain statements that will justify us in saying that Edgar is a crow and one of these statements cannot be "All crows are black".

Crows make a distinctive sound called a 'caw'. We might recognize Edgar as a crow on this basis. The conjunction of "All birds that caw are crows" and "Edgar is a bird that caws" will justify us in saying that Edgar is a crow. Now consider the following:

1. All crows are black.

2. All birds that caw are crows.

3. Edgar is a bird that caws and Edgar is white.

Let us suppose that we know on the basis of observation and incontrovertibly that 3 is true. Given that 2 is also true we can deduce that 1 is false. However, if all we know for certain is that 3 is true all we know about 1 and 2 is that at least one of them must be false. But it could be 2 just as easily as 1. We could take it that all crows are black is, in fact, true in which case the fact that Edgar is a bird that caws and is white only goes to show that not all birds that caw are crows.

If 1 and 2 are both factual (i.e. contingent) statements there is no way to determine on the basis of 3 which is true and which is false; but we can determine on the basis of 3 that at least one must be false. We do not know which has been falsified and this is not a very satisfactory situation. It makes a nonsense of the idea of falsification because it makes no sense to say that certain statements are falsifiable if we never know when to say they are false. Also if falsification is given up then we will also need to give up the ideas of contingent truth and the idea of factual truth as we have defined these in terms of falsification. Furthermore, if we tried to represent this sort of system in software we would have computability problems because the system is not decidable.

The problem is not resolved by adding more statements to the system. Suppose we add:

4. All British carrion eating birds are crows.

5. Edgar is a white, British carrion eating bird that caws.

These added to 1 and 2 still do not show that 1 is false. Given that 5 is true it is still possible for 1 to be true if 2 and 4 are false. That is 5 could be taken as showing that both 2 and 4 are false just as easily as it could be taken as showing that 1 is false. This situation will continue no matter how many factual (e.g. contingent) universals we add to the system.

The only way to make the system coherent and decidable is to introduce logical truth. If we take it that 2 is a logical rather than a factual truth the problem disappears. In this case being a bird that caws is a defining property of crows. From this it follows, by definition, that Edgar must be a crow. And from this it follows that not all crows are black.

3.3 Logical Truth and Definitions

It now needs to be explained how logical truth can be established. Logical truths are true by definition. Statements that are logically true are either full definitions, statements specifying a defining attribute or statements that follow from these by the rules of logic.

It is common sense that we as individuals can define our terms in any way we like. However, if our definitions are going to be part of an information system, that is a system used to communicate with others, then the other people involved will need to know about and accept them. Indeed the amount of communication between individuals could be measured in terms of the definitions they accept. There will only perfect communication between two interlocutors if they accept all the definitions in a universe of discourse.

In information system design, therefore, it is of vital importance that there is a consensus about the definitions in the system among the people using the system.

How this consensus can be achieved using Soft Systems Methodology has been the subject of previous papers (Gregory 1993).

3.4 Logical Truth Alone is Uninformative

Although logically true statements are essential for factual statements they are not in themselves, nor in conjunction with factual particulars, informative about the real world. Suppose that Tiddles is a panther. Then it might seem that by Statement i one can infer that Tiddles is black and that this tells one something one did not already know. But this is an illusion. As Statement i is logically true all it does is say something about how a panther is defined. If Tiddles does not fit this definition then Tiddles is not a panther. If Statement i is logically true one will not be able to infer from it any real world facts, i.e. contingent facts, about Tiddles.

The configuration of most computerized information systems is such that they embody rules that are logically true and only rules that are logically true. The entry of data, which is the equivalent of the introduction of factual particulars, will not change or falsify any of these implicit rules. People expect these systems to be genuinely informative about real world events, however, this would appear to be logically impossible.

It needs to be explained, therefore, how it is that people appear to find them useful. The simple answer is that computer systems do not function in isolation but in the context of a wider system of belief. This is the system of beliefs adhered to by the human operators and users. Their beliefs encompass a plethora of universal factual truths and it is these that complement the logical truths returned by the machine in such a way that they can be mapped on to the real world and produce genuine information.

4   A Model of an Information System

An information system should consist of elements corresponding to logically true universals, factually true universals and factually true particulars. They should work together as follows:

1. Factual particular: Tiddles hunts at night.

2. Factual universal: Only panthers hunt at night.

3. Factual particular: Tiddles is a panther.

4. Logical universal: All panthers are black.

5. Factual universal: All black things are the colour of coal.

6. Factual particular: Tiddles is the colour of coal.

Here the factual universals act as buffers between the factual particulars and the logical universal and allows 6 to be a genuinely informative inference. At the same time, the logical universal is an indispensable part of the system. The users do not identify panthers on the basis of the definition in the computer system, i.e. 4, but on the basis of another criterion, i.e. 2, which they have formulated themselves and which they believe to be true as a matter of fact. These factual universals are inductive hypotheses and can be falsified as the world or knowledge of the world changes. For example, it might be discovered that a certain tiger hunts at night. In this case 2 would be falsified and the user would have to formulate another factual universal as a criterion for the identification of panthers.

This is how a system of logical rules and definitions can be mapped on to the real world. The mapping will break down when the user fails to formulate factual universals relevant to the system. In this case the user will be accused of not understanding the system. However, it will also break down if the logical rules are such that there are no factual universals that could effect a mapping on to the real world. In these cases there will be no interpretation of the system that will correspond with observed events. If the system is not changed then it can continue to operate in a Kafkaesque mode. It will not map on to the real world but it can have an indirect effect, through the actions of the users, on people in the real world.

The fundamental problem is that while the logical elements of the machine can be created by systems designers, the users' systems of beliefs, which are essential for reference to the real world, cannot. However, this can be overcome by designing information systems that include factual universals as well as logical universals and particulars. A method for doing this explicitly has already been developed and sample programs that include factual universals have been written (Gregory 1995).

5   Conclusion

The problem of mapping information systems on to the real world is not as difficult as explaining mathematics. It is mainly a problem because is not recognized as the logical problem that it is. The tools of systems analysis, such as data flow diagrams and entity-relationship models, have very limited logical power. They are not sufficient to produce a system that will map on to the real world. However, most information system designers think they are adequate. Many designers have come to think like the systems they design.

Organic Information for the Organic Organization? An Application of the Work of Talcott Parsons to Information Systems

Richard Kamm

The organic metaphor is an increasingly popular image used in the study of organizations, particularly in the light of the application of information technology networks. It is therefore important to discuss organic views of information and communication. The ideas of Talcott Parsons are examined as a source of material for an organic concept of organizational information. The organic metaphor itself is one which places emphasis on the need for social integration. An appropriate organic view of the role of information systems is as the means by which organizations are integrated. The possibility of defining information as a symbolic medium is discussed and the organic nature of this idea is explained. The limitations of the idea of symbolic media are discussed in the context of a more general criticism of the organic metaphor itself.

1 Introduction

The purpose of this chapter is to develop the implications of a philosophically-informed area of social theory for our definition of the nature and role of information. The organismic metaphor for organizations is the subject of this piece partly because it is one of the most durable views of society, but also because of its particular resonance in the field of information systems. Many of the most influential ideas concerning the development of information systems have been developed within organismic frameworks, most notably systems theory and socio-technical systems ideas, which give the metaphor much of its historical significance (Morgan 1986: 44–6; Jackson 1991: 45; Scott 1992: 84). The continuing attraction of the image is illustrated by more recent attention being paid to the idea of evolutionary forms of systems development and also to styles of management that emphasize flexibility and adaptability in a competitive environment. The idea of the 'organismic organization' was elaborated during the 1960s (Burns 1971) but has current relevance in the arguments that work is becoming less formal and more autonomous in organizations which are held together more by information than by well-defined structures and hierarchies (Drucker 1989a; Bergquist 1993: 123; Marshall 1990: 98–9). It is important to establish the implications of the organic metaphor for communication and information use if the full implications of the metaphor are to be appreciated.

The focus of this chapter is on the ideas of Talcott Parsons because his work is among the most suitable within organismic traditions for the purpose of reexamining the nature of information. Parsons was the oldest of a number of writers who have, since the Second World War, attempted to integrate the philosophical study of language and communication into sociology. Jürgen Habermas (1984: 288) and Anthony Giddens (1984: 21) are two others who have, in very different ways, addressed a similar theme and in doing so have felt it necessary to engage directly with Parsons' framework (Habermas 1987b: ch.7; Giddens 1984: 263–74). Parsons' work therefore offers considerable material for discussing the possibility of developing a consistently organic definition of the nature of organizational information. The priorities of the metaphor will be described and their implications for the use of information developed through reference to some of the most significant concepts developed in his writings.

2   The Organic Metaphor and the Ideas of Talcott Parsons

In examining the organic metaphor we are less concerned with precise analogies between biological and social phenomena than with the nature of organizations as gradually evolving entities comprising interdependent parts. While acknowledging the inspiration provided for some writers by studies of the natural world, an organismic view of social activity is more an acceptance of Aristotle's argument that we are social beings; recognizing and accepting our interdependence is an essential part of our humanity (Aristotle 1962: 59–60). The implication of this attitude is that human activity cannot be judged by objective standards of efficiency but must be evaluated as part of the culture within which it is embedded. 'Organic' links exist not only between members of a society but also between a society and its own past. The most serious problems are therefore those which create social strains by undermining the sense of belonging which individuals need to feel if they are to be integrated within society (Deutsch 1963: 33; Parsons 1969: 174).

The organic metaphor in organizational analysis has taken its cue from Durkheim, for whom society is primarily a moral institution (Durkheim 1984: 300–1). Modern industry has, from this point of view, gained in technical efficiency but has lost the common values which create a sense of belonging (Durkheim 1957: 9; Mayo 1949: 6; Fenton 1984: 60). The full benefits of industrial development can be realized, but only when individuals are fully

A   G

Adaption subsystem Economy i.e. resource distribution	Goal-attainment subsystem Polity i.e. a decision-making for achieving particular objectives
Latency (Pattern maintenance) subsystem Maintenance of instituted cultural patterns e.g. religion	Integration subsystem 'Societal Community' i.e. structures for application of norms and laws

L   I

Figure 1: Parsons' functional subsystems of the social system; adapted from (Parsons 1969, Parsons 1971b).

---

integrated into a wider, purposeful community. A purely individualist philosophy runs the risk of undermining the consensus on which collective identity and solidarity depend (Durkheim 1984: 220 & 339); "the solitary who works alone is always a very unhappy person" (Mayo 1949: 127). Adaptability and flexibility are important to the organic metaphor, but they can only be realized when social activity is founded on shared customs and values.

The treatment of moral consensus is particularly subtle in Parsons' work, where it is associated with the idea that any human system has four functional requirements. Two of these functions are related to the generation and preservation of shared cultural understanding; Pattern-maintenance, or Latency, is the preservation of core values, while Integration subsystems apply them to particular situations via the implementation of norms. The total of four subsystems in the AGIL framework (Adaptation, Goal-attainment, Integration and Pattern-maintenance) must be well-balanced, which implies that the activities of resource distribution and practical goal-attainment need to be underpinned by a normative consensus which gives them meaning (see Figure 1). While values are a fundamental point of reference, they cannot explain everything. They would have little practical effect without a framework of activity which is provided by institutions such as the law and voluntary associations. This normative conception of law as an integrating force suggests that it is best seen not as a series of commands and expected responses (which is closer to a utilitarian view) but as a means of generating legitimacy, demonstrating that values are genuinely shared, giving guidance as to what they mean in particular circumstances and creating an impression of consistency over time (Parsons 1969: 362).

3 Information Systems as Sources of Organizational Integration

Parsons' development of the AGIL framework is most explicit at the level of the whole social system, but there is also work by him and others which applies his ideas to the study of organizations (Hills 1976). The goal-attainment activities are those which are concerned with the implementation of policy. 'Adaptation' in this context refers to the organization of resources; often the management and allocation of finance. The idea of 'Pattern-maintenance' is applied to the generation of values which give the organization a reason for its existence. In current parlance, the importance of a mission statement could be viewed as providing the essential foundation for stability in the organizations which are otherwise subject to constant change (Bergquist 1993: 73).

The pivotal and subtle role of integration at the level of an organization is given to coordination, defined in a way that makes it analogous to the development of norms for an entire social system (Parsons 1960: 37; Hills 1976: 850). Since coordination involves the use of information the implication would be that an organismic view of the development of information systems would see the important questions as those relating to the meaning conveyed by information within the accepted culture of the workplace. Coordination, here, is not simply a matter of organizational structure but also includes relatively intangible concerns such as motivation and the encouragement of cooperation (Parsons 1960: 30 & 34). This suggests that the development of organizational information systems is a normative activity similar to the practice of law or the writing of constitutions. The spirit in which the various items are understood is more important than the content of specific messages.

The contrast here is with a mechanistic definition of organizational information which treats it as a well-structured flow with a quantifiable value (Kamm 1993). Scientific management and formal bureaucracy, both associated with the assumptions of the mechanistic metaphor, tend to treat information as 'data plus meaning', with the greatest attention given to establishing the integrity and security of data. The meaning given to the data should be unproblematic if the structures of data use are well-designed. By contrast, the organic metaphor, with its stress on the need to preserve common norms and assumptions, would not see meaning as something which is self-evident in any particular piece of data. Instead it proceeds from continual developments of human communication and must therefore itself be seen as being in a state of evolution. An organicist view requires that the construction of consensus through the attribution of meaning be seen as a social process which cannot be separated from the provision of data.

In principle, there is little that is contentious in describing the organic view of information as dependent on cultural context. It is accepted in the literature inspired by socio-technical systems ideas that issues such as norms and values should be taken into account when considering changes such as the introduction of new technology, e.g. Miller & Rice (1967). While critics of mechanistic approaches to management and organizational structure, seeing them as essentially outdated, they often retain a mechanistic view of the role and nature of information; that is as a resource for making clear, unambiguous decisions. Much of the management literature which emphasizes the need for adaptable enterprises privileges statistical measures above other types of information (Peters 1987: 488–90). Despite the importance given to group work over hierarchical structure, the aims of Total Quality Management are reinforced by the use of measurable targets against which performance is to be assessed (Atkinson 1990: 36). Even in more reflective works which develop a systems view of organizational information, information is sometimes treated purely as a resource for managerial decision-making (Kast & Rosenzweig 1985: 429). In Parsonian terms, this implies that information serves solely the goal-attainment subsystem, having little to do with the problems of integration.

There are two possible reactions to this. One is to restrict the role of information and accept that it genuinely has nothing to do with the problem of moral integration which is central to the organismic metaphor. While this approach has the attraction of a rigorous, statistical approach to information, it underestimates the problems of identification with the interests of the organization which are raised by the adoption of decentralized, organic structures. The other, more consistently organismic, approach would be to build on the insights of those writers, notably Katz & Kahn, who have warned that treating any aspect of organizational behaviour as if it were a tangible object moves the analyst in a mechanistic direction (Katz & Kahn 1978: 37). They argue that information need not be seen in this light, citing 'job rationale' as an example of a communication which is both intangible and useful, facilitating a systemic view of the organization (Katz & Kahn 1978: 440–1). The argument which follows examines the possibilities for using the analysis of communication within Parsons' organic view of society to produce a more general approach to information analysis within this organic framework.

4 Information and Symbolic Media: Parsons' Analysis of Communication

The following section examines view of communication which Parsons developed to explain the workings of the functional subsystems of the AGIL schema. The idea of the symbolic medium is described as Parsons developed it for the level of whole societies and its relevance to the idea of organizational information is discussed.

4.1 The Idea of a Symbolic Medium of Exchange

As Parsons developed the idea of functional subsystems, it became increasingly abstract. The requirements of Adaptation, Integration, Pattern-maintenance and Goal-attainment will exist regardless of the extent to which they are recognized and formally defined. It has been argued that the idea of allotting each of them a medium of communication allows them to be more easily related to some aspect of objective reality (Alexander 1984: 111). Each subsystem is oriented towards particular values which need to be transmitted to other subsystems if the relevant outputs are to have the effects which they have evolved to produce. For example, economy (the adaptive subsystem of the social system) is oriented towards the values of utility, and the means by which this is communicated is money, a medium which is 'anchored' in its parent subsystem but which is simultaneously active in the other three. The relevant media anchored in the other components of the social system are, respectively, power (in the goal-attainment subsystem), value commitments (in the underlying value system) and influence (based in the integration system) (Parsons 1969).

Parsons' view of communication was that it incorporates not only the passage of symbols but also their reception and interpretation. Language inevitably has a normative content, as explained by the fact that "a message can be meaningful and hence understood only by those who 'know the language', that is, the code, and accept its 'conventions'" (Parsons 1969: 404). Arguing that the media of exchange are special cases of language, i.e. more limited means of communication, implies that they all require a symbolic element which is based on trust between the sender of a message and its recipient. Money, for example, is not simply a tangible token (Parsons 1971a: 27). It also requires confidence to be expressed in its current and future value if it is to be used in economic exchange. Deflation is marked by a collapse in confidence in the ability of money to act as an acceptable medium of exchange and a tendency to revert to the basic level of gold (Parsons 1969: 446).

Similarly, power or law rarely consist purely of force but usually require an acceptance of their legitimacy by the individuals of whom it is exercised. Neither is to be regarded as a set of tangible units with a fixed value, nor will they produce an automatic response (Parsons 1969: 361–2). Trust in a medium can be reduced (signifying 'deflation') or extended beyond its ability to produce results (signifying 'inflation') but the essential symbolic element is the product of historical circumstances rather than inherent in the medium itself. This is an essentially non-mechanistic idea because of its rejection of a stimulus-response or instrumental view of social relations, arguing instead that the legitimacy of a medium is essential to its effect.

4.2 Can Information be Described as a Symbolic Medium?

The prospect of defining information as a symbolic medium appears tempting. As described above, there exists a mechanistic image of information as a tangible entity which is analogous with the utilitarian views of power and money which Parsons argued against. Information has been likened to money as an essentially intangible medium on which increasing reliance is placed to link highly dispersed organizations (Drucker 1990: 8). Parsons' later work, in which neuro-cybernetic ideas were extended to sociology, contains an argument that the equivalent of information-communication within the nervous system is the integrative function of the symbolic media (Parsons & Platt 1973: 23). If information is to be regarded as truly integrative force in organizations, however, the component of trust has to be shown to be relevant to its function and to affect the way in which it is used.

The difficulty with classifying information in general as a symbolic medium is Parsons' own view of it in his analyses of communication at the level of the whole social system. Initially, he found the idea of information as an integrative medium extremely plausible because of its role in inducing norm-governed activity (Parsons 1969: 417 & 424). He came to argue, though, that it is both too general and too specific a notion to carry the entire burden of representing social influence. It is too general in the sense that it was necessarily active in every aspect of human behaviour; i.e. it can be found in each element of the AGIL schema. It is too specific in that it did not convey the multifarious ways in which influence might be exercised (ibid.: 430–2). Influence exercised purely through 'solid, verifiable fact' to the exclusion of ambiguous intentions and opinions would be an impoverished form of the medium (ibid.: 433–4). It is at least as likely to be exercised through prestige as through information; the best-known example being a patient who is likely to follow medical advice mainly because of the status of the doctor providing it than because the details of his condition are laid in front of him (Parsons 1976: 103). The question is therefore raised as to whether the idea of a symbolic aspect of information can be developed within an organismic framework at all.

In principle, this objection would seem to hold for analysis at the level of particular organizations. Information appears to play a distinctive role within each of the functional subsystems; bearing messages of command within the goal-attainment system, facilitating the distribution of resources within the adaptive, communicating the corporate mission as a means of pattern-maintenance and enabling the requirements of coordination to be met by the integrative. If information is defined purely as a statement of fact, its uses within the different areas of organizational activity can be seen as having little in common beyond a capacity to transmit the necessary messages.

It is, though, possible to argue that by confining his view of information to hard fact, Parsons oversimplified to the extent of ignoring the issues of trust and meaning attribution; the essentially organic problems which the idea of a generalized medium of exchange was intended to address. Parsons' own ideas have been extended by others who have suggested that they imply that the very concepts of communication and information should be treated as problematic (Baum 1976: 541). In effect, it is suggested that Parsons' use of the term 'information' is closer to our understanding of data with unambiguous meaning. Baum argues that a consistently Parsonian view of a medium would treat it as a system of communication in which the items of data are bound up with the implications of its use and the relevance and significance to the individuals who interpret it (Baum 1976: 548).

At the very least, it is possible to distinguish a category of 'organizational information' which may be seen as 'communication' in this way. Information is used in organizations to produce particular, often specified, effects. If the intended effects are to be produced, the extent of trust, (or lack of) between members of the organization, or 'solidarity' as 'valued association' (Parsons 1969: 433), becomes a central concern. This quality is the focus of organismic analyses of most aspects of organizational activity, and is produced by a commitment to common values. An absence of trust will lead to the erosion of common feeling and the settlement of disagreements purely by coercion, either by use of the law or through the strength of market position. With regard to information, a mechanistic view of trust will draw attention simply to the extent to which the information is seen to relay an unambiguous and accurate message. An organismic approach, on the other hand, will regard trust as involving an understanding that information is used in a way which does not undermine a sense of shared interest.

The idea of an organismic approach to organization being one which relies on teamwork and group responsibility for the exercise of management functions is an important application of this idea of trust. Where trust between members either exists or has been consciously developed, work groups can invite participation in decisions and can be left to organize production without close managerial supervision because of the common commitment to the values and objectives of the organization (Fox 1974: 40). Without a core of agreed norms, the interests of groups and management will diverge to the point of organizational collapse. Similarly, when information collected to monitor production, say, is gathered in a high trust organization, it is accepted as a valid contribution to objectives by the people whose work it assesses and is used by the assessors in a way which reinforces the prevailing ethos of the organization (Fox 1974: 141).

By extending the idea of trust to organizational information, the concepts of deflation and inflation of a medium (Parsons 1969: 463) become more relevant. A decline of trust in the organization would be accompanied by the erosion of the capacity of information to evoke the desired response. A reduced sense of common interest in the firm or institution will be reinforced by an absence of a feeling of shared ownership of information. Similarly, 'inflation' of information would be marked by an excessive belief in its capacity to produce desired effects. The improvement of organizational performance might rely on the communication of organizational mission or priorities to the exclusion of more material concerns such as working practices. Whatever the problems of incorporating trust within a more general view of information, it is central to the role of information within organizations.

4.3   Information as the Promoter of Organizational Complexity

A further issue concerning Parsons' view of media is their role in facilitating the development of social complexity. As society moves beyond the stage of organization in face-to-face communities, it requires forms of communication which allow common ideas to be expressed in order to prevent it from disintegrating. Money, for example, permits the spread of sophisticated economic exchanges and, for each individual, removes the need to possess physical products to barter for the necessities of life. Social evolution here implies 'the enhancement of adaptive capacity' (Savage 1981: 208); the extent to which a society possesses adaptive and integrative institutions which are distinct from the process of value creation and which allow values to inform individual goal-attainment activities (Parsons 1966; 1971b). 'Differentiation', the name given to the process of increasing scale and complexity of social organization, is dependent on media as specialized languages which help to hold society together by expressing the necessary relations of trust (Parsons 1971b: 27; Haines 1987).

The equivalent of this process of differentiation at the level of organizations can be seen as the development of coordination via the communication of information (Parsons 1966: 22). It would not be difficult to draw on our knowledge of industrial history to describe an evolutionary pattern of organizational growth in which the use and availability of information both creates and resolves the problem of control at each stage (Beniger 1986). The initial phase of this evolution is marked by personal ownership and leadership of the organization, with control exercised by individuals who hold their position by charisma or hereditary right. As organizations become too large for a single person to coordinate, delegation becomes necessary and with it the communication of organizational information. Thus the development of the bureaucratic corporation can be seen as a necessary stage in organizational history which is made possible through the introduction of techniques of financial and managerial control based on a mechanistic approach to information. Such an approach to information use may not, however, reflect universal principles of management but may, instead, lead to the creation of new forms of organization.

There is a tradition of evolutionary assumptions in organicist work on organizations. It is argued that mechanistic approaches, such as scientific management, were appropriate at one stage of the development of corporations but are becoming outdated either because expectations of consultation or participation have arisen in society or economic conditions are forcing businesses and the state to be more flexible and decentralized in their approach (Mayo 1949: 12; Kast & Rosenzweig 1985: 117). Most recently of all, information technology has come to be seen as the integrating force for organizations whose members may work in completely different locations (Daniels 1993). Under such conditions, the organic organization needs an appreciation of the essentially organic point that decisions are not simply an instrumental application of rules but also reflect shared expectations and values (Parsons 1960: 39). The integrative role of information can therefore be seen as a means of giving the organization a shape which is particularly appropriate as the more formal structures decline (Bergquist 1993: 44).

Organizational information can be seen as the bearer of messages for any of the functional subsystems of organizations but it also fulfils a specifically integrative role. Information conveys data within each of the functional

103

subsystems of organizations, but it will also bear meaning which, in a well-integrated organization, has evolved to be understood by all who have an interest in it. Its integrative role is the communication of norms of expected behaviour in which activity is imbued with the values of the organization. It promotes differentiation in that it allows those values to be practically effected by holding together organizations of any size above that in which delegation is unnecessary. The question raised is not whether the integrative function exists, but whether it is reasonable to regard normative consensus as both a useful concept and an unambiguously healthy aspect of organizational behaviour.

5 Limitations of the Symbolic Medium Idea

The insights of Parsons' work on media are extremely important for our understanding of the organic metaphor for organizations. They allow us to distinguish the specifically organic elements of the discussions of information usage in new organizational forms from those which are arguably more closely related to older forms of management thinking. The implications of the idea of the symbolic medium should therefore be evaluated, not simply in their own right but also because of the opportunity they provide to examine the assumptions which lie behind the organic organization. While the idea of information as a symbolic medium is consistent with the organic metaphor, its limitations point to criticisms which might be made of the whole organic approach to organizational development.

Parsons' development of the idea of symbolic media has been subject to a number of criticisms. It has been argued that he relies too heavily on the characteristics of money in expounding the nature of all media; ideas such as 'circulation' and 'banking' are not readily applicable to other media (Lidz 1991: 123; Cartwright & Warner 1976: 651). Such an objection applies to organizational information. Data might be said to circulate and be storable but if, in an organic framework, a variable element of meaning is an integral aspect of information, it can hardly possess a value based on a commonly accepted scale of measurement. It cannot, moreover, be alienated, since when it is passed on, it does not necessarily become unavailable to the provider (Habermas 1987b: 275). Parsons' view of the integrative medium of influence places it in a different category to its more specific counterparts in adaptive and goal-attainment subsystems. Since information is similarly qualitative in an organic view of organizations, likening it to money or power raises the expectation that there might be an information science of comparable rigour to economics and operational research. In an organic context, such a science is probably unrealizable.

A more fundamental argument against seeing information as a symbolic medium relates to the usefulness of the whole idea of integration around a normative consensus. The attraction of an organismic view of information use is the insight that meaning is dependent on cultural context. To build on such an analysis, however, leads to the same difficulty which Habermas (1987b: 260) has identified as being endemic to functionalism as a whole; the ideas can proceed in one of two directions, neither of which consistently preserves the priorities of the metaphor. An organic view of social activity can point towards either a more formal development of systems theory or a move into a form of cultural analysis which is divorced from any material model of human activity.

A neuro-cybernetic development of systems theory has been put forward as a logical step, and was explicitly considered in Parsons' later work (Parsons & Platt 1973: 23). A likening of integrative information flows to neural impulses has the advantage of giving greater precision than is allowed by an organismic view which, as noted above, has a more qualitative than quantitative view of the value of information. A cybernetic treatment of information flows has some similarities to the mechanistic, but preserves the essential systemic ideas of interdependence and hierarchy which inform the organismic approach (Jackson 1991: 129). The difficulty with Parsons' use of cybernetics, it has been argued, is that it leads to control being seen as proceeding purely from society to individual, thus upsetting the balance between functional and cultural analysis in favour of the former (Haines 1987: 32). Norms become interesting less for their content than for the underlying role that they play in maintaining integration. Meaning as a problematic quality tends to be subsumed within a more formal analysis of well-defined responses to particular stimuli and a shift of emphasis from the culture to the structure of organizations.

To provide a more subtle analysis of meaning, however, also departs from the path followed by organicist thinking. For Parsons, the essential feature of a fully developed social theory is that it combines cultural and functional analysis (Alexander 1984: 47). An integrative medium such as organizational information is therefore seen as conveying a rich variety of meanings but also as performing the particular role of reinforcing normative consensus. A fully hermeneutic approach to information systems would have great difficulty in accepting any degree of consensus as natural, or dissension as intrinsically pathological (Walsham 1993: 37). It might instead accept disagreements over the meaning of information as potentially justifiable, and therefore as valuable, thereby moving analysis away from the concept of functional needs which is central to the organismic metaphor.

6 Conclusion

An organismic concept of information is conceivable, and can be clearly distinguished from the conventional mechanistic view. However, to develop an organic form of information use to complement the organic organization not only requires structural and procedural change but also means facing some difficult questions about the nature of integration and collective values. Despite the pervasiveness of the metaphor in organizational thought and the attractions of the more comprehensive view of information that it entails, there remain problems which cannot be dealt with purely within the logic of organicist ideas. Both of these models, the mechanistic and organismic, define the role of information as an organizational resource for particular purposes, and therefore raise significant issues concerning its nature and management. To extend discussion of these issues satisfactorily will therefore require the contribution of further metaphors which draw on the development of social theory in other directions.

Methodology

Introduction

Stephen K. Probert & Ian A. Beeson

The four chapters in this section can be seen as the applications of various aspects of philosophy to some of the central theoretical debates in contemporary information systems research. Although the authors use different philosophical approaches, and address different aspects of the information systems discipline, they are united by a common desire both to instill greater rigour in research and to encourage more reflective approaches to the analyses of current practices.

Brian Petheram considers that work in information systems research — and moreover practice — inevitably leads to the need for philosophical reflections about many of the concepts and issues at the core of the information systems discipline. Petheram begins by considering the relationship between models of information systems and the aspects of the world which they are attempting to be models of. He argues that the quality of the model is responsible, in large part, for the quality of the final information system, as delivered. The quality of the model depends, in turn, on the philosophical assumptions adopted by the analyst. Therefore the analyst is (or should be!) inevitably drawn into philosophical considerations of the most fundamental kinds. Whilst these considerations include, as might be expected, considerations of the relationship between epistemological assumptions (about how it is that we acquire knowledge about the world) and ontological assumptions (about what kinds of things the world fundamentally consists of), Petheram also argues that issues concerned with the relationship between power and knowledge are also of considerable importance. He reasons that the development of successful information systems depends on both the acquisition of knowledge and the taking of appropriate action, and consequently he finds that some of the concerns of post-modernist philosophers may offer useful insights for information systems development teams. Finally, Petheram considers that the philosophical assumptions adopted by the analysts are much a matter of personal choice, and as such the values that analysts' hold are of crucial significance in determining those choices. These values are also embedded in philosophical schemas, which should be critically (and periodically) analysed by those responsible for information systems developments.

Paul Wernick and Russel Winder take a slightly different approach to the relevance of philosophy, preferring to use some aspects of philosophy as a research methodology for the analysis of a number of important issues in information systems (they call their approach 'applied philosophy'). Using the example of software engineering, their work attempts to apply Thomas Kuhn's conceptions of 'the structure of scientific revolutions' as a methodology for analysing the structure of changes in both the theory and practice of software engineering in recent years. Although they fully recognize that software engineering can hardly be held up as an example of a 'normal science', they nevertheless hold that the application of Kuhn's ideas to the analysis of this discipline will bring about a better understanding of many of the problematic aspects of the discipline for both researchers and professionals alike. To this end, they begin by considering those elements of software engineering most amenable, analogically, to an analysis of the Kuhnian kind. They go on to specify what they consider to be the relevant aspects of Kuhn's analytical technique, and to apply this technique to analyse the discipline of software engineering. They pay careful attention to the unusual properties of the community of software engineers, insofar as this community — unlike its pure scientific counterparts — has a responsibility not only, or not predominantly, for knowledge-production. Software engineers actually construct information systems; this places them somewhat at the mercy of market forces, in that the systems they construct have to be delivered within tight cost and time constraints. As such, Wernick and Winder argue that software engineering can be best construed as a Kuhnian 'pre-science', and they find many important facets of a pre-science, as identified by Kuhn, are represented in the current 'craft' of software engineering. Consequently, having decided to analyse software engineering as a Kuhnian 'pre-science', they are able to draw several interesting conclusions. Firstly, they argue that many of the terms currently in use within the software engineering community, such as 'object-oriented', are in need of greater conceptual clarification and standardization. They conclude that, if this were to be achieved, then this would improve the professionalism of the discipline and go some way to removing the 'sales gimmick' tag applied, by hard-headed sceptics, to many of these terms! Secondly, they argue that more astute philosophical analysis of some of the concepts currently employed within this discipline would provide greater clarity of the meaning of such concepts. This in turn would help to provide a frame of reference in which research questions concerning both the effectiveness of different methodologies used for developing systems, and the analysis of reports of real world software developments, could be better conducted. Such conceptual clarity, at which Wernick and Winder aim, would also help to improve both the education of future generations of software engineers, and the professionalism of those engineers thereafter. Finally, they argue that such a framework as they would like to see in place would also be of benefit to the software engineers who work in small teams (often those not using a formalized methodology). This group could benefit from the guidance such a framework would provide in helping to choose appropriate tools.

Steve Probert's chapter explores the metaphysical and epistemological assumptions inherent in Soft Systems Methodology. He finds some confusion in the accounts offered by SSM's proponents, noting allegiance to two opposing theories of enquiry, one deriving from Kant and the other from Locke. Despite claims from Checkland and his co-writers that their systems thinking is essentially Kantian (or indeed Husserlian), Probert finds their epistemological assumptions closer to Cartesian rationalism (although sometimes they are closer to Lockean empiricism). Checkland also appears to espouse a Popperian orientation, despite Popper's rejection of subjectivist ('bucket') theories of knowledge. Probert's chapter provides a summary chart of some key philosophers' positions to steer us through these difficult waters and throws light on the problematic relationship between ontology and epistemology in SSM. One key conclusion from the analysis is that SSM, although it subscribes to holism at the ontological level (especially in the notion of 'autonomous observers'), turns out to be reductionist in its epistemology.

In the final chapter in this section, Marcus Lynch attempts to provide greater conceptual clarification as to the fundamental nature of an information system. Lynch finds that there is considerable conceptual confusion as to the precise nature of an information system, and attempts to provide an essentially notional model of the logically necessary features of such systems, considered as human activity systems. To this end, a formal model is developed, and various logical consequences are derived from this model. Interestingly, Lynch argues that all information systems are recursively embedded in an hierarchy of information systems. Lynch therefore concludes that the support for decision-making provided an information system must, if it is to be genuinely useful, pay careful attention to the decision-making needs of the wider information system in which it is embedded.

All four chapters in this section show a keen awareness of the need for greater conceptual clarification of some of the key concepts in information systems methodologies. However, all of the contributors also show an appropriate sensitivity to the need for information systems professionals to operate in an highly competitive marketplace, and as such they demonstrate that, whilst there is little scope for idle speculation within information systems philosophy, there is little to be gained (and much damage to be done) from adopting a cavalier attitude to the philosophical aspects of information systems methodologies. Indeed, it could be argued that it is the tacit acceptance of the 'fact' that there are no important philosophical aspects of information systems methodologies that gives rise to current trends for innumerable 'fads' in information systems — all of which would no doubt claim to be exclusively aimed at 'getting the job done'! Whilst not arguing resolutely for the adoption of a particular set of conventions to govern the information systems concepts discussed, each contributor — in his own way — furthers a valuable debate as to the precise nature of what needs to be done at a philosophical level before better information systems methodologies can be developed at a practical level.

Backing into Philosophy via Information Systems

Brian Petheram

This chapter takes a pragmatic stance on the relevance of philosophy to information systems practice. By focusing on modelling as a key process of information systems development, it attempts to show how the deployment of something akin to a 'philosophy' is inevitable. This may be conscious or unconscious; implicit or explicit. It argues that a reflective practitioner will tend to develop an interest in philosophy since its appropriateness determines the quality of models which in turn determine the usefulness of the new or changed information system.

It is accepted by many that the current state of the art in information systems is unsatisfactory, arguably a mess. Symptoms of this include the high failure rate reported by users, and the proliferation of methods accompanied by a lack of agreement over the criteria which should be used to match a method or methods with a given situation. It is also widely accepted that the issues addressed by information systems are so complex that effective understanding and deployment of methods can only be achieved if underpinned by a powerful body of theory. If the aim of information systems is taken to be effective action in a problematic situation, then a useful area to investigate may be the relationship between action and situation. The discipline of information systems draws on a wide range of theory to assist in understanding the nature of the situation in which intervention is contemplated. This chapter focuses on the processes by which such understanding affects the actual practice of information systems. It is argued that information systems is essentially a pragmatic discipline in that knowledge is not valued for its own sake but for its contribution to improved practice. A more explicit account of the ways in which knowledge informs action may identify those areas or types of knowledge which are most useful. It may also support the understanding and evaluation of the processes which form the link.

Figure 1 gives an overview of the relationship between situation and action. The processes involved — abstraction, representation, and translation, can be conveniently summarized as 'modelling'. It can be argued that action in any context is based on a model of the relevant 'real world' situation. The model

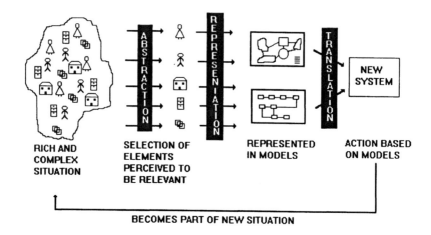

Figure 1: Processes linking situation and action.

may be mental, as in personal construct theory (Bannister & Fransella 1971) — thus a decision about what to do this evening would be influenced by mental models of what the alternatives would be like. The development of information systems involves a large number of modelling processes, many of which may be more formal and/or more explicit. They may be used to represent the current situation; as tools to assist in design; as a basis for debate with stakeholders; and ultimately as specification documents for the hardware and software elements of the new system. Thus the systems that are implemented can be seen as essentially translations of the specification models into another form. This also applies to human procedures or data definitions; the non-technical aspects of the new system will be interpretations of some kind of models that emerge from the development process even if the 'model' is in the form of a verbal agreement. It then follows that the quality (or appropriateness) of the system is dependent on the quality (or appropriateness) of the model. As can be seen from Figure 1, a model is by definition a selection or abstraction from the richness of the 'real world' and the quality (or appropriateness) of a model is therefore dependent on the quality (or appropriateness) of the basis of that selection. That basis of selection could be thought of as a 'philosophy'. This chain of reasoning shows why reflective practitioners might find themselves 'backing into' a concern with philosophy.

This essentially pragmatic approach to philosophy has led to a working definition of philosophy as 'a set of assumptions about relevance and purpose'.

'Relevance' relates to the process of the necessary reduction of richness and complexity ('abstraction' in Figure 1). 'Purpose' relates to the form and intended usage of the model. The set of assumptions would include fundamentals such as ontology — some types of action are more effectively carried out using realist assumptions, a nominalist stance may be more useful in other contexts; and these would underpin the processes of enquiry adopted. There would also be elements of theory from a wide variety of sources such as organizational sociology, psychology, management science, and even computer science. The one assumption that seems to be a constant is that of the usefulness of 'system' as an intellectual construct (Woodburn 1988). This notion of system transcends 'soft' and 'hard'.

Such an approach to philosophy implies that its components will change according to the context in which action is contemplated, since concepts of 'relevance' and 'purpose' are dependent on the particular situation. This places a burden on the would be actors in that they have to reflect on, and make a conscious choice about the nature and components of their philosophy rather than select from a limited range of 'packages' or adopt a single approach. I see this process as inevitable given the current limitations of Information Systems as a discipline. Thus 'philosophy' in this sense is more of a process than a body of knowledge. A consequence of this is that issues such as 'truth' and 'belief' become relative rather than absolute. This does not mean, however, that 'mainstream' philosophy has nothing to offer. The emphasis placed on reflection about assumptions inevitably leads to a concern with both a widening of the range of possible sources and a deepening of understanding of those that are considered. Thus there are aspects of philosophy, which whilst not being apparent candidates for application to action, are of great interest due to the light they may shine on options that are currently more favoured. For example, ideas propounded under the heading of 'post-modernism' have been found to be useful; mainly as a stimulus to the kind of dialectical debate advocated by Churchman (1971), but even on occasion as a directly useful insight. Some of Foucault's concepts of local power (Smart 1983) would be examples of the latter. Similarly the notion of autopoiesis (Mingers 1989) may have some potential for enrichening systems thinking. Furthermore many of the methods used in information systems development are strongly rooted in one or more branches of traditional philosophy — Checkland (1981) makes this most explicit in relation to Soft Systems Methodology (SSM) — and an understanding of the philosophical underpinnings is arguably necessary for effective deployment of the methods.

Those who have read this far may by now be thinking that this position has much in common with that of complementarism as expounded by Flood & Jackson (1991) within Critical Systems Thinking. This is true up to a point. Whilst there is a need to match philosophies and methods with situations, there is a third factor that is just as important, that of the actor/analyst/problem solver. The values and intentions of the holder of this role will have arguably the most significant impact on choice since he or she is the chooser, or at least has power over it due to superior knowledge of the options. For example 'emancipation' can be seen as a value which the actor brings to the situation rather than an intrinsic imperative within the situation. Hirschheim & Klein (1989) explores in some depth the impact of the actor's values.

From the above it follows that the position outlined here differs from the traditional view of philosophy as a search for absolute 'truth'. The aim is rather 'usefulness in context'. However it must be acknowledged that such a position is itself a kind of truth statement since it is clearly rooted in a nominalist ontology and embodies an interpretivist epistemology. On reflection, philosophy is pervasive!

Software Engineering as a Kuhnian Discipline

Paul Wernick & Russel Winder

There is a very strong analogy between Kuhn's model of scientific endeavour and software engineering. In this chapter, we explore this analogy in an attempt to characterize and understand software engineering as a discipline. The impact of the model of software engineering thus derived is then discussed.

1 Introduction

1.1 Background

During our appraisal of the current state of computer-based systems development, we have considered a variety of predefined 'methods' which have been proposed and/or used for developing software. The different sets of assumptions implicit and explicit in these methods have caused us to consider the meaning of software engineering, in the sense that the term is used to denote a unified discipline. Additionally, we have been particularly concerned to observe the lack of impact of a discipline rich in predefined formalisms and ways of developing computer-based systems on those systems developers who work as individuals. These people seem from our investigations often to ignore all of the predefined development mechanisms proposed by the software engineering community.

In this chapter, we present an explanation of the philosophical underpinnings of our on-going examination of this situation, in which we are trying to explain the current fragmented state of software development theory and practice. As a starting point for this examination, we have been using Kuhn's (1970) models of pre-scientific and scientific disciplines.

The choice of Kuhn's work was based on two analogies:

1. an analogy drawn between some attributes of the current state of software engineering and Kuhn's models; and

2. an analogy between the design of models using analysis and design notations and computer programming, leading, via the effects of the notations and

117

mental models used to develop a program on the program design (Petre & Winder 1988, Petre 1989, Petre & Winder 1990), to a concern about similar effects being implicit in software engineering practice.

This chapter sets out our basis for applying the first analogy, that between Kuhn's vision of a scientific discipline and software engineering.

It is important to recognize the basis of our use of the philosophy of science for software engineering. We are *not* saying that software engineering is a science, it is a design discipline. There is a fundamental difference between the search for universal laws in a science and the search for 'the next specific solution' in a design discipline. However, taking a pragmatic approach, and essentially ignoring this distinction, we will take advantage of the similarities between Kuhn's model and the current state of software development.

Kuhn can be thought of as taking a sociological rather than epistemological or logical view of science, basing his ideas on identification of the 'scientific community' of researchers working in a discipline, and exploring the effects of the underlying beliefs of the members of that community. He notes that this approach may be applicable to other types of discipline than that of science (Kuhn 1970: 209).

Taking this as a basis, we have been trying to isolate some of the elements of the paradigm* of software engineering, to open up the fundamental explicit and implicit beliefs and models to examination and questioning. We believe, for reasons which we will set out below, that this will be a useful and fruitful line of research.

This chapter focuses on the work of Kuhn as the basis of an analogy between his model of science and software engineering, to the exclusion of the work of other philosophers of science, although an example is given later of how the latter may be of use in the future. This is intentional since we believe Kuhn's to be the only work based on a sociological approach rather than an epistemological approach. This may be naïvety on our part. Some people may feel that our approach to philosophy bears some resemblance to the hackers' approach to software development and indeed some of the subtleties of the philosophies which we are using as analytical tools may have been lost in our analysis. However, our research is in the realm of 'applied philosophy', that is, we are looking in the short term for advice which can be useful to and directly applied by software practitioners, and we feel that the immediate practical value of what we are doing will offset any loss of philosophical precision. Indeed, some of the deeper questions behind what we are doing have been deliberately omitted from our consideration. For example, will software engineering ever be united under a single paradigmatic disciplinary matrix, as Kuhn expects of a mature scientific discipline, or will the differing schools of theory tend to remain split under academic or commercial

---

*We use the term 'paradigm' here to mean what Kuhn explains using an alternative term, which we will also follow, 'disciplinary matrix', or 'constellation of group commitments', a many-faceted belief system.

forces? We do not know the answer to these questions, and for the moment we regard it as outside the direct line of our enquiry, although we do touch on it later. Such speculation, in the context of our model of the discipline, may, however, form a useful backdrop to the development of software engineering.

1.2 Defining Software Engineering

We have taken the use of predefined, documented methods, tools and techniques to be an informal definition of the term software engineering for the purposes of this chapter. Our pragmatic definition of 'method' is a 'process model and a set of techniques and notations'.

We note that such definitions always carry with them a number of implicit assumptions, and therefore may weaken a pure philosophical approach to these matters. We also note that some current attitudes affect the way in which some practical aspects of software development are seen, such as opinions concerning the Waterfall Model, which is comprehensively rubbished by some advocates of prototyping, who seem sometimes not to admit that there are any advantages to it at all.

Such beliefs and assumptions form bases for dividing the software engineering community into differing *schools* of thought, which are strikingly parallel to Kuhn's version of a similarly divided pre-science discipline.

2 Kuhnian Models of a Discipline

Kuhn (1970) has identified three types of discipline; the pre-science, the science and the non-science.

2.1 The Pre-Science Discipline

A pre-science discipline is one which is capable of developing into a science, but has not yet got there. Kuhn (ibid.: 12) gives the example of optics prior to the eighteenth century, before the emergence of the first universally-accepted model of light. A pre-science discipline is characterized by division into schools (ibid.: 16), which:

- disagree over the nature of the phenomena with which they are dealing and how to interpret their observations (ibid.: 17) — in Kuhn's example of optics, light was seen by different groups as particles emanating from material bodies, modification of the medium between the body and the eye, or interaction of the medium with an emanation from the eyes (ibid.: 12);

- are unable to agree on definitions of key concepts, and therefore talk at cross purposes (ibid.: 198) — key concepts which have been the subjects of such disputes include definitions of a chemical 'element', and the distinction between chemical 'compound' and 'physical mixture', without which the Law of Definite Proportions cannot be derived; and

- each have their own disciplinary matrices (Kuhn 1977), including different metaphysical bases and separate sets of exemplars which each of their theories do most to explain (Kuhn 1970: 12–3).

119

An important consequence of the lack of a certain belief system across the different schools of thought shared between all of those examining a class of phenomena is the *incommensurability* of the differing set of beliefs and models or paradigms. They see the same phenomena in different ways, using different terms (or, worse, the same terms with different meanings) to explain them. This results in the need to translate between the work of different practitioners, and a critical loss of synergy between the different groups.

It is interesting to note that Kuhn accepts 'the more creative' members of these groups as 'scientists' (ibid.: 13), even if a unified 'science' has not yet emerged!

Kuhn gives examples of other disciplines which have exhibited this early stage during their history — including chemistry, heat and motion — before becoming 'sciences' with a universally accepted paradigm; he notes that other disciplines remained (in 1963) to have their 'paradigm' accepted by all practitioners.

2.2   The Scientific Discipline

In contrast to the fragmented school-based aspect given by a pre-science, a science is, to Kuhn, based on a single disciplinary matrix, which has emerged as the winner from the matrices of a set of pre-science schools, and which is now for most purposes agreed to by all practitioners. However, Kuhn (ibid.: 209) notes the 'relative scarcity' of competing schools in the 'developed sciences' indicating that some fragmentation into schools still occurs and that some current 'sciences' have not yet completely achieved their own paradigms.

To Kuhn, the paradigm within which normal scientific work proceeds arises as a nexus of the sharing of beliefs, models and so on among those people active in the field in question. This group is the 'scientific community', and is usually between 25 and 200 strong. Larger groups do exist however; the astronomy community and the particle physics community, for example, are international communities estimated to have between 300 and 1,000 active researchers. It could be argued, however, that these communities are not coherent disciplines, rather that they are collections of mutually exclusive sub-disciplines. For example, in astronomy people studying stellar evolution could be seen as a different community to those studying galactic clustering. These smaller communities do in fact fall within Kuhn's size estimates. This view can be backed up with the evidence that different models and theories apply in these different communities. A similar argument can be applied to particle physics where people studying the properties of neutrinos could be seen as a different community from those studying hadron–hadron collisions. However, in this field, there is a drive for a 'Grand Unified Theory', a single theory describing all interaction between any collection of particles. The fact that there is a single model implies that there is a single community, that what might be seen as boundaries between disciplines are actually just sub-communities within a single discipline.

In a science, the nature and effect of its disciplinary matrix is changed from those of pre-sciences; the disciplinary matrix of a science presents challenging puzzles, supplies clues to solutions and guarantees the clever practitioner success

— which those of the pre-science schools do not (ibid.: 179). The paradigm gives a firm metaphysical basis for work, and a common language. It defines which questions can reasonably be asked, and which do not make sense — for example looking for definite proportions for components of chemical compounds did not make sense whilst the difference between 'solution' and 'compound', i.e. physical mixing and chemical reaction, were not accepted. Whilst they were seen as the same thing, any combinations of mixable components seemed to 'work' until some saturation level was reached. The view of what was happening, even though it could not be seen, changed when the difference between 'mixture' and 'compound' was brought into the model of reality.

A major advance in the change from pre-science to science is that a pre-science's fact-gathering is replaced by a more purposeful experimental activity in the science, because the paradigm sets the problems and acceptable solutions, although some 'scientific' work is occurring in pre-sciences.

The life of a science is not a smooth path of advancing theory and practice; it is characterized by phases of 'normal science' punctuated by 'scientific revolutions'. *Normal science* is the devising, performing and analysing of the results of experiments within an accepted paradigm. However, over time, problems emerge with the theories enshrined in the paradigm. These problems sometimes become so great that they lead eventually to a sense of scandal and 'something must be done' in the community of scientists. As the scandal of the current paradigm's insufficiencies grows, and in an effort to explain the anomalies, competing paradigms emerge. At some stage, one of these — or the original paradigm re-stated or embellished — emerges as the new, generally accepted paradigm; this is a *scientific revolution* or *paradigm shift*. After the revolution, the new paradigm becomes the basis for another period of normal science. Textbooks are rewritten from the new perspective explicit and implicit in the new paradigm, the old paradigm is forgotten and the revolution becomes invisible. The cycle of normal science and revolution can now begin again.

The classic modern example of a scientific revolution is physics at the end of the 19th century. Empirical observations, such as the precession of Mercury, were not explainable within Newtonian mechanics. Within a 30 year period, 1895–1925, relativity theory and quantum mechanics were born, requiring a complete re-write of vast sections of the physics literature.

2.3 Non-Science Disciplines

Chalmers (1982: 108–9, quoting (Kuhn 1970: 22)) states that non-science disciplines are those disciplines which do not conform to Kuhn's account of a science, i.e. those disciplines which are not capable of being united under a single paradigm.

It can be observed that Kuhn's model of a science seems to be based on the physical sciences, such as physics, chemistry or geology. However, disciplines may exist which, although they are not labelled as 'sciences' by society, nonetheless conform to the 'science' model. Although Kuhn wrote his work primarily as an explanation of science, he himself noted in the postscript to the second edition of his major work that the concepts which he had introduced might be applicable to other types of discipline (Kuhn 1970: 209). He saw the primary use of his work in such disciplines as being to explore the nature of their operational communities as a parallel to scientific communities.

Our work outlined here has been carried out in the spirit of Kuhn's idea of applying it to other disciplines, but with an emphasis on operationalizing the paradigm to support advances in its theory and practice rather than on delving into the community structure. The latter is employed as a support for the analogy; that is, as a means rather than an end.

3   How Does Software Engineering Fit the Kuhnian Model?

3.1   Introduction

We describe here the way in which the current state of software engineering can be fitted into Kuhn's models of a discipline. Specifically, we consider the way in which Kuhn's ideas fit into the current state of that part of software development which is based on predefined methods, tools and techniques.

Pragmatically, Kuhn's works looks like a good fit for what we have observed in software development. The current state of methodology development shows many of the attributes of a set of pre-science schools, such as seeing the same phenomena from differing viewpoints. Considering the way in which a software development methodology is used, the 'puzzle solving within a philosophical framework' nature of Kuhnian normal science is a good analogy for software development under the control of a pre-defined methodology.

3.2   Methodology and Technique Development

The theoretical side of software development can be considered as an analogue of a Kuhnian pre-science. It shows many of the attributes of the pre-science model, in particular, it is composed of many schools, each of which has:

- *Its own way of seeing the world* which is embodied in the notations and modelling techniques advocated.

  Consider, for example, differing computational models: procedural, object-oriented, functional, logic-based, rule-based, data flow, , , , , .* Each of these computational models can be used as the basis of a series of notations for describing problems or solutions. Different computational models underlying the notations available may cause the analyst or designer to see the world in different ways; the dataflow modeller will see flows of (passive) data to and from stores, being modified in processes; the object-oriented modeller will see numbers of objects, each with its own set of allowable actions.

  Does this difference result in any fundamental differences in the models produced? This is a question which needs to be asked and answered other

---

*Sometimes an individual methodology will mix and match multiple computational models but usually a specific modelling technique will espouse a single one.

than by metaphysical appeals to 'naturalness' which are common in current literature. This is the kind of work which we hope to perform or encourage by advancing the models of software development presented here.

- *Its own set of beliefs and assumptions* concerning such fundamentals of systems development as the process models to be employed (for example, waterfall vs. incremental vs. prototyping) and the importance attached to involving the user in systems development.

- *Its own definitions of key terms* such as 'object-oriented', on which members of differing schools of 'object-orientedness' are unable to agree, or 'quality' in a software process or product.

In the context of the current state of theories of software development, as instantiated in methodologies and techniques, we must note Kuhn's criticism of the operation of pre-science disciplines, i.e. that progress is sapped by disagreements over philosophical bases (Kuhn 1970: 13) — is methodology and technique development suffering from the same problem for the same reason?

In seeking for reasons for these strength-sapping divisions, we can refer to such issues as different requirements of systems, different environments of operation, different constraints, and so on. We might also consider the effect of the commercial world and academic pressures, which combine to press for product differentiation. How often does one hear a consultant saying proudly that his or her organization has 'its own methodology'? This reflects an attitude in which difference is distinctive and good, rather than representing a failure to combine, as might be felt in a mature area of a science. The effect of market forces must also be taken into account, requiring saleable, working answers before the relevant questions have been answered by theorists in term agreed by all (as sometimes expressed in other fields by standards set by bodies established for the purpose — but who would set the international standard for the object-oriented computational model?).

3.3 Methodology and Technique Use

In the context of using a given methodology, we can consider the practical side of software development — actually developing and implementing computer-based systems — equivalent of Kuhnian 'normal science'. There is often no (or not much) questioning of the philosophical basis of the mechanisms which are employed during the process of developing a system under the control of a pre-defined methodology or set of techniques. Developers of software use the mechanisms which they know best, or which they are told to use, and these contain their own versions of the world.

It is interesting to note Kuhn's justification for this lack of questioning of bases in a mature science — it allows rapid development of the practice of a discipline without the need to rebuild the philosophical basis each time (Kuhn 1970: 42). Rapid development without much debate on the philosophical basis of the methodology employed (once the methodology is chosen) is exactly what is needed to develop computer systems! It does not need further justification; it is the right thing to be doing.

However, practitioners need to be sure that the wider philosophical basis of the methodology selected is reasonable (a term which will also require definition!) for both the system to be developed and the context within which that development will take place. Software engineering cannot yet guarantee this, because not all of the beliefs forming the philosophical basis have yet been found and examined! We also feel that there is a need for the practitioner to be able to consider the effects on his or work which arise implicitly or explicitly from the methods, tools and notations used in that work. Without that information, it is impossible either to assess any influences on the work done or to decide on which of the many methods available may be most applicable in the circumstances.

The disciplinary matrix within which the software development work (to which 'normal science' is equivalent) is performed consists of elements derived from a number of sources including: personal, organizational, role, project and discipline. The emphasis in our research so far has been on the parts of the paradigm which are common across people, organizations and projects, i.e. those related to role and (particularly) discipline.

3.4   Imperfections in the Analogy

There are some areas in which Kuhn's models of a discipline do not fit into the current state of software development. These include the following:

- We are not saying that software engineering is a scientific discipline. We believe it is currently a craft within Long & Dowell's conceptions of a discipline as craft, applied science or engineering discipline — see Wernick & Winder (1993). The work presented here may shift it a little towards the more controlled status of an engineering discipline, but it is not a 'science' in the sense that Kuhn uses the term (i.e. something like physics).

  As a result, we may ask whether software engineering will ever achieve the status of the analogue of a Kuhnian science, with one disciplinary matrix uniting and accepted by all practitioners. We might ask whether seeking this unifying belief system would be a useful goal for software engineering theorists, or an unattainable holy grail, another magic bullet? Such a quest assumes that all problems for which solutions provided in software are subject to the same set of universal laws; is this true even for all important aspects of software developments? It is in our view better to assume that, at the current state of development of software engineering, there is only an analogy to be drawn between method-based software engineering practice and Kuhn's view of a science, rather than suggesting an identity between the two.

- Although Kuhn has stated that the contents of a disciplinary matrix are invisible, we have had some success in finding some of the contents of that of software engineering — see, for example, Winder & Wernick (1994).

- One type of element which Kuhn states will appear in the disciplinary matrix of a science, the symbolic generalization (a law sketch, often in the form of an algebraic formula, which both allows calculation of values and defines the terms used* — see (Kuhn 1970: 182), seems from our work to date not to be present in software engineering. We currently believe that this lack may be due either to the current state of the knowledge forming the scientific base of software engineering (mostly computer science), which is mostly qualitative rather than quantitative, or to the fact that few such elements are there to be found in this particular discipline. Theories concerning complexity and computability are well accepted but there seem to be few accepted theories otherwise. Perhaps the lack of symbolic generalizations may reflect the disparate and early state of computer science itself.

- The size of the community involved in the activity. As we have stated, Kuhn suggests that the body of active researchers forming a scientific community is 25–100 people strong. Looking to software development, this number of active workers may be about right for the developers of a particular method, but *not* for the practitioners who use it. A possible response to this is to relate the research scientists in, say, one branch of chemistry with the (much larger) group of chemical engineers who *apply* any of the work developed by the theorists.

4 Applying the Analogy

4.1 Introduction

Having decided that the analogy between Kuhn's views of a science and software development is supportable, our next task is to determine the work required to make the analogy useful and derive some benefit for those who work in the field. Having described this, we can consider the possible benefits of performing this work.

4.2 Making the Analogy Useful

In order to make the analogy drawn between a Kuhnian science and software engineering of direct use to practising software engineers, we need to identify the structure and elements (beliefs, models, assumptions) which form the disciplinary matrix of software engineering.

The current view of the structure is as a network, with some elements being common to all software engineers and defining the discipline, and values for other elements being selected or weighted to form the different sets of schools. Some of the common elements may be implicit — such as the Principle of Uniformity of Systems (Winder & Wernick 1993). Some elements may be ignored at times, for example: some definitions of 'quality' often exclude some aspects which may be

---

*Kuhn (1970: 183) provides an example of this from Newtonian mechanics, the relationship between force, mass and acceleration: $F = ma$. This simultaneously shows how the values are to be calculated and defines the terms employed.

considered important by others; portability is not important in some applications, but vital in others. Some elements are more important to some of the actors in a software development than to others, for political, cultural or pragmatic reasons. We are currently working on the identification of elements; the mechanisms we are using include trawling through literature, interviews with software developers and research into philosophy and the philosophy of science.* We have concluded as a result of these investigations that these disciplinary matrix elements do exist, and influence the work of the software developer (Winder & Wernick 1994, Wernick 1996).

All of the elements of the matrix are weighted, and traded off against each other, in order to form the disciplinary matrix which is employed under an individual set of circumstances. This may, for example, result in a trading off of implied or explained aspects of the definition of software quality against speed-enhancing short cuts (hacks) if management insist that a tight deadline be adhered to.

As an example of how we intend to extend our work, we are planning to consider how the work of other philosophers of science can inform our work. For example, the thoughts of Feyerabend may be useful as a starting point in considering those software developers who use informal analytical and design mechanisms. His idea that 'anything goes' (Feyerabend 1983: 19) by which he actually means 'use what seems to be the best method under the circumstances', underlies in particular the work of some experienced developers who work on their own; with a library of techniques, and an understanding of how they work under particular circumstances, they will select what appears to be the best under those circumstances. In effect, they have made explicit at least some of the trading off of disciplinary matrix elements mentioned above. However, this activity will still be less effective than it could be until the complete set of effects of each technique or notation are understood and made explicit; this is the long-term objective of our work.

We will also need to draw conclusions as to what the effects of these elements of belief, individually and in combination, on the part of methodology developers is in practice on software developers. We believe that some of these effects may differ from those expected by proponents or developers of specific methodologies, approaches or models, which makes the research programme outlined here more urgent as the number of methodologies continues to increase. For instance, does the lack of feedback in a waterfall process model result in less innovative software designs?

4.3 Advantages of Applying the Analogy

We describe here the advantages which we see for method and software developers, both in general and in each specific area. We also consider the possible advances which we believe our approach might allow to those who develop software without the benefit of predefined methods or techniques, or apply these in an ad hoc fashion.

---

*See, for example, Winder & Wernick's (1993) work on the effects of software engineering's inductive basis and the measures which can be taken to minimize these.

4.3.1   In General

The examination of the underlying belief systems of methods would help to define the discipline and practice of software engineering by reference to a common set of underlying beliefs — the shared disciplinary matrix of all of those who would be defined as members of the software engineering community. This could be stated in the form of a syllabus for what the professional software engineer should know about the tools of his or her trade, and thus be applied directly to the teaching of future generations of software engineers to give them an understanding of what the knowledge base of their profession is.

The development of the underlying beliefs of software engineering would assist in the development of definitions of key terms which can be agreed by all software developers, by bringing out differing assumptions implicit in the current controversial definitions; consider for example definitions of the term 'object-oriented'. It might also help to demolish attempts to turn technical terms into sales gimmicks. By promoting better understanding of what each term actually means, and what one would expect to see implied or explicit in an implementation laying claim to it, impostors would be more easily spotted — a step towards a greater degree of professionalism in the discipline of software development.

4.3.2   Methodology Development — Software Engineering Theory

We believe that a research programme based on making explicit the elements forming the disciplinary matrix of current software development would provide a means of giving a greater understanding of the principles underlying the tools and techniques which are embodied in the methods which they design, and developing an ability for people to reason about, and test, these principles. This testing might relate to how these principles affect software development, looking either at one in isolation or at how more than one interact with each other. Additionally, it would provide a framework for method developers to examine how effectively their methods implement their desired belief system.

For example, in the context of looking at the disciplinary matrix of software development, it is legitimate to ask what effect the computational model of a notation has on the models produced using it. It is a truism that any language can express only a limited set of concepts (consider Orwell's (1949) *Nineteen Eighty-Four!*). The inclusion of the computational model of a notation in the disciplinary matrix underlying the development of a particular computer system provides a framework with which this sort of question can be asked, and the basis of an experimental mechanism for answering them.

The joining of the explicit philosophical aspects of a method to the implicit ones will enable methodology developers to reason about, and test the effects of, the principles in combination. For example, if different elements of the disciplinary matrix each modify the way in which a system is developed, what effect do these elements have in combination? Certain process models may support some types of techniques better, such as an iterative model supporting prototyping. The concept of the disciplinary matrix provides a framework for these aspects to be investigated.

The existence of a 'reference collection' of influences on software development would also allow methodology designers to test the effectiveness of different methodologies in converting these principles into working systems. It would provide a basis for framing and answering questions in an experimental environment, and in considering reports of real-world software development experience allow the consideration of the results of software developments in the context of the influences on the developers. This would speed up and inform the process of methodology development.

Overall, we feel that, once the relationship of underlying influences on practical aspects of how systems are developed is better understood, this will help method developers understand the implicit and explicit mechanisms behind the methods they design and therefore understand the effects of the design decisions they make in developing methodologies.

4.3.3   Applying Methodologies — Software Engineering Practice

The advantages which we see for the software developer who chooses and/or uses a predefined method reflect the greater availability of information to support method choice and use. The practitioner would also be able to consider the effect of his or her personal ways of working on the results of development projects. Finally, the teaching of software development tools could be made more general, and therefore longer-lasting.

An examination of the disciplinary matrix underlying methods would provide better information for those selecting methodologies on the effects of the selection decision on the systems developed. An understanding of the underlying paradigm will enable developers to predict the influences of different methods on the project, and therefore to select a method which is a good fit with what is required.

By giving systems developers who use methodologies an understanding of influences on their practice, examination of even a partial disciplinary matrix would begin to answer the question of how what they currently do affects the results they get.

Teachers would be provided with a basis for teaching the effects of the use of methodologies to new and existing practitioners in terms of the generalized syllabus mentioned previously.   By teaching the effects of methodological principles, rather than particular methods, a more portable and durable learning process will be created. It will allow the teaching of software engineering to be improved, by explaining what the implicit as well as explicit effects of different software development tools are. This knowledge, if properly described, will not become obsolete as might teaching the intricacies of a particular method, and will replace much on-the-job, informal learning which happens in the student's first job after a software engineering course.

4.3.4   The Non-Methodological Developer

From anecdotal evidence, and our semi-formal interviews with software practitioners (Wernick 1996), it appears that those who develop computer systems without reference to a predefined method, often in small teams or as individuals, feel ill-served by the current range of formalized software development tools. They see these as tools for managing and coordinating large development teams rather than for supporting the imaginative and communicative processes of software development, as tools for managers rather than for design. Such formalisms are therefore seen as being irrelevant to their work. They prefer to use informal analysis and design mechanisms and notations to the formalized mechanisms advocated by the authors of textbooks and courses.

The investigation and description of the implicit and explicit contents of the disciplinary matrix of software engineering would promote an understanding of the fundamental reasons for methodology, technique and notation design decisions. Testing the implementation of such decisions in different methodologies would enable the analysis of effectiveness and side-effects on the design process. Modification of methodologies based on this information may allow them to be made more relevant to the individual or small team development environment, in a formalized manner, by modifying the design decisions to fit the different set of goals and criteria held by such developers.

More immediately, the publication of the underlying models, values and influences on software development would assist informal developers in selecting and applying tools relevant to their situation. This information, which would in many aspects be as applicable to informal development mechanisms as to formal ones, would provide an understanding of how the tools selected affect the products of the development process. Well presented, the information could be seen as an aid in the informal process of selecting the tools to be used by the ad hoc developer. We therefore see such information as a support for informal developers' experience and understanding rather than a replacement for it, providing a framework within which these developers can make more rationally-based choices of development mechanism.

5 Summary

To summarize, we believe that the analogy of Kuhnian disciplines can be justified for software engineering. On this basis, a good model for method development is a pre-science — at least currently. Method use is similar to normal science activity. We also feel that the effort required to pursue this analogy to find explicit and implicit elements of the disciplinary matrix underlying current software development theory and practice would be justified in terms of the benefits to be gained.

Can we develop method development into the equivalent of a science united around a single disciplinary matrix? Our work makes no claims to this having happened, although we have noted the similarity between Kuhn's normal science and method-based software development, but neither does it absolutely confirm its impossibility. Even if this objective is not achieved (or even looked for), the elicitation and questioning of the belief system underlying software engineering will undoubtedly be a valuable research activity leading to a greater understanding of the influences on software development theory and on practice.

The Metaphysical Assumptions of the (Main) Soft Systems Methodology Advocates

Stephen K. Probert

The purpose of this chapter is to examine the basic epistemological assumptions of the Soft Systems Methodology (SSM) advocates, as these are relevant to understanding the nature, scope, and coherence of SSM. A number of writers have discussed the philosophical underpinnings of SSM; the general conclusion being that SSM embodies the philosophical assumptions of (some form of) subjectivism, e.g. Mingers (1984). Unfortunately, in recent years, two sorts of accounts of the basic process of human enquiry have been put forward by the SSM advocates. Although these two sorts of accounts are ultimately contradictory they are similar in that they are both highly psychologistic accounts of epistemology; they both focus on the process of enquiry. *The two accounts will be termed:*

1. the so-called Kantian account; and

2. the Lockean accounts.

It will be argued that whilst the advocates of SSM subscribe to a subjective mode of enquiry, such a mode has its history — and its rationale — firmly grounded in the early modern philosophies of the natural sciences. It is also argued that the SSM advocates (in fact) subscribe to the thesis of epistemological reductionism, *and this thesis will be contrasted with that of* epistemological holism.

1 SSM and Subjectivism

It has been claimed that SSM should be considered as *an epistemology*:

> "The essence of soft systems thinking ... [is] that it provides a coherent intellectual framework ... as *an epistemology* which can be used to try to understand and intervene usefully in the rich and surprising flux of everyday situations." (Checkland & Scholes 1990: 24)

In recent years, a number of writers have discussed the philosophical underpinnings of Soft Systems Methodology (SSM); the general conclusion being that SSM embodies the philosophical assumptions of (some form of) subjectivism, e.g. Mingers (1984). Mingers (1984) notes that Checkland offers us the following assertion:

> "... we have no access to what the world *is*, to ontology, only to descriptions of the world ... that is to say, epistemology ... We should never say of something in the world: 'it is a system', only: 'it may be described as a system'." (Checkland 1983: 671)

Discussing this notion of subjectivism, Mingers states:

> "Two things are worth noting. Firstly the statement itself is epistemological rather than ontological. It neither asserts nor denies what might exist but directs itself solely to our knowledge. This is as it must be. The view that we cannot know what exists logically precludes any such assertions or *denials*. Secondly the statement applies to the whole of reality — the physical, as well as the social world — and so equally applies to natural science." (Mingers 1984: 90)

So it appears to follow from the subjectivist epistemological assumptions embraced by the SSM advocates that, in a sense, epistemology (and not ontology) is the *only* field about which definite assertions can be made.

2 The Basic Ontological Assumptions of the SSM Advocates

In this respect, and despite Mingers' succinct remarks, it should be noted that SSM advocates generally appear to hold that there are crucial *ontological* differences between the *subject matters* of the natural and social sciences (*natural phenomena* and *human activity* respectively):

> "Any approach to rational intervention in human affairs has to accept that in studying purposeful human action and in trying to bring about change in human situations, it is not simply a matter of setting to work to discover 'laws' governing the phenomena in question. Autonomous human beings could, in principle, deliberately act in a way which could either confirm or refute any supposed 'laws' of human affairs." (Checkland 1991a: 59)

The argument that autonomy is an emergent property of human beings can be described as *ontological holism*. Put simply, SSM advocates hold that the *natural* world consists of a rule-obeying domain and that the world of *human activity* consists of a self-determining domain. That different domains of explanation are possible is explained by this idea of *ontological holism*:

> "'The whole is more than the sum of its parts'. My student had understood the idea exactly when I heard her say to a fellow student: 'You are

certainly more than the sum of your parts, you're an idiot!' She was
saying that the description 'idiot' *has no meaning* at any level below that
of her companion regarded as a single entity." (Checkland 1983: 669)

Now it could be argued that SSM advocates in fact believe that the concept of
ontological holism is merely part of their *epistemology* — which might be relevant
to aiding understanding and so on. However they do consider it to be a *plausible*
ontological account. In any case it should be pointed out that the epistemological
assumptions of the SSM advocates *as propounded by those advocates* contain
certain ontological commitments:

> "Perceiving the systems movement as a whole ... and examining the
> work that goes on within it, draws attention to the fundamentally different
> types of entity (things, phenomena or situations) which the researcher or
> practitioner may deem to be 'systems'. Three fundamentally different
> types may be discerned ... *Type 3*: situations in which interconnections
> are cultural, situations dominated by *the meanings attributed to their
> perceptions by autonomous observers*. Most real-world situations are of
> this type ..." (Checkland 1983: 670)

The interesting point here is not that there are things which the researcher
may be deeming to be systems but that there are *autonomous observers* in
the description. This is an ontological statement. The SSM advocates do
not seem willing to advocate solipsism as a plausible philosophy; there are
other autonomous observers in the world besides themselves (or, strictly
speaking, besides *themself*!). For the SSM advocates, autonomous observers
are fundamental ontological *givens*: i.e. they exist — and this is made explicit
in the metaphysical assumptions embedded in *Type 3* of the proposed taxonomy
of systems enquiry — provided in (Checkland 1983: 670). This is stated more
baldly thus:

> "Situations of type 3 derive from the autonomy of the human observer,
> from his or her freedom to attribute meaning to perceptions." (Checkland
> 1983: 670)

Furthermore knowledge or belief must be *located* somewhere — and Karl Popper
(a philosopher of science) propounded some interesting arguments on this issue
(to be discussed shortly).

So despite the SSM advocates' definite assertions to the effect that statements
about ontology are unjustifiable, it is reasonable to argue that SSM advocates in
fact hold ontological holism to be the case. In fact, this position is both a *sine qua
non* for SSM to be considered as 'an epistemology' and, many might consider, the
raison d'etre of SSM. In recent years, two sorts of accounts of epistemology have
been propounded by the (main) SSM advocates. Although these two accounts are
ultimately contradictory they are similar in that they are both highly psychologistic
accounts of epistemology; they both focus on the *process* of enquiry. These two

accounts will be termed the *so-called Kantian account* and the *Lockean accounts*, and these will now be characterized.

3 The So-called Kantian Account

In the most recent and detailed account of the developed form of SSM, Checkland & Scholes (1990) see their epistemological tradition as stemming from Immanuel Kant (1724–1804):

> "When the Spanish conquistadors arrived in what is now Mexico, the indigenous people, unfamiliar with horse riding and seeing riders dismount from horses, thought that creatures had arrived on their shores who could divide themselves in two at will. This story provides a good illustration of the way in which we have in our heads stocks of ideas by means of which we interpret the world outside ourselves. Philosophically the story supports the view of Kant, that we *structure* the world by means of already-present, innate ideas, rather than the view of Locke [John Locke, 1632–1704] that our minds are blank screens upon which the world writes its impressions. But it seems clear that the supposedly 'innate' ideas may have two sources. They may indeed be part of the genetic inheritance of mankind, truly innate; or they may be built up as a result of our experience of the world ... What is being argued is that we perceive the world through the filter of — or using the framework of — the ideas internal to us; but that the source of many (most?) of those ideas is the perceived world outside ... As human beings we enact this process everyday, usually unconsciously." (Checkland & Scholes 1990: 19–20)

(It should be noted immediately that Locke's theory of perception is not as vacuous as the SSM advocates suggest in this quotation, as will become clear shortly.) The essence of this account is that perception is representational, but representations are only possible via the mediation of ideas prepossessed by the perceiving subject. As ideas are the necessary prerequisites of coherent perceptions some ideas must be *innate* — they are born with us as part of our genetic inheritance.

Kant's transcendental idealism is far too complex to be explored in this chapter, so suffice it to point out that Checkland & Scholes' (1990) account of epistemology should not be construed as Kantian:

> "No name can do justice to this profound and complex philosophy which arose out of the two most important philosophical theories of his time: the rationalism of Descartes and Leibnitz and the empiricism of Locke, Berkeley, and Hume ... *Kant agreed with the empiricists that there cannot be innate ideas in the sense of anything known prior to any sense experience, but he was not prepared to say that therefore all knowledge must be derived from experience* ... Kant's procedure differed significantly from the generally psychological empiricist method, for

rather than seeking for the impressions upon which certain ideas are based, he investigated the relationship that exist between the fundamental concepts related to a subject's having experience of objects. He was concerned with theoretical questions of a sort he calls 'transcendental', such as 'under what conditions is experience of an objective world possible?'." (Flew 1979: 175–6, emphasis added)

Kant was not really interested in the processes of perception — he was primarily interested in what must be necessary for a subject to be capable of having *any* perception; not how it is that one has a perception *of* things like an horse and rider.

There are two main aspects to the so-called Kantian account. Firstly, the observer is seen as trying to make sense of his or her perceptions of the world by applying ideas to his or her *raw* perceptions; some of these ideas are innate. The claim that observers try to make sense of the world in this way most closely resembles accounts put forward in the tradition of the Cartesian project of pure enquiry — first articulated by Descartes (1596–1650) around 1640. There are three related features of Descartes' account of epistemology (all of which are central features of the of the SSM advocates' so-called Kantian account). These are:

1. the doctrine of innate ideas;

2. the subjective representation of reality; and

3. the intellectual construction of models.

These features will now be discussed.

3.1 The Doctrine of Innate Ideas

The notion, advanced by Checkland & Scholes, that our thinking is 'structured' by innate ideas also hails from Descartes' rationalism (rather than from Kant's transcendental idealism):

"Another controversial tenet of Descartes' position is that some of our ideas are innate ... [One reason] for the necessity of innate ideas is that we can apprehend the specific quality of our experience only if we possess ideas with which to interpret it." (Aune 1970: 28–9)

Descartes himself argued:

"I cannot doubt but that there is in me a certain passive faculty of perception, that is of receiving and taking knowledge of the ideas of sensible [physical] things; but this would be useless to me, if there did not also exist in me, or in some other thing, another active faculty capable of forming and producing those ideas." (Descartes 1912: 133)

Checkland & Scholes clearly root the 'active faculty' both in our 'genetic inheritance' and in the psychological processes of the individual subject.

Descartes also argued that this 'active faculty' does not just arbitrarily make up these ideas:

> "[And] what I here find of most importance is ... that I discover in my mind innumerable ideas of certain objects, although perhaps they possess no reality beyond my thought, and which are not framed by me though it may be in my power to think them, but possess true and immutable natures of their own. As, for example, when I imagine a triangle, although there is not perhaps and never was in the universe apart from my thought one such figure, it remains true nevertheless that this figure possesses a certain determinate nature, form, or essence, which is immutable and eternal, and not framed by me, nor in any degree dependent on my thought ... and which accordingly cannot be said to have been invented by me."
> (Descartes 1912: 121)

It should be noted that Descartes ultimately argued that these innate ideas are transferred to us from the mind of God, whereas Checkland & Scholes' account is entirely secular, and is generally expressed in terms of our 'genetic inheritance'.

3.2 The Subjective Representation of Reality

For both Checkland (and Scholes) and Descartes, knowledge is to be produced or created *in the mind of an individual subject*; the basic epistemological notion is of an attempted representation (or interpretation) of the world by a subject, and this is clearly a Cartesian legacy:

> "Descartes' account ... is expressed in terms of a representational theory of perception. We are given a picture of the mind in direct contact only with its own experiences or ideas, *outside* which there are objects, causing these experiences and imperfectly represented by them. Descartes thinks that, strictly speaking, the purely mental ideas involved in perception do not *resemble* the world at all, and even with regard to the corporeal representations of the world in the brain, which he believes to occur as part of the perceptual process, he emphasizes that the important point is that they should be capable of conveying the required complexity of information about external things, not that they should resemble them (*Dioptric vi* 113)." (Williams 1978: 239–40),

Checkland's account of the purpose of building the conceptual models (used extensively in SSM) is strikingly similar in important respects; for both Descartes and the SSM advocates, the same implications are drawn from this *subjective representation* approach to human enquiry: the need for *models* of reality. Of course the SSM advocates are primarily concerned with modelling *social reality*, which they believe to be (strictly-speaking) 'unmodellable' owing to the free-will that they attribute to actors in the real-world (Probert 1992; 1994):

> "The important point is that, in using SSM, we must never lose sight of the fact that the models are *not* would-be descriptions of parts of the world.

They are abstract logical machines for pursuing a purpose ... which can generate insightful debate when set against actual would-be purposeful action in the real-world." (Checkland & Scholes 1990: 311)

However this aspect of SSM is not strictly relevant to the discussion herein.

3.3 The Intellectual Construction of Models

Bernard Williams has recently summed up Descartes' contribution to epistemology in the following manner:

"Descartes is, rightly, said to be a rationalist philosopher ... But it's sometimes supposed that he was such a strong rationalist that he thought the whole of science was to be deduced from metaphysics by purely mathematical or logical reasoning ... He thought no such thing. In fact, he is absolutely consistent in saying that experiments are necessary to distinguish between some ways of explaining nature and others. You can build different models. This is a very modern aspect of his thought. You can build or construct different intellectual models of the world within his laws, and experiment is needed to discover which truly represent nature." (Williams 1987: 90)

(Note that this account is only related to the natural world, and not the social world.) Checkland's philosophy of (natural) science is quite definitely of this sort:

"Natural scientists cannot fail to be aware of two fundamental considerations: first, that in the professional talk concerning the work, words are used as carefully defined technical terms ... second, that the words so carefully defined refer to models, to intellectual constructs rather than supposed physical reality. The natural scientist is well aware that he or she is playing a game against nature in which the intellectual constructions are used to predict physical happenings which can be checked experimentally." (Checkland 1988: 235)

Just how Cartesian the SSM advocates' so-called Kantian account of epistemology is can be shown by the following observation:

"... many passages showed that he accorded a crucial role to experiment. Descartes' actual conception of scientific method often resembles ... the model where an hypothesis is advanced, and the results logically deduced from it are then compared with actual observation." (Flew 1979: 86)

The conclusion to be drawn is that the epistemological assumptions of the proponents of the so-called Kantian account of epistemology are those of *Cartesian rationalism*.

Two objections might easily be made to the account of the epistemological assumptions of the SSM advocates' so-called Kantian account that I have provided. Firstly, Checkland (1981) explicitly rejected the idea that any form of *systems thinking* could be rooted in a Cartesian epistemology. Secondly, and related to the first point, this whole epistemological approach (Cartesianism) is somewhat surprising, given Checkland's (1981) Popperian orientation. These objections will be discussed shortly.

3.4   Cartesian Reductionism

Before exploring these possible objections fully it will be necessary to briefly examine the SSM advocates' use of the term 'reductionism'. Checkland's use of the term 'reductionism' is non-standard in modern epistemological terms, but standard in the (looser) general philosophical sense and this can be (potentially) misleading. Flew defines 'reductionism' as follows:

> "REDUCTIONISM (or Reductivism). 1. The belief that human behaviour can be reduced to or interpreted in terms of that of lower animals; and that, ultimately, can itself be reduced to physical laws ... 2. More generally, any doctrine that claims to reduce the apparently more sophisticated and complex to the less so." (Flew 1979: 279)

It is the latter, philosophically looser, sense that the SSM advocates seem to intend. However, in modern epistemology, a more usual definition would be:

> "REDUCTIONISM: the belief that each meaningful statement is equivalent to some logical construct upon terms which refer to immediate experience." (Quine 1980: 20)

Note that 'meaningful' (above) means, basically, *grammatical and intelligible*, e.g. 'Barking dogs bark.' is meaningful (but vacuous), as is 'Paris is the capital city of Antarctica.' (this is meaningful, but false).

Quine's argument is that statements, and not exclusively scientific statements, do not refer to particular sensory experiences in isolation. Consequently particular experiences will not always give rise to particular statements:

> "The totality of our so-called knowledge or beliefs, from the most casual matters of geography and history to the profoundest laws of atomic physics or even of pure mathematics and logic, is a man-made fabric which impinges on experience only along the edges. Or, to change the figure, total science is like a field of force whose boundary conditions are experience. A conflict with experience at the periphery occasions readjustments in the interior of the field ... But the total field is so under-determined by its boundary conditions, experience, that there is much latitude of choice as to what statements to reevaluate in the light of any single contrary experience." (Quine 1980: 42–3)

An example may help here. Prior to conducting chemical experiments we may be told that if sulphur is present on a splint then a bright yellow flame will be present if the splint is immersed in a Bunsen burner flame. If we were to do such an experiment and a bright yellow flame did not appear (although there was good reason to believe that sulphur was present on the splint) we might conclude that there was something wrong with the whole of chemical theory, but *pragmatically* we would probably search for a simpler explanation — say that some other chemical was present which inhibited the experiment from working properly, or that there was an insufficient amount of sulphur for the experiment to work properly, and so on. We would not immediately rush to the conclusion that we had *falsified* the chemical theory that gave rise to the periodic table of elements. As such Quine's *epistemological holism* stands as a rebuttal to Popper's *critical rationalism*. Somewhat ironically Checkland claims to support a Popperian philosophy of science, which is ultimately dependent on the validity of *epistemological reductionism*, and which (for example) Quine explicitly rejects:

"If an hypothesis implies observations at all, we may stand ready to drop the hypothesis as false as soon as an observation that it predicts fails to occur. In fact, however, the refutation of hypothesis is not that simple ... there is the matter of the supporting chorus. It is not the contemplated hypothesis alone that does the implying, but rather that hypothesis and a supporting chorus of background beliefs." (Quine & Ullian 1978: 102–3)

Popper was fully aware of the need for the acceptability of epistemological reductionism for his philosophy of science to be satisfactory:

"... though every one of our assumptions may be challenged, it is quite impractical to challenge all of them at the same time ... Quine formulates (with reference to Duhem) [a view that] ... our statements about the external world face the tribunal of sense experience not individually but only as a corporate body ... it should be said that the [Quine's] holistic argument goes much too far. It is possible in quite a few cases to find which hypothesis is responsible for the refutation ..." (Popper 1972: 238–9)

It is very important to note that Checkland (1981) supports Popper's reductionist view of epistemology.

Checkland (1981) argued that Descartes' epistemology was based on *reductionism* in the looser philosophical sense, and was therefore not *systemic*:

"The core of Descartes' approach to science ... was 'reductionist', in the sense that science should describe the world in terms of 'simple natures' and 'composite natures', and show how the latter could be reduced to the former. The process of identifying the simple natures in complex phenomena was what Descartes meant by 'analysis' ..." (Checkland 1981: 47)

The above *may* be the case, but there is some considerable evidence that Descartes was not as naïve as such accounts make him appear:

"... it is an important feature of his [Descartes'] physics that ... We cannot consider how a body would ideally move if it were not in an environment of other matter influencing its motion, since such a state of affairs, through the equation of matter and physical space, is absolutely unintelligible. For Galileo, by contrast, the consideration of how a body would move under ideal conditions (for instance, a body falling in a vacuum, or a ball rolling on a surface under zero friction) was fundamental to his analysis of motions, and could be coherently employed." (Williams 1978: 255)

Knowledge, for Descartes, was a unified system. For Descartes:

"All the sciences are interconnected and dependent on one another ..." (Flew 1979: 83)

So there is some evidence of a systemic orientation to Descartes' account of epistemology. However this point is not central to the conclusion that the basic epistemological assumptions of the SSM advocates' so-called Kantian account of epistemology are those of Cartesian Rationalism.

3.5   Popper's Epistemology and the So-called Kantian Account

Checkland subscribes to a thesis described in Section 2 as *ontological holism*. Similarly for Popper:

"If the situation is such that, on the one hand, living organisms may originate by a natural process from non-living systems, and that, on the other hand, there is no complete theoretical understanding of life possible in physical terms, then we might speak of life as an *emergent* property of physical bodies, or of matter." (Popper 1979: 291–2)

Quine does not endorse such a view:

"Better to drop the [ontological] duplication [of mind and body] and just recognize mental activity as part of the activity of the body ... I have been accused of denying consciousness, but I am not conscious of having done so." (Quine 1987: 132)

In this respect it should be noted that Quine ultimately advocates *ontological reductionism* (put crudely, the strict reduction of *mind* to *body*); this is reductionism in sense 1 described by Flew above (in Section 3.4).

Popper espoused the virtues of rationalism:

"Now I want to make it quite clear that as a rationalist I hope to understand the world ..." (Popper 1979: 292)

However, the SSM advocates generally accept the principle that epistemology is primarily the study of the processes of enquiring and learning:

"... there are no absolutes in our epistemology; as systems thinkers we are virtually driven to a process view of the world." (Checkland 1992c: 1026)

Although such a view is entirely compatible with Cartesian epistemological assumptions, Checkland has made the (implausible) claim that this view is compatible with Popperian epistemological assumptions:

"[A] number of very distinguished scientists ... have attested to the importance of Popper's ideas in their thinking ... We have a picture of science, then, as a method of enquiring or learning, which offers us, at any moment of time a picture of our understanding of the world's reality which consists of certain conjectures, established in reductionist repeatable experiments, which have not yet been demolished ... [This] outline of science ... will be relevant to later discussion of whether or not systems thinking can contribute to the difficult problems which face a social science which aspires to be scientific in the full sense of that word." (Checkland 1981: 57–8)

However, Popper was quite explicit that he considers science to be objective (knowledge) precisely because it does *not* reside in a knowing subject,

"Epistemology I take to be the theory of *scientific knowledge* ... Traditional epistemology has studied knowledge or thought in a subjective sense — in the sense of the ordinary usage of the words 'I know' or 'I am thinking'. This, I assert, has led students of epistemology into irrelevancies: while intending to study scientific knowledge, they studied in fact something which is of no relevance to scientific knowledge. For *scientific knowledge* simply is not knowledge in the sense of 'I know'. While knowledge in the sense of 'I know' belongs to what I call the 'second world', the world of *subjects*, scientific knowledge belongs to the third world of objective theories, objective problems, and objective arguments ... Knowledge in this objective sense is totally independent of anybody's claim to know; it is also independent of anybody's belief, or disposition to assent; or to assert, or to act. Knowledge in the objective sense is *knowledge without a knower*: it is *knowledge without a knowing subject*." (Popper 1979: 108–9)

Therefore, the emphases placed by Checkland on *enquiring* and *learning* are somewhat puzzling as Popper rejects the idea that scientific progress (i.e. the growth of knowledge) has anything to do with learning — because learning necessarily involves a (learning) subject:

"The common sense theory is simple. If you or I wish to know something not yet known about the world, we have to open our eyes and look round. And we have to raise our ears and listen to noises, and especially to those made by other people. Thus our various senses are our *sources of knowledge* — the sources or the entries into our minds. I have often called this theory the bucket theory of the mind ... The important thesis of the bucket theory is that we learn most, if not all, of what we do learn through the entry of experience into our sense openings; so that all *knowledge consists of information received through our senses*; that is, *by experience* ... My thesis is that the bucket theory is utterly naïve and completely mistaken in all its versions, and that unconscious assumptions of it in some form or other still exert a devastating influence ... the bucket theory is a theory of our acquisition of knowledge — and thus it is a theory of what I call the *growth of knowledge. But as a theory of the growth of knowledge it is utterly false* ... The common sense theory of knowledge ... took it for granted that there was only one kind of knowledge — knowledge possessed by some knowing subject. I will call this kind of knowledge 'subjective knowledge', in spite of the fact that ... *genuine or unadulterated or purely subjective conscious knowledge simply does not exist.* The theory of subjective knowledge is very old; but it becomes explicit with Descartes: 'knowing' is an activity and presupposes the existence of a knowing subject. *It is the subjective self who knows."* (Popper 1979: 60–73)

The key point, again, is that Checkland & Scholes' so-called Kantian account of epistemology is Cartesian, rather than Popperian, in character (although no implicit advocation of Popper's epistemological arguments is intended). This is somewhat surprising given the espoused early research aims of SSM:

"These are early days in the systems movement, and the stage reached is that the movement is still testing the proposition that systems concepts can be the basis of a fruitful epistemology. Eventually we may reach the stage at which there are examples of well-tested 'public' knowledge which is *systems* knowledge, knowledge which could only have been gained by means of systems thinking. When this happens we shall have objective systems knowledge in what Popper calls ... 'world 3' ... When this stage is reached we shall have a recognized systems epistemology *without a knowing subject*, and achieving it ought to be a prime objective of the systems movement." (Checkland 1981: 100–1)

However, in more recent accounts it is clear that the epistemological problem, as discussed by the SSM advocates is always discussed in terms of 'What *can* I know?', and this is a Cartesian legacy:

"... it was Descartes, and almost Descartes alone, who brought it about that the centre of Western philosophy for these past centuries has been the theory of knowledge. He brought it about that philosophy started from the question 'What can I know?' rather than questions such as 'What is there?' or 'How is the world?' Moreover, the question is not 'What can be known?' or even 'What can we know?' but 'What can *I* know?' That is, it starts from a first-person egocentric question." (Williams 1987: 94)

A more detailed discussion of the issues concerning epistemology without a knowing subject lies outside the scope of this chapter, but Haack (1979) has carried out a thorough analysis of these issues.

4 The Lockean Accounts

These accounts of epistemology are entirely Lockean in character, and appear both before, after and simultaneously with the publication of Checkland & Scholes' (1990) account (the so-called Kantian account). Their main difference lies in the outright denial of the possibility of innate ideas:

> "I shall drastically summarize the development of systems thinking ... an human observer tries to make sense of his or her perceived reality ... by means of some intellectual concepts used in some mental process or methodology ... 'System' is one of the concepts used in this process, but considerable confusion is caused by the fact the word is used not only as the name of an abstract concept which the observer tries to map onto perceived reality, but also as a label word for things in the world — as when we refer to 'the education system' or 'the legal system'. The confusion is of course not helped by the fact that the ultimate source of 'concepts' ... is (can only be) perceived reality; that is the ultimate source of the concepts through which we try to make sense of perceived reality in a never-ending cyclic process of learning ... Perceived reality and the intellectual concepts steadily create each other." (Checkland & Scholes 1990: 305–6)

A similar account has been propounded in a more recent article:

> "... we may note that in the end the ultimate source of abstract notions ... is the perceived world itself ... the world as we perceive it yields concepts by means of which we perceive the world; there are no absolutes, only a continuous process in which the concepts create the perceived world which creates the concepts." (Checkland 1991b: 27)

These are Lockean accounts because Checkland quite explicitly states that the only source of ideas (or concepts) is perceived reality — and therefore ideas (or concepts) cannot be innate — and this is one of Locke's most important and influential theses:

> "... Locke argues in detail in book 2 [of (Locke 1977)], we can account for all of the ideas in our minds by *experience*. Experience is of two sorts. There are ideas of sensation, derived from the outer senses, and ideas of reflection, which are those ideas of which we become aware by introspection ..." (Flew 1979: 190)

143

In Locke's own words:

"Whatever *idea* is in the mind is either an actual perception or else, having been an actual perception, is so in the mind that by memory it can be made an actual perception again ... ideas are no more born with us than arts and sciences ..." (Locke 1977: 27–9)

However, it will be worthwhile to indicate the full extent of the Lockean nature of the epistemological assumptions of the SSM advocates (as propounded in the non-Cartesian accounts). The main difference between the Lockean and the so-called Kantian accounts is their denial of innate ideas, however it has been noted that there are considerable similarities between Descartes' and Locke's accounts of epistemology:

"Locke's theory of thought and knowledge, too, can look superficially like Descartes'. He takes thought to involve a series of ideas which exist 'in the mind', or 'before the mind', and which represent things outside the mind. Reasoning is a sort of mental operation on ideas which leads to knowledge or belief." (Ayers 1987: 121)

Put this way it may seem that the SSM advocates' account of the relationship between ontology and epistemology is more sceptical than Locke's — that mental ideas do not strictly represent the natural world:

"... the world is taken to be very puzzling: there is no reason why we should have evolved brains beyond those needed to survive on the planet's surface; there is no reason to suppose our senses and brains can tell us what reality is really like." (Checkland 1983: 672)

But Locke's argument was that our senses only give knowledge that there are some things outside ourselves (which is clearly assumed above). Locke did not argue that our senses can tell us what those things are really like:

"... Locke developed a ... line of thought ... Although the senses give us knowledge, they give us limited knowledge — knowledge of the existence of things, not knowledge of their nature or essence. And because all our thought is restricted to the concepts that we have acquired through our senses, even our speculations about the world are restricted. He thought that there was no method by which scientists could expect to arrive at the underlying nature of things. So, despite his rejection of absolute scepticism about the external world, he was himself a sort of modified sceptic. We know that the world is there, but we don't know what it's really like." (Ayers 1987: 123)

The SSM advocates are (sometimes, but not always!) also 'sort of modified sceptics', as can be seen when they are articulating their ideas that holons (*systems* in everyday parlance) somehow 'reside' in the enquiring subject, rather than being *in the world.* For the SSM advocates, systems modelling is a mental activity; its validity is therefore something *internal* to us — something constructed by the enquirer. We can apply systems thinking to 'perceived reality', in an unfolding flux of events and ideas. This notion is entirely Lockean in character:

> "His [Locke's] explanation of the possibility of mathematical science, and geometry in particular, is importantly different from Descartes'. For ... Locke it's an abstract science which is created by us. We so to speak pick geometrical properties of things, and we can go on to construct such properties ad lib beyond the limits of our experience. In this way we can create the subject matter of a sort of non-empirical science. Such a science is possible because it's not really concerned with the nature of things at all. It's simply concerned, as Locke puts it, with our own ideas." (Ayers 1987: 130)

Although at no point do the SSM advocates involve themselves in discussions about primary and secondary qualities (these are Lockean notions); the conclusion I draw is that, broadly speaking, the epistemological assumptions of Checkland's 1990 and 1991 accounts are those of *Lockean empiricism.* It should be noted that such accounts were precisely the sort of accounts that Kant was keen to deny:

> "The illustrious Locke ... meeting with pure concepts of the understanding in experience deduced them also from experience, and yet proceeded so *inconsequently* that he attempted with their aid to obtain knowledge which far transcends all limits of experience." (Kant 1933: 127)

Kant's argument is that Locke's ultimate mistake was to conduct his analysis by reflecting on the process of perception, rather than on the *conditions of its possibility.* It is *not* argued here that Locke's, or Kant's, accounts of epistemology are superior or inferior to other accounts of epistemology; this is a question for philosophical discussion that lies outside the scope of this chapter.

To use a theatrical metaphor, where Popper displaced the subject to the fringe of the epistemological scene, in the Lockean account the SSM advocates place the subject back into the centre of the epistemological stage. Such an account is one that Popper would have surely denied, as it is rooted in the subjectivism characteristic of both Descartes and Locke — which Popper called 'the bucket theory',

> "Among the many things which are wrong with the bucket theory of the mind are the following: (1) Knowledge is conceived of as consisting of things, or thing-like entities in our bucket (such as ideas, impressions ...). (2) Knowledge is, first of all, *in* us ... To sum up: what I call the common sense theory of knowledge is something very close to the empiricism of Locke, Berkeley and Hume and is not far removed from many modern positivists and empiricists ... Almost everything is wrong in the common sense theory of knowledge." (Popper 1979: 62–3)

	Descartes	Locke	Popper	Quine	SSM (Kant)	SSM (Locke)
Location of knowledge	subj	subj	obj	subj	subj	subj
Mind body reductionist	no	no	no	yes	no	no
Theory testing reductionist	yes	yes	yes	no	yes	yes
Rationalist vs. empiricist	rat	emp	rat	emp	rat	emp
Source of innate ideas or dispositions	God	n/a	genes	genes	genes	n/a

Table 1: Metaphysical differences.

The SSM advocates' Lockean account of epistemology can neatly and accurately be characterized as a (Popperian) *bucket theory* — and as such, Popper would have surely denied that such an account has anything whatsoever to do with the study of epistemology.

It should be noted that the so-called Kantian account is characterized only once in a major work, i.e. Checkland & Scholes (1990), whereas the Lockean accounts can be found in several journal articles, and some passages of Checkland & Scholes (1990) are quite definitely in the Lockean mould. A recent article is also biased towards the Lockean account:

> "... it is useful to remember that ultimately the only possible source of ... ideas is our perception of the world outside ourselves ..." (Checkland 1992c: 1026)

5 Collating the Results of the Analysis

The results of the preceding analysis will now be collated. Table 1 puts these findings in a tabular form. Explanations will be provided for the vertical headings, and brief résumés — plus some additional supporting arguments — will be provided for the horizontal categorizations.

5.1 Location of Knowledge

This category concerns where the account claims knowledge is *located*: which for all of the accounts discussed will either be in the mind of the subject or in some objective realm. All the philosophers — except Popper — were concerned with what can be known by a subject. Popper's *objective knowledge* thesis has been characterized. It is clear that neither of the SSM advocates' accounts attempt to build on Popper's thesis. It should be noted that Quine prefers to discuss *belief* rather than knowledge:

> "We do better to accept the word 'know' on a par with 'big', as a matter of degree. It applies only to true beliefs, and only to pretty firm ones, but just how firm or certain they have to be is a question, like how big something has to be to qualify as big ... I think that for scientific or philosophical

purposes the best we can do is give up the notion of knowledge as a bad job and make do rather with its separate ingredients. We can still speak of a belief as true, and of one belief as firmer or more certain, to the believer's mind, than another." (Quine 1987: 109)

Quine's account is, however, clearly subjective (*belief* is a subjective notion).

5.2 Mind Body Reductionist

This category concerns the ontological accounts propounded. *Reductionist* here refers to the notion that explanations of human activity can be reduced to physical or natural explanations. Descartes, Popper and both the SSM advocates' accounts are all characterized by the need for explanations of human activity to be about a different ontological realm from explanations of natural phenomena (albeit for different metaphysical reasons). Popper and the SSM advocates prefer the notion of emergent properties of human activities, whereas Descartes utilizes the notion of a strict dualism between mind and body. Locke is slightly problematical as there is some evidence that he advocated the possibility of a unitary ontology:

> "[Locke is] ... inclined to think that the world is composed of matter and minds, but he's consistent enough to say that since we don't know the nature of either we can't even be sure of that. So he is ready to accept the possibility that materialism is true and that we thinking things are in fact complex and subtle machines, although how we work we have no idea at all ... one wonders why on other occasions he says that dualism is probably true. He never justifies the 'probably'." (Ayers 1987: 131–2)

Although Locke never justifies the probably, I have concluded that there are insufficient grounds to claim that he was a mind body reductionist.

5.3 Theory Testing Reductionist

This category refers to a dispute which has only arisen in the twentieth century, although it was presaged by the work of Pierre Duhem (1861–1916). The question revolves around whether or nor it is possible to subject *any* theory to reductionist tests. Quine argues that theories face the tribunal of sense experience as a corporate body (in fact he ultimately argues that the unit of meaning is the whole of science). Popper defended the notion of epistemological (theory-testing) reductionism. Previously philosophers had not raised the question. Popper's main aim was to supplant epistemological induction with falsificationism, although inductive accounts of epistemology — such as those of the logical positivists — implicitly accept the thesis of epistemological reductionism (on a probabilistic model). The SSM advocates generally claim to support a Popperian account of epistemological reductionism — which is interesting because of its implicit (and Popper's explicit) rejection of Quine's thesis of epistemological holism.

Note that, in this respect, there is some evidence of a systemic orientation to Descartes' epistemology (see Section 3.4).

5.4   Rationalist vs. Empiricist

This is the classic philosophical dispute between those who argue that knowledge is primarily to be gained from experience (empiricists) or from reason (rationalists). Descartes was a paradigmatic rationalist whilst Popper was a critical rationalist. If the SSM advocates seriously subscribed to Popperian epistemology they would be rationalists also. However this is one of the areas where the accounts they provide equivocate. Any theory which depends on the existence of innate ideas will be rationalist (to a greater or lesser extent) — because knowledge will be expressed (at least in part) in terms of such ideas and the ideas themselves are not given in experience, whilst any theory which denies the existence of innate ideas will be empiricist — because all knowledge will therefore, ultimately, have to be derived from experience.

Note that Quine is sometimes referred to as a 'pragmatist' as opposed to an 'empiricist'. The term 'pragmatist' has a special epistemological meaning, and this should not be confused with the sense in which the term is used by, for example, Flood & Jackson (1991). However as the SSM advocates do not discuss *epistemological pragmatism* this issue will not be discussed further.

5.5   Source of Innate Ideas or Dispositions

Obviously this category does not apply to those accounts which deny the possibility of innate ideas or dispositions. For Descartes the source of our innate *ideas* was God, whereas for the more modern philosophers innate *dispositions* are linked to the concept of Darwinian evolution; they are said to evolve. To abbreviate this notion the term 'genes' has been used as the source of innate ideas or dispositions. Innate ideas and innate dispositions are really two quite different notions; Popper and Quine were concerned with similar notions, i.e. 'expectations' (Popper) or 'dispositions' (Quine). Neither philosopher has advocated the existence of innate ideas in the Cartesian sense. The *flavour* of their evolutionary accounts is similar in some respects, although they differ crucially with respect to their *epistemological* significance. Popper argued that innate dispositions have survival value:

> "The theory of inborn *ideas* is absurd, I think; but every organism has inborn *reactions* or *responses*; and among them, responses adapted to impending events. These responses we may describe as 'expectations' without implying that these 'expectations' are conscious. The new-born baby 'expects', in this sense, to be fed (and one could even argue, to be protected and loved). In view of the close relation between expectation and knowledge we may even speak in quite a reasonable sense of 'inborn knowledge'. This 'knowledge' is not, however, *valid a priori*; an inborn expectation, no matter how strong and specific, may be mistaken. (The newborn child may be abandoned, and starve.) Thus we are born with expectations; with 'knowledge' which although not *valid a priori*, is *psychologically or genetically a priori*, i.e. prior to all observational experience." (Popper 1972: 47)

It should be noted that Popper did not believe that such subjective 'knowledge' provided by innate dispositions is of any real *epistemological* significance. It would appear that the SSM advocates' so-called Kantian account subscribes to a more Cartesian notion of innate ideas — a notion that Popper found 'absurd' — rather than to Popperian or Quinian notions of innate expectations or dispositions. Popper thought that knowledge literally evolved in an objective realm (World 3):

> "Popper makes use of a notion not only of an objective world of material things (which he calls 'World 1') and a subjective world of minds (World 2) but of a third world, a world of objective structures which are the products, not necessarily intentional, of minds or living creatures; but which, once produced, exist independently of them." (Magee 1975: 60)

Quine's evolutionary notions are similar in some respects to Popper's, the main differences being that Quine has no corollary of Popper's World 3, and that for Quine innate dispositions are of *epistemological* significance. In Popperian terms, Quine's thesis is about World 2, which — owing to Quine's ontological reductionism — will ultimately be about World 1.

Quine argues that genetic inheritances are responsible for (amongst other things) our choosing the *simplest* theory to refute in the face of recalcitrant experience:

> "Darwin's theory of natural selection offers a causal connection between subjective simplicity and objective truth in the following way. Innate subjective standards of simplicity that make people prefer some hypotheses to others will have survival value insofar as they favour successful prediction. Those who predict best are likeliest to survive and reproduce their kind, in a state of nature anyway, and so their innate standards of simplicity are handed down." (Quine & Ullian 1978: 73)

Quine's theory is not about Cartesian-style innate ideas; in fact he prefers to avoid discourse about ideas:

> "... the way to clarify our talk of ideas is not to say what our ideas are, but to show how to paraphrase talk of ideas into talk about language. It is ironical, then, to find the idea idea officiating in the purported clarification of linguistic matters, when the viable direction of clarification is the reverse; but we do find just that." (Quine 1987: 88)

Finally it should be mentioned that the SSM advocates' so-called Kantian account posits the existence of Cartesian-style innate ideas, however these ideas supposedly (might) result from the process of evolution of the human brain (our 'genetic inheritance') rather than from being transferred from the mind of God to our minds.

6 General Conclusion

It is clear that at least as regards epistemology, SSM does not embody a mode of enquiry that could be construed as Popperian in character, except insofar as the SSM advocates accept the notion that the strict reduction of sentences to sense-data is achievable (epistemological reductionism) and in so far as the SSM advocates embrace the same thesis as Popper with respect to the ontological holism implicit in the thesis of there being emergent properties of human activity. Such *epistemological reductionism* can be clearly contrasted with *epistemological holism*.

It seems definite that the SSM advocates subscribe to the thesis of *ontological holism*, whilst simultaneously subscribing to the thesis of *epistemological reductionism*. What is less definite is whether they subscribe to epistemological reductionism on the model of *Cartesian rationalism* or on the model of *Lockean empiricism*, as there is conflicting evidence in their texts. SSM may increasingly be used as a methodology for undertaking information systems design (Checkland 1995). Therefore it seems apparent that the SSM advocates should seek to establish their epistemological principles in a more definite manner than has hitherto been the case:

> "The researcher must set out the *epistemology* in terms of which research findings will be expressed. This is essential if others are to critically appraise the work. Indeed, it is what makes accounts of action research potentially more than the equivalent of 'a letter home to mum'." (Checkland 1995: 2)

At a basic level, this task remains to be done.

Towards a Paradigm of Information System

Marcus Lynch

This chapter explores a possible paradigm of information system, using the Soft Systems Methodology (SSM) to structure development of the definition. Context and purpose are considered in a way that extends previous definitions of information system.

1 Introduction

Having read the special edition of the *Systemist* on information systems (Systemist 1992), and inspired by Peter Checkland's *Information systems and Systems Thinking: Time to Unite?* (Checkland 1992a), I felt spurred to use the Soft Systems Approach in a way that none of the contributors seemed to have done. Basically, this meant using SSM as a system of inquiry to obtain some potentially relevant answers to some initial questions about information systems.

In carrying out this analysis, I kept in mind that systems are intellectual constructs and I have used SSM very much in this vein with the concept of 'system' as an overarching metaphor for guiding my inquiry into the information systems situation.

2 SSM Analysis

I started with a representation of the information systems situation (part rich picture, part in my head). This representation included my working definition of information as 'data plus meaning', as well as the view that information systems are necessarily human activity systems (Checkland 1992b). A fundamental assumption throughout this analysis has been that the attribution of meaning to data is a uniquely (and therefore defining) human property. I intend to return in a later paper to the question of whether meaning is an individual or a linguistic/social phenomenon.

Some of the issues I identified in the information systems situation are:

- disagreement about what constitutes an information system;

- confusion about the nature of information systems and their relationships to other systems (e.g. goal-setting systems);

- argument about the relevance of various perspectives and methodologies for information system description and development;

- dogmatic positions (my own included!) about the 'right' approach(es) to adopt for information system description and development; and

- misunderstandings about usage of terms such as 'information' and 'data' (and even 'system').

I attempted to find ways of generating a coherent approach to the discussion of information systems, taking just one issue to begin with, namely the definition of an information system. This is the place to begin any system of inquiry, i.e. first defining the focus of inquiry. I felt that previous definitions (Checkland 1992b, Wilson 1991) could do with some clarification and expansion in order to illuminate and further current debates about information systems.

This led in turn to a pretty thin, if fairly uncontroversial, relevant system, as below:

A system that attributes meanings to data in a context, in the furtherance of a purpose.*

As this relevant system was deficient of all but the 'T' of the CATWOE criteria, I then attempted to define (still at a general level) what those criteria might be, as below:

Customers	Purpose-setters & others
Actors	Information system operatives
Transformation	Attribute meaning to data in a context
Weltanschauung	Purpose set (i.e. it is meaningful for this information system to exist!)
Owners	Purpose-setters
Environmental constraints	Clarity of purpose, data input

This resulted in a more extensive root definition, as below:

A system:

- Owned by purpose-setters.

- Operated by information system operatives.

- On behalf of purpose-setters and others.

- In the belief that it is meaningful for this system to exist.

---

*Thanks to Steve Probert for pointing out the importance of the relationship between information systems and the purpose they are designed to further.

- Constrained by clarity of purpose and data input.
- To attribute meanings to data in a context, in the furtherance of a purpose by:
  - filtering data input;
  - deciding criteria for filtering data input;
  - knowing the limitations of information system capacity;
  - selecting data for meaning to be attributed;
  - defining the context of selected data;
  - knowing the range of meanings which can be attributed to data;
  - attributing meanings to selected data;
  - monitoring the attribution of meanings to data;
  - generating additional possible meanings which can be attributed t   a;
  - deciding criteria for the attribution of meaning to data; and
  - knowing purpose(s) to which resultant information will be put.

From here, I then derived a conceptual model of an information   tem, as shown below. I realized as I did this that I was using this stage of SS   with the formal systems model as a meta-paradigm to generate a paradigm of   rmation system. A further iteration might involve using a different meta-par   ;m such as the viable systems model (Beer 1985) to explore other possible p   igms of information system.

It must be stressed at this point that the conceptual model shown is   i design for an information system, but rather a logical development of the spar   :finition given. The conceptual model makes no distinction between human at   :chnical activities, nor should it. That said, the central transformation of the   em, i.e. 'attribute meanings to data' is unequivocally an human activity, by d   tion.

The logically derived activities that the conceptual model represer   irprised me in that this model has much more detail than previous des   ions of information system, e.g. Checkland (1992b) and Wilson (1991), w ⟆ ı I have seen. I presume that this is due to my trying to depict the logically necessary steps in attributing meaning to data in a context, in the furtherance of a purpose.

3   The Model

Figure 1 shows the conceptual model resulting from the analysis.

Testing against the formal systems model yields the following:

- A continuous purpose/mission. To attribute meaning to data in a context, in the furtherance of a purpose.

- Measure(s) of performance. Implicit in Activity 5.

- Decision-taking processes. Many of the activities in the conceptual model are decision-taking processes.

- Components which are themselves systems. All of the components are systems, and could be further 'unpacked'.

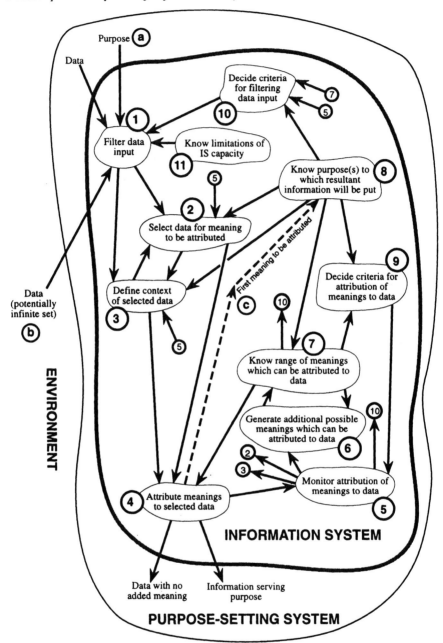

Figure 1: A conceptual model of a system to attribute meanings to data in a context, in the furtherance of a purpose (i.e. a generalized information system).

- A degree of connectivity/interaction between components. The activities are a densely coupled ensemble of systems as shown on the conceptual model.

- An environment with which the system interacts. The 'E' in CATWOE — clarity of purpose and data input.

- A boundary, separating it from the environment, and defining the area within which decision-taking process has the power to cause action to be taken. This is shown on the conceptual model.

- Resources at the disposal of the decision-taking process. Data and possible meanings seem most pertinent here.

- Some guarantee of continuity, and ability to recover after disturbance. The continuing existence of the purpose-setting System, as well as the densely coupled nature of the activities in the conceptual model.

Note (a) The purpose does not feed directly into Activity 8, but via Activity 4.

Note (b) Data always has to be filtered, but the level of 'granularity' or 'chunking' is possibly an issue here.

Note (c) This is the primary start-up activity of an information system.

4 Conclusion

Reflection on the model shows that there must also be recursive levels of information system at the wider system level and within some of the individual activities in the conceptual model. Use of the viable systems model (Beer 1985) to explore the area further seems to be congruent with this realization, as does the exploration of the 'mycelium model' (Todd, unpublished communication) of organization.

One thing that is noteworthy about this conceptual model of information system is the number of decision making activities involved. It may seem trite to say, but the attribution of meaning to data in a context means making lots of choices! These decision making activities also reflect the purpose of the wider system, including the inclusion or exclusion of 'permitted' meanings. Which agencies determine which meanings are acceptable will be the subject of a future paper about the relationship between information systems and power.

Organizational Issues

Introduction

Ian A. Beeson

The three chapters in this section share a common interest in the organizational context of information systems and the articulation of information systems practice within a broader process of organizational change. In two of the chapters, the primary organizational focus is the National Health Service (NHS); the third is concerned with information systems in community organizations. All three discuss appropriate forms of system development practice, and all three see 'information management' as an important issue for organizations. Questions are raised about the conduct of technical work in a social and political environment, and about how organizational activity can be represented and controlled as or through information processing.

Nick Plant explores prospects for sustainable information systems in community organizations. He locates these within the Voluntary Sector, and more specifically in the area identified as the 'Social Economy' in a model due to Paton. Such organizations can be characterized as value-based: people in them work from personal commitment towards the public good. Information systems and information technology are for various reasons relatively undeveloped in and between organizations of this kind, and there is only a weak theoretical base for understanding the role of information systems in this context. Plant suggests sustainability as an important goal and criterion for information systems in community organizations: information systems are needed which are themselves relatively stable and which together promote organizational success (as locally defined) and autonomy. In building such information systems, attention will have to be paid at the same time to strategic purposes and to issues of empowerment. Brian Wilson's model of information management activities might be adaptable to the community organizations context, but there are issues to resolve in the tension between system management and power sharing.

Stuart Maguire looks ambitiously towards a 'market-led' (as opposed to a 'product-led') philosophy emerging for information systems development, arguing that the success of information systems depends more critically on management of organizational change than on technical innovation. His analysis is aimed at complex organizations (and specifically at the NHS), but is more generally applicable. Information systems development has concentrated on delivering particular concrete results (working programs, documents, interfaces) and paid insufficient attention to the cultural context of information system introduction and implementation. Alienation and resistance may be the result, especially where technical change is viewed as disrupting previously satisfactory and coherent practice. In his current research at NHS sites, conducted according to a participative action research model, Maguire is investigating how the general goal for information systems of producing high quality information can be achieved by broadening the technical/financial agenda which normally dominates development, so as to bring previously peripheral staff groups into the change process, and to include consideration of organizational culture, work arrangements, and educational and personnel matters.

The chapter by George Bakehouse, Chris Davis, Kevin Doyle and Sam Waters also draws on an NHS setting — in this case a project to specify an integrated workstation for use in the neurosciences department of a hospital. The report on the fieldwork for that project is preceded by a comprehensive overview of systems thinking, theory and models, triggered by some reflection on difficulties in requirements determination, and leading in turn to some consideration of anthropological and sociological methods for the analysis of 'social systems', and of Loftland's analysis of the social setting of information systems. The research method adopted by the team (which included intensive fieldwork shadowing the clinicians) was informed by these theoretical perspectives; their observations have been focused on social rather than technical or instrumental action. The data gathered in the investigation of current practice revealed a number of information weaknesses or problems; many of these were of common occurrence, the most prevalent being incompleteness of information for the task at hand. Results so far provide a basis for consideration of how information management and access might be reorganized to give better support in operational circumstances, as well as at the same time feeding usefully into the data modelling part of the workstation specification process.

Sustainable Information Systems in Community Organizations

Nick Plant

Research in progress on information systems in community organizations is described. Such organizations are placed into context using a model of the UK 'social economy', and the notion of 'sustainability' is introduced as a device for improving on the limited understanding of information systems in community organizations that has been established to date. An overview of project methodology, influential reference disciplines and current modelling is provided, and finally some pointers to further research, together with reflections on the philosophical implications for information systems practice, are offered.

1 Introduction

This chapter provides a report on work in progress on a applied research project looking at the development and management of sustainable information systems in community organizations. My approach to this work is very much oriented around information systems practice. Other personal biases and starting premises may be summarized as follows. Theorizing does not come to me as naturally as does practice, but I use action research cycles in developing and then applying abstract understanding of concrete problem situations. Through my work I seek to be able ultimately to deliver practical, realizable, benefits to community organizations, a sector of society with which I have been strongly associated throughout my working life, and to which I remain deeply committed.

My own values also include a fascination with what might loosely be termed 'knowledge transfer', and a strong sense of the importance of the information systems practitioner actively considering the role of knowledge, expertise or technology transfer as part of their routine interventions in real-world problem situations. Indeed, in this chapter I will attempt to demonstrate why self-conscious attention to such concerns raises important philosophical issues for information systems theory and practice, especially in the light of societal and technological changes. It should be self-evident by this point that I stake no *other* claims to being qualified for entry to more abstract philosophical discourse!

The Voluntary Sector	
Estimated number of voluntary organizations, using a broad definition:	500,000
Number of registered charities:	170,357
Estimated number of adults involved in volunteering:	23,000,000 (about 1 in 2)
Number of people given formal advice each day:	35,000
Number of employees (highest of several estimates, full- and part-time):	500,000
Total income of registered charities in England and Wales:	£16.18billion (3.1% GDP)
Central government funding to voluntary organizations:	£3.4billion

NB. Figures cover different periods and multiple sources of original research, thus
comparability and rigour should not be assumed.

Table 1: Some key figures — (Fries & Randon 1993) and (NCVO 1991).

In presenting this report, a brief picture of the domain of investigation is
provided, followed by a summary of the limited understanding of community
information systems that exists so far. The notion of 'sustainability' and its
application to information systems practice is then introduced, and an account of
my early search for appropriate theoretical underpinnings and tools to support the
research methodology leads in to some final reflections.

2   The Social Economy

The scale and influence of the voluntary sector in society today is by no means
negligible. As Table 1 shows, registered charities alone contribute a significant
proportion to the UK's gross domestic product, an high proportion of individuals
are actively involved in voluntary organizations regularly (either as helpers or
clients), and the sheer number of organizations is notable.

However, consistent research data and clear terminology is elusive. Different
authors focus on different facets of the voluntary sector as a whole, and use a
wide variety of terms. Terminology depends sometimes on the research context,
the values and purpose of the organization or individual using it, and sometimes
it appears to depend merely on convenience. Furthermore, some definitions
appear interchangeably, thus adding to the confusion about exactly what is a
'voluntary organization', 'voluntary agency', 'community group', 'non-profit
organization', 'charity', 'charitable organization', or which organizations or
groups could be identified with the 'voluntary sector', the 'third sector' or the
'non-statutory sector'. Even the most eminent specialists in the field, such as
Wolfenden Committee (1978), Handy (1988), Butler & Wilson (1990) and Leat
(1993), have faced, documented, and resolved only with some trepidation, such
problems.

It is not even clear that any grouping of such organizations could together be described with any degree of confidence as forming a 'sector'. Voluntary organizations range from large national charities with household names to fledgling local campaigning groups, and from those with a clear welfare remit to those, like building societies or motoring associations, who are today barely indistinguishable from ordinary commercial organizations.

Paton (1992) recognizes that homogeneity is a myth, and that a new understanding of the voluntary sector is needed in order to convey both its distinctiveness and variety without misleading associations. Drawing on European traditions, he uses the label 'social economy' by viewing voluntary organizations in the context of society as a whole, and arguing that attempts to identify strict categories and boundaries between sectors of society might be productively replaced with the notion of two *dimensions*. These are respectively the dimensions of complexity and purpose, as shown in Figure 1, overleaf.

A six segment model results from this analysis, with the corporate and public sectors being similar to each other in complexity but distinct in purpose, and the 'natural economy' of informal family or friendship networks having lowest complexity alongside the hidden economy, but again being distinguishable in terms of purpose. Between these extremes lie small and medium enterprises and the social economy, the latter being distinguishable by the value-based purposes of its member organizations.

Paton claims that this approach highlights common features of organizations within a sector, and — perhaps more importantly — illuminates the character of organizations falling between sectors. It also represents a powerful model by encouraging an understanding of the transactions between social economy organizations and those in other sectors, the migration of organizations from one sector to another over time, and the influences that other types of organization have on social economy organizations. Contemporary developments and trends that can usefully be viewed in this light include: the move away from local authority grant aid for community organizations to the contracting out of service provision; the pressure on charities to refrain from 'political' activity and the changing nature of lobbying and pressure group work; and the continuing reduction in the role of the welfare state and society's greater reliance on the social economy to deliver basic services.

Whilst useful, the social economy model requires an higher level of resolution in order to act as a foundation for empirical research at an operational level. Kazi et al. (1990) have addressed this in suggesting some indices of complexity and purpose, and there are established and theoretically-grounded taxonomies such as that which distinguishes three broad types of voluntary activity, namely: mutual support and self-help organizations and networks; service delivery organizations visibly providing services to those in need; and campaigning organizations and pressure groups (Handy 1988). This taxonomy could be superimposed on the Paton model, and furthermore, it may be that rigorous functional classifications such as that being established on an international basis (Salamon & Anheier

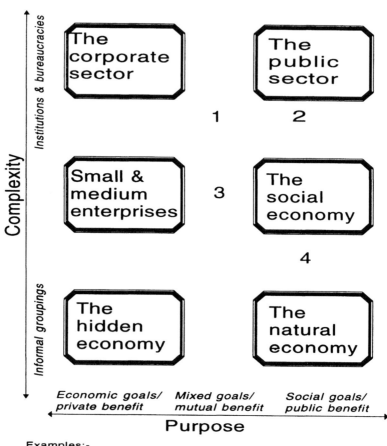

Figure 1: Types of organization in and around the social economy, with examples, based on (Paton 1992).

1993) could be added as a third dimension to the social economy model. This could, arguably, dilute the original systemic intent, so further investigation of an enhanced model is required and forms a component of the current research project.

Meanwhile, the current project is intentionally focused on organizations at the low complexity end of the social economy sector, yet is concerned with formal organizations and not the informal groupings that the 'natural economy' typifies. The tag 'community organization' seems intuitively appropriate to such a subset of the social economy, and a working definition of this term (based on a qualified version of Paton's characterization of the social economy as a whole) is *a small value-based organization founded on commitment (arising from devotion, compassion, enthusiasm, solidarity, defiance, etc.) and working for a common or public benefit at a local (typically county or city) level.*

3 Community Organizations as a Domain for Information Systems Research and Practice

Before outlining the key hypothesis at the centre of the present research project, it is necessary to summarize some of the salient features of community organizations as a domain for information systems research and practice, including their information systems characteristics.

In addition to their value-based orientation, community organizations can be characterized as being reliant on the commitment and shared values of their human resources through use of high levels of volunteer labour and relatively poorly-paid staff. They are frequently under-resourced, and yet are remarkably resource-efficient, are often unstable, can only set short-term planning horizons, and tend to lack strategic management and planning. Given the contemporary social policy climate, bringing with it a reducing role of the welfare state and increasing attention to charity, community organizations are facing significant role changes and ever-tightening funding constraints, yet display continuing resilience and innovative capabilities. Management styles are often humanistic, open and collective, and increasingly professionalized.

Though it is beyond the scope of this chapter, this crude characterization warrants deeper examination, for as Diana Leat (1993) has pointed out, the differences between non-profit and for-profit organizations may not in fact be so great as it may seem, though other management writers show they are distinct. For example, Drucker (1989b) suggests that for-profit organizations have much to learn from best practice in management exhibited by non-profits.

Whilst the literature on management in voluntary organizations has developed considerably in recent years, the literature on information systems in community organizations (and indeed in the broader social economy) has remained remarkably sparse, especially in academic domains. Nevertheless, the distinguishing features of community information systems are worthy of note, although again rigorous analysis is warranted but is beyond the scope of the present chapter.

Studies such as Rowan (1994), Boyle et al. (1993) and Plant (1992) are consistent in suggesting that the role of information systems in community organizations is largely confined to the service of low level efficiency objectives (through use of, often only one or two, office automation applications), and movement towards the service of effectiveness or inter-organizational objectives is highly limited so far (despite the recent growth of, for example, online and email services provided by and for the voluntary sector specifically). There is a significant presence of information technology, but an absence of concern for information *systems* considerations, with technology-focused practices, 'quick-fix' projects, and lack of thorough staff participation in information systems development and management, being typical.

Equally typically, staff in community organizations rarely have significant levels of expertise in, yet retain high expectations of and hopes for, their information systems. Perhaps more problematically, severe resource limitations impose major constraints on the ability of community organizations to utilize external expertise, and outside expertise does not always exhibit the characteristic of being 'in sympathy with their aspirations' that has been argued as a precondition to success, for example IT and Communities Working Party (1992) and Plant (1992). Moreover, such expertise that is recruited from outside rarely offers more than technical support at operational or tactical levels of community information systems, and information systems planning is not regarded as important. In one recent study, only nine organizations were interested in information technology needs analysis or information technology strategy development in response to 20,000 advertizing flyers and other publicity for a community computing grant aid scheme (Rowan 1994).

At a structural level, social economy organizations appear to have far less support for information systems concerns than others. Even brief scrutiny of documents, reports or journals emanating from the social economy, or from writers on the social economy, reveals an highly diverse and multi-faceted general support infrastructure. One listing of resources for community development identifies about 17 national organizations whose primary or sole purpose is providing infrastructural support for community organizations (Taylor 1992), and on a local level a myriad of centres for voluntary service, self-help networks and other support organizations exist for the same reason.

However, as Boyle et al. (1993) have concluded, there is little or no infrastructure for supporting community information systems either locally or nationally, and furthermore cooperation between community organizations appears to exist at a lower, more piecemeal, level than their value-based stance might suggest. Researchers have identified a forbidding range of information systems support needs, including development of self-help strategies, and made suggestions on how they might be addressed (IT and Communities Working Party 1992, Plant 1992, Plant 1994), yet there is as yet little insight into how such propositions might be realized, particularly (though not solely) in the light of serious resource constraints. Furthermore, doubts remain on whether general-purpose national or local support organizations have the capacity to develop or sustain information systems support initiatives in the light of resource pressure on their existing operations, though again there are occasional (but all-too-often one-off) breakthroughs in the form of guidance booklets and resource guides such as Charlton et al. (1988) and Smith & Plant (1994).

Community organizations could therefore be said to represent a particular challenge for information systems research and practice, in that their organizational and management characteristics are unique and complex, and because of their ambitiousness and large-scale deployment of information systems (albeit primarily utilizing small-scale, mainly PC-based, information technology). Furthermore, the challenge is extended through the lack of appropriate models for positioning and organizing information systems expertise at an infrastructural or strategic level, compared with, say, the corporate Information Centre or the central or departmental information systems units of public sector organizations.

4   Can Community Information Systems be 'Sustainable'?

The mission of the present project is to tackle some aspects of the community information systems challenge, and to make an original and significant contribution to knowledge in the process. A starting premise is that adoption of information systems may be less successful in community organizations than elsewhere, and that in order to make improvements in the light of low levels of internal information systems expertise and the lack of an external support infrastructure, there is a need to focus on the scope and nature of interventions by information systems practitioners. The research is also premised on the lack of directly relevant theory, together with the possibility of applying to this domain theoretical insight developed in other domains, using the interdisciplinary field of information systems as an overall guiding framework, and an action research approach to the development of theoretical understanding through abstract reflection on practice.

The project aims therefore include the development and demonstration of good practice in the introduction and management of sustainable information systems by community organizations or their service providers, having established the need for the notion of 'sustainability' to be taken into account as part of this practice. Work in progress so far towards these aims includes literature review and analysis, an initial phase of fieldwork, and preliminary development of a 'sustainability hypothesis'. This hypothesis lies at the heart of the research, so its initial formulation will now be described.

'Sustainable information systems' are defined, according to this initial formulation, as promoting organizational autonomy, successfully contributing to the pursuit of the organization's goals, and exhibiting reasonable longevity. The term refers not to individual information systems, nor solely to information systems as objects, but to the totality of information systems activity, including its objects and processes, within an organization. The three components of

Figure 2: Sustainable information systems: initial definitions and influential factors.

this definition (autonomy, success and longevity) are each conceived as being influenced by three respective sets of factors, as modelled preliminarily in Figure 2.

The development of the model itself, and the identification of the contributing factors, has drawn on previous work related, in a variety of direct and less direct ways, to the current research. A similar three-segment framework is offered by Hirschheim (1987) in representing his definition of information management, and his information systems design, information technology design and 'implementation approach design' segments map broadly on to the success, longevity and autonomy segments of the sustainability model respectively. Equally, an analysis of the factors influencing success in small business computing led to the formulation of a three-pronged model of influential forces involving organizational, computer system and development process clusters (Wroe 1986, Wroe 1987), which also map broadly on to the success, longevity and autonomy segments respectively.

Now examining briefly in turn the three segments of the preliminary sustainability model, the overall success of information systems in contributing to the goals or objectives of the organization could be argued, firstly, to depend on management factors. A theme that appears in the literature on information systems planning is that there should be strong linkage between business planning and information systems planning (Galliers 1987a), and in the case of the social economy this factor itself suggests that relative stability of the organization itself, and thus its general planning processes, is a prerequisite (though as noted above, a non-trivial one). Another common theme in the literature is the need for information systems management to involve systemic attention, i.e. attention to a broad range of interacting social, technical and organizational concerns, not just a narrow focus on information technology and system development issues. In the case of the social economy, cultural appropriateness and resource efficiency can be added as related but separate factors, given respectively the commercial world-view associated with many information systems products and processes, and the sometimes-supervening limitations imposed on community information systems by severe resource constraints.

Factors influencing the longevity component of sustainable information systems are focused more on technical concerns, and include the hypothesized need for balanced attention to both 'top-down' (strategically led) and 'bottom-up' (infrastructure led) methodologies for information technology identification, design and evaluation, with perhaps an additional 'inside-out', or opportunity-driven innovation-oriented, dimension to complete the approach suggested by Earl (1989). High maintainability and flexibility, together with appropriate complexity, may be said to be desirable characteristics of information systems in any sector, but may need to be given particular attention in the social economy, given critical constraints such as the need to avoid lock-in to external expertise, the need to maximize resource utilization and the need to avoid over-complex, over ambitious, information technology projects. A final factor influential in this area, though by no means orthogonal to others, is the notion of 'human scale' technology, a concept which has appeared in information systems literature (Nurminen 1988) and outside (Sale 1980).

The third and final set of sustainability factors is associated with empowerment issues, and which together contribute, in this model, to the degree of information systems autonomy in social economy organizations. It could be argued that to maximize the prospects of success and reasonable longevity of community information systems, there is a need for long-term control by the organization itself to be maximized and for dependency on external expertise to be minimized. Such goals are themselves influenced by other factors identified in their own right, including the nature and scope of interventions by outsiders and the development of an appropriate level of skill, knowledge and expertise of members of the organization's staff. In this context the term 'appropriate' should be emphasized, as it is recognized that users do not necessarily want or need to take on board the expertise of information technology, information systems or information management analysts themselves. The term is intended to suggest that explicit awareness of and attention to such distinct, wide-ranging and complementary roles is necessary, that technology, knowledge or skill transfer (Shields & Servaes 1989, Waters 1994) will necessarily occur in most situations, but that the degree to which it occurs will vary according to each unique combination of situational variables. Participation by appropriate organizational actors, and organizational rather than personal 'ownership' of information systems initiatives and artefacts, is thought to be another empowerment factor. Finally, in the light of the critical dependency on empowering interventions from outside, the sustainability of expertise delivery mechanisms must be added, thus introducing an element of recursion to the sustainability model.

The concept of sustainable information systems in community organizations can therefore be seen to involve a rich interplay of factors and characteristics, which have been derived hitherto from personal intuition, past practice as a consultant, and analysis of early attempts to generate general guidelines and abstractions from such practice (Plant 1991), as well as from the available literature and through discussions with colleagues. However, as already stated, the current formulation of the sustainability hypothesis is highly preliminary, and is expected to evolve further as the research progresses. The mechanism by which this evolution is being nurtured will be discussed in the context of the project methodology more generally.

5 Development of the Research Methodology

After establishing that an elaborated social economy model was an appropriate background tool for understanding community organizations in a broad context, identifying as a starting point some of the distinguishing management and information systems characteristics of community organizations, and arriving at a preliminary sustainability hypothesis, a methodology for the project as a whole was falling into place. A commitment was made to an early phase of (non-interventionist) fieldwork which will qualify and elaborate the initial models, provide a reference point against which to evaluate and make explicit personal biases, and establish the need for the notion of sustainability to be further investigated.

This initial fieldwork involves semi-structured interviews with a sample of local community organizations who could be regarded as primarily 'consuming' information systems services, and a sample of other organizations or individuals who primarily act as 'providers', together with a third sample of others who occupy both 'consumer' and 'provider' roles. In addition to addressing the above aims, this fieldwork is expected to identify bases for action research consultancy aimed at bringing about improvements in the sustainability of community information systems in sample organizations. The second, interventionist phase of fieldwork will also drive the development of further theoretical modelling and will be followed by a final sustainability evaluation phase after a time delay, thus addressing the obvious need for a longitudinal component to the research methodology.

Arising perhaps from a personal philosophical position on sharing skills and knowledge with others, another early commitment was to concentrate attention on the autonomy component of sustainability, and to focus the investigation on empowerment factors, whilst retaining a broad, holistic approach to the rich interplay of factors in all areas. Viewing the information systems practitioner, then, as (potentially at least) a facilitator of sustainable community information systems, a decision was made to concentrate on the relationships between community organizations and outside expertise.

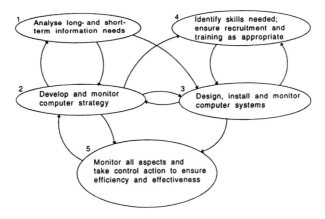

Figure 3: Information management activities, based on (Wilson 1991).

However, an established theoretical framework in which to locate, even if only temporarily, early investigations at the most general level possible was needed, and Brian Wilson's model of information management was adopted for this purpose, as its scope appeared suitably broad. Furthermore, some operational aspects of this model not only resonated with personal experience, but could also be rendered reasonably accessible to non-experts in community organizations during fieldwork. Wilson suggests that the three main tasks for information management are to:

> "... identify the information support and communication needs of the particular organization; satisfy those needs by using the appropriate technology through appropriate processes of implementation and change and, as a support to that activity, to know about the opportunities provided by technological developments." (Wilson 1991)

In the same paper, Wilson goes on to describe a more detailed mapping of information management activities that was carried out (in an end user department of a commercial organization), and offers a complex but powerful model which was then used to explore possible boundaries to various different job definitions of end user information management subset roles. A simplified version of this model appears in Figure 3, in the form prepared (using lay language) as an exhibit to support fieldwork interviews, although its very simplification risks loss of richness and meaning. Furthermore, it is clear that the culture in which Wilson's research is embedded is very distinct from that in which the present research is taking place, and so the implications of this domain-change require deeper exploration.

171

Nevertheless, it was felt that Wilson's model of information management activities could be a valuable tool, in this research, to support a similar exercise, namely the exploration of different role allocation possibilities involving non-expert members of community organizations, outside expertise and a range of combinations of the two. More specifically, if it is assumed that all of the activities modelled need to be carried out in any given community organization, research questions generated include: what activities are within the capabilities of non-expert individual users and can be allocated internally; what activities are likely to remain external due to internal skill or resource limitations or other factors (including preference); what internal capabilities can in principle be enhanced through technology/skill/knowledge transfer activities; and what relationships between community organizations and outsiders can be developed within which such transfer opportunities can be realized whilst taking account of practical constraints (including the need, argued earlier, to ensure the sustainability of delivery mechanisms)?

Thus it can be seen that this model provokes a diversity of issues which when addressed will improve our understanding of community information systems and its sustainability. Other questions are perhaps more fundamental: is the whole range of information management tasks appearing in the model being addressed currently by community organizations in practice; is there adequate external expertise readily available in order to fill gaps in service provision; and is 'end user information management' empowerment a realizable or desirable goal? Referring back to the sustainability hypothesis of Figure 2, such questions enable the two models to be cross-referenced, particularly in terms of the long-term control factor in the autonomy cluster, the systemic awareness factor in the success cluster, and others. This might suggest that there is scope for integrating the two models, an option which itself remains at present one of the many areas to be tackled during further research.

6 Conclusions

This chapter has provided an account of a specific research project whose methodological and theoretical underpinnings are still evolving, and whose applied nature renders its philosophical connotations relatively minor. However, Petheram's comments (in this volume p.113) on "Backing into Philosophy via Information Systems" strike a chord, given that my own experience could be characterized as 'backing into' information systems from a position of having recognized the poverty of information *technology* practice in tackling concerns around community information systems and sustainability, and further investigation of philosophical aspects is both warranted and expected.

Nevertheless, I believe that some of the issues raised in this chapter have philosophical implications for the information systems community generally, particularly issues like whether 'end user information management' is a realizable or desirable goal. The chapter will therefore conclude with a number of diverse remarks related to this belief.

Firstly, it is not clear to me whether we yet have adequate models of the information systems practitioner as educator and enabler. Emancipatory practice is overtly espoused by the critical systems thinking movement (Flood & Jackson 1991), but most reports on action research in information systems appear to see an information systems methodology as the object of the research, or imply that it is the researcher/practitioner in the role of beneficiary of the action, and not the information systems user. Transfer of power would appear to be an explicit motive in other disciplines such as community development, being "concerned with change and growth — with giving people more power over the changes that are taking place around them" (Taylor 1992). Parallels with this field need to be explored, and connections with methodological work in the community operational research movement (Jackson 1988) could also be made, though the extent to which power issues are addressed here are not clear to me at this time.

Secondly, even if power transfer is overtly and self-consciously placed at the centre of attention, the task of information management transfer in the context of small organizations is likely to pose significant challenge. Guidance offered by end user *computing* theory and practice is limited, though there are transferable models such as those of user ability/skill/education levels (Panko 1988), and end user information systems literature does not appear to offer adequate systemic/holistic frameworks, though again some insights at a lower level such as an "End User information systems Project Methodology" (Regan & O'Connor 1994), and a classification of types of end user computing by degrees of user autonomy (Robson 1994) could be useful. information management is not itself a well-defined, established discipline, so if it is poorly understand by its experts, can it be well transferred? The addressing of this conundrum might find useful philosophical inspiration in the human-centred systems movement, given that this field recognizes the creative power of ordinary people and the folly of the separation of theory and practice, experts and practitioners (Gill 1991).

This relates in turn to the third remark, that as the millennium approaches, the near-ubiquity of information technology (even in small organizations), and ever-increasing penetration of computer, communications and other modern technologies into the daily lives of more and more people, might reinforce a machine-centred view of information systems, not assist in the development of an human-centred view. Increasing computer literacy, confidence and fluency in information technology might, paradoxically, lead new generations to enter the same technologically-focused, positivist paradigm unaware that recent history has seriously questioned its merits. This places humanistic information management awareness and education in an high priority position, and arguably it might be particularly important in connection with individuals or very small organizations, as an information management agenda is least likely to be found in such situations, being close to the consumer culture and accustomed to personal information systems but perhaps less aware of organizational and social information systems concerns. Is the information systems research community ready for community information systems practice, or indeed information management practice as a whole, to consider a "market-orientated conceptualization of the profession" like community operational research (Jackson 1988)?

Fourthly, the changing nature of organizations, of work, and of the relationships between individuals and organizations, provides further challenge still, as established information systems approaches have been developed for established forms of organization. As Land (1992) has pointed out, information systems theory and practice should support informal systems and infrastructure-led approaches as well as formal top-down support, and yet as argued above strategic alignment needs not to be lost as well. This paradox will be addressed, initially in small social economy organizations, through the exploration of the sustainability hypothesis that has been outlined. However, the paradox may apply just as strongly in larger organizations, and results may ultimately be transferable from small to large domains. Equally, the social economy may be an excellent domain for post-positivist investigation, as its cultural baggage may be less weighty due to the humanistic, value-based tradition of this sector, and therefore again it might offer a pilot of a more general application of sustainable information systems.

Acknowledgements

I would like to thank my colleagues, particularly Anne Moggridge and Brian Petheram, for their support for this project, and for the many ideas that they have contributed to the research.

A New Philosophy, a New Agenda: Introducing Information Systems into Complex Organizations

Stuart Maguire

This chapter tries to identify a number of issues that information systems professionals may be addressing in the next millennium. It puts forward the proposition that a new philosophy within information systems should incorporate a 'market-led' rather than 'product-led' approach — this should apply to both the information systems developer as well as any methodology adopted. It expresses the view that systems development is primarily the handling of the management of change. This chapter concentrates on a multi-site research project undertaken within the National Health Service.

1 Introduction

It is an interesting task trying to identify the range of subject areas that should be included within information systems development. The range of experiences required to introduce information systems into organizations is wide and varied. If we agree that the range of stakeholders and agendas is also wide and varied we are confronted with a very complex situation. There is no doubt that the National Health Service (NHS) is a rich area for experimenting with the different approaches to system development that have been prevalent over the last thirty years. I must make it clear at this stage that I am interested in introducing information systems into organizations rather than implementing them.

This chapter reviews the issues and outcomes from a national project undertaken over a four year period within the National Health Service (NHS). The project was named Oases and was based on work done at 5 different organizations in the NHS. The original aim of the Oases project was to support the development of effective information systems within suitable organization structures, supported by appropriate information technology, in turn underpinned by effective and efficient management of information.

2 The Research Project

The speed and complexity of the development of information systems within the NHS is having an adverse effect on those groups interfacing with them. It has been recognized within the NHS that:

> "any attempt to install sophisticated information systems before the Service has the skills to implement and operate them and exploit their potential, would only impeded the very changes they were aimed at assisting." (NHSME 1990)

There is an urgent and large scale need for NHS professionals to understand the introduction of information systems whether they are to be developers or users of systems. Working Paper 11 also talked of a substantial cultural change in, "working practices, attitude, and organization in every part of the National Health Service" (NHSME 1990).

There is a tight link being made between the implementation of information systems/technology within the NHS and an improvement in health care. The vast majority of large information systems which have been implemented within the NHS have been developed using 'hard', structured techniques. They do not address the major social, organizational and legal implications arising from the introduction of information systems (Welke & Konsynski 1982, Guiterrez & Greenberg 1993). The methodologies used have been based on the system development life cycle. Most of these take a very simplistic view of a number of key issues, namely:

- Training.

- Documentation.

- System Evaluation and Review.

- User/Analyst Interface.

- Management of Change.

- Problem Identification.

If this major area of change within the NHS is not handled properly it will have dysfunctional effects on the organization in the areas where most efficiency and effectiveness gains were expected (Pettigrew et al. 1988).

Large numbers of NHS Staff have become disillusioned with the use of information technology/information systems within their specific areas because of the way the introduction has been mishandled. This implementation has been undertaken by the group referred to as the Information Specialists. This user dissatisfaction should necessitate a change of attitude in those introducing information systems within the NHS. The existing system methodologies have not worked.

It is very important that any methodology used within the NHS addresses the culture therein. The NHS has a very close analogy to the planning orientation that Ackoff (1970) described as Inactivism. Inactivists are described as being satisfied with things as they are but who do not like the way things are going. Therefore, they try to prevent change. This resistance to change must be seen as a major issue and not a minor hindrance to system development. Involving the user as part of the system reduces alienation and leads to a more successful implementation of computer systems (Lucas 1985).

System developers are often guilty of selling system implementation to users/managers. There is often very little questioning of whether the introduction of information technology into organizations is effective or not. Peter Keen talks of counter-implementation:

> "Believers in rationalism generally view resistance to change and protection of vested interests as faults to be ignored or suppressed. The tactical approach to implementation sees resistance as a signal from a system in equilibrium that the costs of change are perceived as greater than the likely benefits. The bringers and sellers of change — academics, computer specialist and consultants — assume that what they offer is good." (Keen 1981)

This has important implications for organizations when a second system is being developed — and the first attempt has been a disaster. The development of information systems within the NHS is currently dominated by the use of methodologies based on the idea of purposive/rational action. The underlying knowledge base of many of the methodologies is technical knowledge interest. One reason for the failure of information systems within the NHS is that their design has conflicted with the prevailing organizational culture and attitudes. This has highlighted the failure of the scientific approach in information systems development (Checkland 1981, Anderson 1985).

The Oases project tackles a number of important system development issues in a way that focuses on the need to understand the whole range of behavioural, organizational, change management and information quality problems that may confront NHS staff. It would be wrong to assume that because the development and implementation of an information system has been successful in a manufacturing company that the same process will work within the NHS, which has special problems such as size, the variety of interacting agencies, culture and reporting mechanisms.

Oases has highlighted a variety of systems issues in an attempt to improve the quality of information used within the NHS. Effective information systems can provide quality information (a scarce resource made scarcer still by frequent and major change within the NHS). The need to carefully manage resources and be aware of business opportunities makes the provision of quality information to NHS decision-makers a critical issue. Recent changes in the structure and operation of the NHS have resulted in a greater emphasis on the management of information, especially at local level (albeit within an overall strategy). There is so much data and information within the NHS that it is important to disseminate it effectively and efficiently.

3 Methodology

Accepting the fact that the selection of a best methodology for any particular research project is critical to the resulting quality and value of that project I discounted several modes of study. These included case study, archival research and opinion research. The favoured methodology was participative/action research. I accept the fact that information systems development is a matter of expert knowledge which has to be applied from without or as a matter of participation from within (Klein & Lyytinen 1985). The latter is obviously supported by the socio-technical or critical success theory advocates.

It is extremely important that the users of information systems are able to play a positive role in any new systems methodology. The majority of the current methodologies cannot deal with conflict situations and social debate on ambiguous goals — very often users are in conflict not only with the providers of information systems but with other users themselves (Nissen 1985).

The lack of adequate numbers of skilled information systems staff within the NHS coupled with an high percentage of inexperienced users has left the way open for expert power to control system development. A typical scenario would be a large acute hospital with one or two information technology professionals procuring both hardware and software from a large supplier. In this situation a common simplifying mechanism is to allow the suppliers and information technology staff to set the agenda in terms of system implementation. It is not the purpose of this chapter to isolate the procedures undertaken within and around the system development life cycle — these have been well documented. In the vast majority of system implementations the 'what' is not questioned and the 'how' is often not investigated. It can be viewed as a closed system.

At the present time there is no pressure on the system implementors to change their philosophy towards system development. Measures of effectiveness have been slow to develop — in most cases none exist. Organizational pressures have made implementation deadlines very tight. A common success criteria would be that a system is developed on time. Developing a system within a budget is another criteria, though a stringent cost/benefit analysis is often omitted.

One of the key areas of this research was that the projects overlapped and there was interaction between the various sites. This allowed good practice to be shared between the sites. This was important as many of the NHS organizations were experiencing major change and had limited resources.

4 Progress to Date

The project has highlighted a large number of very different systems issues in an attempt to try and improve the effective use of information within the NHS.

Effective information systems can provide what many NHS managers believe to be in short supply — quality information. The whole process of supplying this scarce resource, information, is further complicated when one considers the frequent major changes that occur within the Health Service. The need to carefully manage resources and also to be aware of business opportunities combine to make the provision of quality information to NHS decision-makers a crucial issue.

Getting all staff to view the provision of quality information systems as part of their overall responsibility is very important. The research aims to demystify a number of key areas and to try and include a number of staff groups who may have considered themselves on the periphery of information systems development but without whom the whole process will fail.

The timing of the project could not be better. It is expected that the total NHS spend on information technology will reach one million pounds by the mid-1990s. This has coincided with a growing concern that there is a widespread failure to deliver benefits on the part of information technology based information systems.

The project has identified a number of key areas that will be of importance to managers, users, systems staff, trainers and human resources management personnel within the NHS namely:

1. Return on Investment.
2. Business Awareness of Staff.
3. Organizational Strategy.
4. Political Environment.
5. Resistance to Change.
6. Strategic Alignment.
7. Environmental Scanning.
8. Systems Education.
9. Systems Training.
10. Information Management.
11. Managing the Information Technology Resource.
12. System Methodologies.
13. Flexibility of Systems.
14. Maintenance of Systems.
15. Information Quality.
16. Users in System Development.
17. Evaluation & Review.
18. Benefits Realization.

From these areas a number of important issues have been identified as being of special importance to information systems development within the NHS:

1. Identification of the need to have a clear understanding of matters to do with change management are crucial if effective information systems are to be developed within the National Health Service.

2. Understanding and applying the basic requirements, such as accurate and efficient data capture and the relationships between information provision and its uses.

3. Understanding the implications of information systems for changing and reshaping working practices.

4. The identification of information quality and organizational culture as key issues.

5. The need to raise education and training to new heights of prominence to combat the inevitable increase in sophistication and complexity that is being brought in by system changes.

6. The need to develop a methodology for the introduction of systems that endorses participation, communication and openness.

5 Conclusions

Current changes in the structure and operation of the National Health Service have resulted in a greater emphasis being placed on the management of information especially at the local level, albeit within an overall strategy. There is so much data and information within the NHS that it is important to disseminate it effectively and efficiently. It is one issue to collect data and information — but it would be a futile exercise if it did not reach the right person at the right time in the right format to be used effectively. Care must be taken to ensure that information flows through the key decision points within the organization. This will only happen if managers and users play a prominent role in system development to identify clearly the information and hence the information systems that they require.

Organization structures and systems are changing rapidly within the National Health Service and this places an extra burden on management to identify not only the information they may require today but also what they may need in several years time. Recent estimates have revealed that 80% of NHS Staff are either information providers, operational information users, information managers, managerial information users or information specialists (NHSTA 1989).

With this number of staff being affected by system developments a participative, flexible approach is of paramount importance. This will require system developers to identify issues relating to the environment in which the system is going to reside. It will inevitably mean that system developers will have to take a market-led, rather than a product-led philosophy towards system development. It will also require human resource management staff within the NHS to take a more proactive role within system development. Business managers will also need to see the potential as well as the dangers of implementing information systems within complex organizations. In the future systems experts may well be seen as change managers rather than system implementors.

Anthropological Reflections on Systems Engineering: Seeing is Believing

George Bakehouse, Chris Davis, Kevin Doyle & Sam Waters

This chapter introduces a programme of action research which involves the pre-competitive specification of an integrated clinical workstation (ICWS) for the Neurosciences Directorate of Frenchay Healthcare Trust. The research team involved includes several members of UWE academic staff and a range of hospital specialists including: consultant neurosurgeons, neuropathologists, neurologists, neuropsychiatrists, neurophysiologists, senior registrars, registrars, senior house officers, nurses, administrators and managers. Academic team members have roles in the project such as the specification of its 'information base', human–computer interaction (HCI), information management (in the organizational context), monitoring and control of activity, and development methods. The chapter outlines the rationale for an organic and evolutionary approach to the development of the ICWS and reports some of the results of recent fieldwork.

1 Introduction

It is a salutary fact that despite the experience and increased sophistication of medical technology over the past 44 years it has made little or no impact on improving global efficiency of clinical medicine. During the last twenty five years information technology has been increasingly used and computers of ever-increasing power have been brought into medicine in ever-increasing numbers. The increase in the number of patients treated, however, has been largely achieved by increasing the number of doctors, nurses and paramedics and other resources. Treatment has certainly become swifter, more accurate and generally more comfortable for the patient and much more can be done for the patient with each year that passes, but only at an increased cost (Griffith 1992).

Experience in the United Kingdom has shown that there is a seemingly immutable curve of patients vs. resources. New and improved medical techniques have increased the demand for medical treatment, the increased demand for medical treatment is a powerful motivator for improving medical technique; and so the cycle continues. The National Health Service Management Executive (NHSME) are now seeking a break in the patient/resources curve. Technology has so far failed to deliver this break economically, information technology doubly so.

Historically, little in the way of information technology has been focused on the clinical process, especially the doctor/patient/nurse interface. The production and handling of a patients medical record has changed very little over the years, with huge volumes of paper and film proving cumbersome and difficult to manage. Major advances in Pathology, Radiology and patient monitoring techniques have all added to the information set presented to the clinician to help in formulating a diagnosis, planning surgical or medical treatment and monitoring outcomes. A large number of computer based systems have been introduced into hospitals in recent years. These systems are wide in variety but tend to serve discrete applications such as CT and MRI image reconstruction, automating laboratory functions, admitting and discharging patients and maintaining hospital accounts. Such systems are extremely valuable in their own right, but rarely do they fit into a well managed information portfolio.

The grand vision of a fully integrated (patient-centred) information base is not new. The enormous waste of money and effort associated with the attempts by Wessex Health Authority to provide a fully integrated computer based health care information system provides a sobering reminder of the complexity of health care requirements (BBC 1993). Cognisant of the magnitude of the problems inherent in specifying a fully integrated information system for UK health care, hospital management, or even patient care the NHSME has developed a research and development strategy in an attempt to strengthen collaboration between the National Health Service (NHS), the Medical Research Council and other research councils, the universities, the medical charities and industry (NHSME 1991).

Part of the portfolio of NHSME supported projects is a project based at Frenchay Healthcare Trust to develop a multi-modality health informatics resource (the integrated clinical workstation — ICWS) to support the clinical, diagnostic and management information requirements of the neurosciences at Frenchay Hospital. This project seeks to refocus technology upon the doctor/patient/nurse interface so as to involve clinicians, nurses and support staff, actively and more efficiently, with a real incentive gain to each individual. In building a full clinical information system (the ICWS) the designers must address the problem of integration of data from the established clinical and managerial sources and the creation of a system with the ability to store, manipulate, transmit and display the right information to the right person in the right place at the right time (Waters 1994).

2   The Integrated Clinical Workstation Project

The aim of the project is:

> "To develop within the multi-disciplinary area of the neurosciences directorate at Frenchay Hospital (Neurosurgery, Neurology, Neuropathology, Neuroradiology and Support Services) an integrated multi-modality information support system (the integrated clinical workstation) to provide a shared information resource accessible to clinicians, nursing staff, radiologists, therapists and managers to support the clinical treatment of neurosurgical patients and the commercial activities of the department." (Mackintosh 1992)

The key objectives of the project are:

1. To enable Neurosurgery to work better by changing the way it uses information.

2. To review the present information usage and operational practices, as the basis of a comprehensive information needs analysis.

3. To define, develop and introduce operational information systems which enhance both the delivery and the quality of the Neurosurgery service.

4. To ensure that all developments are fully documented, monitored and their outcomes audited.

3   The Process of Requirements Analysis

The common way of approaching the early phases of a project intended to produce a computer based information system is to conduct an analysis based on the determination of information requirements. This is a difficult task (Valusek & Fryback 1985, Brookes 1987). Hard systems methods tend to focus largely on existing data requirements by considering data stores and data flows.

The notion of data-centred design is founded upon the premise that models of the 'real world' (typically manifest in data) are more stable than the functions which interpret and use these models (Codd 1986, Jackson 1983).

Martin has extended this notion to information-centred design using entity relationship models (Chen 1979) and the process of normalization (Codd 1972) to structure and represent data, meta data (data about data) and the fundamental structure and form of the organization for which the information engineering activity is being undertaken (Martin 1986).

The aforementioned premise appears logical and can be argued for rationally especially in the area of transaction processing systems where requirements for data are fairly easily defined. In commercial data processing it is also often the case that the complexity of software is linked directly to the complexity of the data structures that it has to manipulate. Where this is true, a clear definition of the necessary structures for input, output and storage of data offer a good basis for the design of the necessary accompanying software (Gane & Sarson 1977, Jackson 1975).

The concept of data independence is central to both data analysis and information engineering. The data requirements of a variety of applications can be established as local logical models and merged (as in Martin's canonical synthesis) into a global logical model. The basic integrity and security of each of the application views is typically supported through facilities provided by a data base management system, supporting views or subschemas.

These views or subschemas are, however, merely wholly contained subsets of the global model or schema with attributes, relationships and entities being excluded and re-ordered as appropriate. In this respect the global model or schema represents a unique objective and supposedly sufficient abstraction of the 'real world' that it seeks to model.

In conducting an analysis of the information requirements of the very disparate stakeholders involved in, and intended to be served by, the ICWS it is recognized by the project team that while there is considerable overlap in information usage by the actors concerned, there are also considerable differences in emphasis, focus and practice. The differences become apparent, for example, when reviewing the split between clinical notes and nursing care plans.

In seeking to develop a shared information resource which provides a real benefit to all its users, the research team has recognized the paucity of conventional information systems development methods in relation to concepts such as meaning, value and priority. Recognizing also the value and the limitations of the use of blended methods (Doyle & Wood 1991) the approach taken seeks to draw upon and learn from the foundations of the systems approach as well as ideas from anthropology and sociology.

4   (Some) Foundations to Systems Thinking

An information system has at its core, by definition, a model of some aspects of the real world. It should be capable of providing consistent, meaningful and useful answers to questions directed at it. This ability is clearly dependent upon the skill of its creators in predicting the likely form of such questions.

It is probable that such a system will have to cope with historical, contemporary and speculative issues, and must therefore be capable of both the retrieval of historical and current data, and in some measure the support of prediction. For example, an integrated information system designed to assist the management of an acute hospital is likely, in a crude sense, to contain at least a partial model of such an institution, those aspects of the environment which are deemed to be important and the interactions of interest (Feibleman & Friend 1945).

In order to produce a useful model from the real world, features relevant to the questions currently being asked or which at some stage may be asked, must be abstracted and in some way represented. The means of representation may vary from a set of very precise mathematical equations such as used in the technique of linear programming, to a purely narrative description, a plethora of representation techniques falling between these two extremes.

These abstractions (models) will naturally be biased towards the weltanschauung of their creator, a fact which must not be overlooked when utilizing them, especially for prediction (Hoos 1972).

In order to produce an abstraction of the real world it is self evidently necessary to understand the things which are being abstracted, and the uses to which the abstractions are to be put. What then, is Frenchay Hospital? It has a name and must therefore be a thing in its own right, but what sort of thing is it? It is clearly a concrete object, a building, and yet it is in another sense a whole, with many constituent parts, some of which are tangible like doctors and theatres, and some of which are abstract such as medical protocols and departments.

Each of the constituent parts are arranged in a specific and potentially discernible manner, and are naturally interrelated and also related in some way to the whole. The term 'potentially discernible' is used because the richness of interrelation is such that the task of describing it is non-trivial. One might well term it a system, but what does that mean?

Prior to the 1940's, the exploration of complex phenomena using the predominant paradigms of science and engineering involved the logical manipulation of component relationships. This was found to be inadequate for the representation of the structure of complex wholes, required by biologists, psychologists and the designers of complex engineering systems. A new approach was called for, and the foundations were laid for General Systems Theory (Emery 1969, Angyal 1941).

> "While accepting the premise that holistic connections cannot be resolved into relationships, some authors have implied that the pattern or structure of wholes does not lend itself at all to logical manipulation. We suggest, however, that the structure of wholes is perhaps amenable to logical treatment after all. That though it may not be described in terms of relations, it may be described in terms of some more adequate logical unit, representing an entirely different logical genus. Here an attempt will be made to demonstrate that there is a logical genus suitable to the treatment of wholes. We propose to call it system." (Angyal 1941)

5 A Systemic Paradigm

Relations require an attribute out of which they are formed, such as colour, position or status, the relationship being based on some similarity or diversity. It was Angyal's contention that members or parts of a system should be thought of as arranged in an important or significant way within the system itself. The relationships between individual parts being a secondary consideration. The difference between a system and a complex relation was, in Angyal's terms, that complex relations could be decomposed into meaningful pairs of simple relations, but a system, which exhibited emergent qualities, could not be decomposed to form simple sets of linear relations.

Angyal argued that the phrase attributed to Aristotle:

"The whole is more than the sum of its parts." (Angyal 1941)

was misleading, because in aggregates it is significant that the parts are added or connected by some inherent quality. In systems, he argued, the parts are arranged or composed:

"The system cannot be derived from the parts. It is an independent framework in which the parts are placed. The concrete organized object is the whole, and the method of organization, the system." (Angyal 1941)

This systemic paradigm was pioneered during the 1940's, predominantly by biologists such as Von Bertalanffy, and developed further during the 1960's by control engineers and cyberneticians. In its early days concern focused on two fundamental pairs of ideas: emergence and hierarchy; and communication and control (von Bertalanffy 1969).

The notion of emergence and hierarchy is broadly an attempt to explain the pattern or structure of wholes in terms of an hierarchy of levels of organization. Each level (subsystem) being something more than can be explained by reference to its component parts, and displaying emergent properties which do not exist at a lower level. It is important to recognize that any one subsystem may belong to more than one higher order system, and thus the structure is more than a simple root/branch hierarchy.

Communication and control is clearly of great importance with regard to purposive/purposeful systems, in order that the behaviour of subparts can be controlled and coordinated towards the achievement of some wider goal. Much important control theory has developed on this theme, such as Ashby's law of requisite variety, which states that the variety of a regulator must equal that of the disturbances whose effects it is to negate, and Bertalanffy's law of equifiniality that open systems can reach the same final state from a number of different initial conditions (Ashby 1956, von Bertalanffy 1973).

A number of systems based methodologies have more recently been developed. For example control theory has been applied to the management of human activity in the form of Cybernetics. Stafford Beer's work on the Viable Systems Model builds upon the concepts of systems viability, feedback, requisite variety and recursion to propose a general cybernetic model for human activity systems (Beer 1985).

Peter Checkland's Soft Systems Methodology uses an action research approach to learning about a problem situation, rejecting the conventional hypothetico-deductive methods favoured by science in favour of a cycle of exploration, understanding and change (Checkland 1981, Checkland & Scholes 1990).

The hermeneutic approach exemplified by Checkland's methodology does not attempt to deal in absolutes when dealing with human activity systems. Rather, it seeks to move towards a satisfactory solution using a process of continual exploration, understanding and change. This activity is undertaken to effect change (hopefully of a desirable nature) in the system, the method of change and the interpretations upon which change is founded. The desirability of change and the point at which the 'problem situation' can be said to be resolved is taken to be the point at which the client deems it to be so, at least temporarily.

5.1 Systems and Science

"The inability to decompose a complex system, and having done so to treat each component in isolation, renders the method of science with its emphasis on reduction, repeatability and refutation, impotent." (Checkland 1981)

The method of science may be characterized by considering Descartes' four rules for "properly conducting one's reason":

1. Avoid precipitancy and prejudice. Accept only clear and distinct ideas.

2. Divide each of the difficulties under examination into as many parts as might be possible and necessary in order to best solve it.

3. Orderly progression from the simple to the complex.

4. Complete analysis, nothing omitted.

Application of these rules assumes that the division advocated in 2 will not distort the phenomenon being studied, and that the components are the same when examined in isolation as they are when playing their part in the whole. It also assumes that the principles governing division of the components are straightforward. The case against this has already been stated.

5.2 Complexity in Systems

When the phenomenon under study is complex in nature with dense connections between components the method of science may provide a means of gathering knowledge but is likely to do little to further understanding. This is especially true when considering the 'unrestricted sciences', such as anthropology and sociology (Patin 1968). Designed experiments in these unrestricted sciences are often made impractical due to the difficulty in establishing adequate controls. In a sociological context, for example, any experiments will be subject to a wide variety of variables, and many unknown factors. In addition to this, social actors can exhibit freedom of choice. By comparison the restricted sciences such as physics, suffer less from the problems of complex interaction, less still from the capricious behaviour of people and generally study only a limited range of phenomena at one time. Under these circumstances the paradigm of science, with its carefully controlled reductionist experiments, is acceptable. This rigorous approach enabling the testing, and perhaps refutation of firmly stated hypotheses by any experimenter. Two identical experiments should yield the same results under these circumstances because the laws governing the universe are not in general capricious (Checkland 1981).

According to the famous philosopher of science, Karl Popper, the process of experimentation and refutation is fundamental to science, a term which he restricted to the consideration of laws and theories which are by their very nature verifiable or refutable (Popper 1963). He applied the term Pseudo-science to disciplines which did not fall into this category because hypotheses were neither provable nor refutable. Systems involving human activity are largely dependent on the behaviour of actors, which may vary from logical to totally outrageous. Consideration of complex social issues, where prediction is difficult and post-hoc explanation subjective, does not seem to be, in Popper's terms, scientifically oriented. He does however observe that when concerning oneself with social engineering "incrementalism and trial and error are the wisest approach" (Popper 1963).

5.3   Human Activity Systems

A taxonomy which illustrates the 'status' of systems involving human action is that ascribed to Blair & Whitston (1971). The categories they describe are:

1. *Natural systems*: these are systems which could not be other than they are. Their origin is in the universe and the processes of evolution, examples being the Earth, man, etc.

2. *Designed physical systems*: designed as the result of some human purpose, for example, chain saws and television.

3. *Designed abstract systems*: the ordered conscious product of the human mind, examples being mathematics, poetry and philosophies.

4. *Human activity systems*: human endeavour, more or less consciously ordered in wholes as the result of some underlying purpose or mission. This, the most complex class of system in the taxonomy, covers all aspects of purposeful behaviour from driving a nail to international politics.

It is interesting to note that the second and third classes would not exist (as defined) if it were not for the fourth, which makes the process of design possible. This holds even if one considers Alexander's notion of 'unselfconscious design' where fitness between form (that part of the world over which we have control and which we decide to shape) and context (the part of the world which places demands on form) is achieved, not through the rational application of design principles to a defined problem, but through an evolutionary or homœostatic process in which tradition is modified by immediacy (Alexander 1964).

5.4   The Systemic Paradigm and Ill-structured Problems

The danger with taxonomies is that they are rooted in the very reductionism that systems thinking purports to avoid. This reductionism causes all systems collected

188

into the same category to be described in the same terms and ascribed the same properties, even when such terms and properties are inappropriate.

A major difficulty for the systems movement is its apparent reliance on the paradigm of science, with its emphasis on reduction, inductive and deductive reasoning to explain, understand and develop the systemic paradigm. One might argue that the development of a new approach requires a meta-approach, and that it is towards this, that effort needs to be directed, thus allowing a wide range of approaches at a lower level to be developed. This almost recursive undertaking is likely to achieve little, especially if treated in the abstract, as a purely methodological conceptual framework. If the systemic approach is to offer a viable alternative to science it must, like science, be demonstrably successful in real world applications.

The scientific approach has dominated the way that we see and think about the world both outside and inside ourselves to such an extent that the term 'scientific' has become synonymous with good practice. It has developed over many generations, through many schools of philosophy, and alongside differing religious and political regimes. It has helped us to understand our world and others which are more distant, to build artefacts and change the face of the landscape from barren to fertile and vice versa. While accomplishing these tasks the method of science has grown and developed, its application promoting better understanding of and providing further insights into its function.

Its success in tackling well bounded, structured problems has naturally led it to be applied to more complex issues, and it is in this respect that it has often proved less than entirely fruitful.

The reductionist approach and a reliance on causal thinking has proved adequate for the exploration of deterministic or stochastic phenomena, but inappropriate where there are problems of dense connection and the phenomenon under study is teleological in nature. It has proved powerless to provide understanding of human activity systems, which by definition contain several, possibly conflicting, goal seeking (Ackoff & Emery 1972) or relationship maintaining (Vickers 1970), subsystems, and are therefore probabilistic at best. The behaviour of human activity systems is linked inexorably to the interpretation of actor and observer. Understanding behaviour is not possible without understanding, and perhaps even empathizing with these interpretations and the weltanschauung from which they derive (Checkland 1981).

The causal thinking common amongst the engineering fraternity assumes that systems can be viewed as a simple transformation process, with inputs and outputs, such that:

"If we have a full description of the input signals and a full description of the system, it is possible to derive a full description of the output signal. Thus dynamic systems analysis remains a determinate discipline. Perhaps it is even more significant that any two of the three descriptions can be used to derive the third." (Heise 1975)

189

This view of systems is only of utility in the analysis of non-purposeful, non-adaptive systems. An human activity system can not be described so fully that its response is determinate, its behaviour is 'probabilistic' in nature. This is always the case where there exist many and varied perceptions of role and purpose, value judgements, personality issues and interpretation of events, all of which have a major bearing on human behaviour. Furthermore, because a human activity system is adaptive in nature, a description of the system as a transformation process is out of date as soon as it is complete. Indeed even the very act of producing the systems model may, by the increased understanding, or altered perception, of its actors, change the behaviour of the system (Checkland 1981).

It is in attempting to understand and control purposeful (or purposive) systems that the systemic approach offers a viable and more appropriate alternative. Its twin concepts of emergence and hierarchy and communication and control together with its notion of a permeable boundary separating the system from its environment, forming a more realistic model from which to achieve both knowledge and understanding, and to promote desirable change.

Some forty years of exploration and debate has led to the following conclusions:

1. The systemic paradigm is primarily concerned with the understanding of wholes which cannot be meaningfully decomposed into simple linear relationships, and is founded on the twin concepts of emergence and hierarchy, communication and control.

2. Systems exist in and generally respond to their environment, environmental factors which directly affect or are affected by a system are of great importance.

3. Systems react in different ways to resist, accommodate, encourage change from outside.

4. Organizational behaviour is affected by external events. Behaviour may be reactive (control) or proactive (planning).

5. The most complex systems of which we are aware are human activity systems precisely because of human involvement.

6. Human activity systems can only be described in terms of the views of actors/observers.

7. There may be as many views of an human activity system's role, value, success, functionality etc. as there are actors/observers.

8. Organizations do not have the goals people may have.

9. Problem situations in human activity systems may be complex with no apparent solutions.

10. Reductionism offers little help where there are complex problem situations with no apparent solutions, hence traditional structured methods (hard systems engineering) are likely to prove inadequate on their own.

6   An Anthropological and Sociological Perspective

Some of the early pioneers of anthropology and sociology developed theoretical and methodological tools which they believed would enable them to deal with the inter-relatedness (wholeness) of various 'traits', institutions and groups within a total social system, and to overcome the atomistic and descriptive methods which had previously prevailed. This approach is commonly referred to as 'functionalist' or 'structural-functional'. Although differing theories emerged, the consensus of opinion within this paradigm, is that 'structure' refers to a set of relatively stable and patterned relationships of social units, while 'function' refers to those consequences of any social activity which make for the adaptation or adjustment of a given structure or its component parts.

The first systematic (and even more importantly, systemic) formulation of the logic of a functionalist approach in sociology can be found in the work of Durkheim (1895). In his works he distinguished between causal and functional types of analysis and concluded that these two methods, far from being antithetical were in fact complementary. Durkheim's definition is that the 'function' of a social institution is the correspondence between it and the needs of the social organism. Many interpreters substitute the phrase 'necessary condition of existence' for 'needs'.

Radcliffe-Brown (1935) believed the concept of function applied to human societies was based on an analogy between social life and organic life. This analogy and the concept of function appear frequently in social philosophy and sociology. In Radcliffe-Brown's analogy between organic and social life, the organism is not a structure; it is a collection of units (cells or molecules) arranged in a structure, i.e. a whole, the parts of which are arranged in a complex holistic set of relations. The life of the organism is conceived as the functioning of its structure. It is through and by the continuity of the functioning that the continuity of the structure is preserved. If we consider any recurrent part of the life process, such as respiration, digestion, etc., its function is the part it plays in, and the contribution it makes to, the life of the organism as a whole. As the terms are being used here, a cell or an organ has an activity and that activity has a function. In the case of the whole organism, activity may be purposeful and goal seeking or relationship maintaining. The parallels with systems theory and its focus on the nature of holism are quite clear.

Radcliffe-Brown (1935) used this theory in his anthropological studies in Africa and Australia where he studied 'primitive' tribes. He noted that individual human beings, the essential units in this instance, were connected by a definite set of social relations into an integrated whole. The continuity of the social structure, like that of an organic structure is not destroyed by changes in the units. Individuals may

191

come and go, the continuity of structure is maintained by the process of social life, which consists of the activities and the interactions of the individuals and groups into which they are united. They are, in other words (rather unsurprisingly), human activity systems.

A key concept of 'function' as here defined thus involves the notion of a structure consisting of a set of relations amongst unit entities, the continuity of the structure being maintained by a life-process made up of the activities of the constituent parts.

A major point where the analogy between natural-organisms and social-organisms breaks down is that in the former it is possible to observe the organic structure, to some extent, independently of its functioning. It is therefore possible to make a morphology which is independent of physiology. In the case of the social-organisms a whole can only be meaningfully observed in its functioning, some features can be directly observed, but most of the social systems which in their totality constitute the structure cannot be observed except in the social activities in which the relations are functioning. It follows that social morphology cannot be established independently of a social physiology.

A second difference is that an animal organism cannot in the course of its life change its structural type, although of course social organisms can and do (this notion will be developed in a paper in preparation: working title "Bowmen, Bobbies And Brain Surgeons").

As Malinowski stated:

> "The modern specialist field-worker soon recognizes that in order to see the facts of savage life, it is necessary to understand the nature of the cultural process. Description cannot be separated from explanation, since in the words of a great physicist: *explanation is nothing but condensed description.* Every observer should ruthlessly banish from his work conjecture, preconceived assumptions and hypothetical schemes, but not theory." (Malinowski 1936)

Immersion in the cultural process is particularly useful in the analysis of complex social settings where goal incongruence might occur as the result of competing objectives: this was found to be an issue during the early fieldwork at Frenchay Healthcare Trust (Mackintosh 1992). Adoption of a similar approach minimized the effects of the political complexities of organizational structure and status of the professions on the researchers: these phenomena are found within all organizations but tend to be particularly problematic in hospitals.

From the outset, the researchers have sought to examine the clinical process and the actors (or 'functionaries') within it: they concentrated their attention on the social physiology, using qualitative observational techniques to record activities as a means to understand the social morphology and thus the 'facts of savage life'.

A second, equally important, requirement for understanding was that the inter-relatedness of the components in the social setting be addressed.

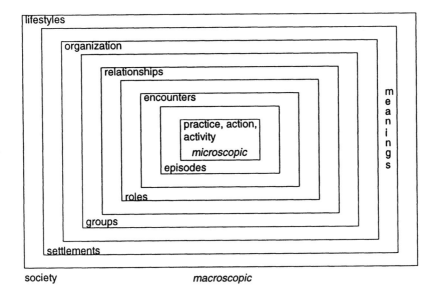

Figure 1: Summary of Lofland's categories.

7 Analysing the Social Setting of Information Systems

Lofland (1971; 1984) identifies the three C's of inter-relatedness:

1. Characteristics.

2. Causes.

3. Consequences.

Understanding of the first C, the characteristics of social settings, demands qualitative analysis to delineate their forms, kinds and types: these range from the macroscopic (societies) to the microscopic (practice, action or activity).

The diagram in Figure 1 seeks to summarize Lofland's categories.

In line with systems thinking, these categories can be contemplated as an hierarchy of social settings, each exhibiting their own particular emergent qualities and existing in the environment of the next order of category. Their function relies heavily on good communication and control mechanisms which rely in turn on the availability of good information for activity, planning and control.

Having identified a social setting as the locus of research by its characteristics, defining what exists and how it varies (e.g. consultation, examination, diagnosis, therapy, ...) we move on to examine the causes and consequences of the variations by measurement of their operationalization — by observing individual actors and acts. Thus, Lofland's second and third C's address the complementarity of function and cause highlighted in Durkheimian sociology, and recognize the primacy of the actors, their roles, values, goals and views, in any social setting.

During the second phase of fieldwork at Frenchay Healthcare Trust our aim was to observe and analyse the information management activities of all actors in the clinical process: adoption of a functionalist approach at this microscopic level of social setting allowed us to relate our findings more readily to the clinical process generally and, as a result, to hospital and NHS-wide information resources.

It is interesting at this point to consider the categories of social setting which seem to be dominant for the various individuals who comprise the clinical process. For example, we might make the following equations:

UGM/Trust Chief Executive	organization
FHSA/Healthcare purchasers	settlement
Consultants	episode
GP	encounters
Patient	roles

8 Method

Between July and November 1993, sixteen members of staff in the Clinical Neurosciences Directorate at Frenchay and three patients were overtly shadowed by four members of the research team: a minimum of two observers were used at all times so as to allow comparison of observation notes. The actors were shadowed for at least one full working day: frequently, the duration of the shadowing exercise was extended, particularly in the case of the patients and the surgeons, to allow continuity of observation of their episodic care and practice, respectively. The timing of the shadowing exercises was also varied so as to sample routine and non-routine activity at various times of the day and night.

Field notes were made openly at the time of the observed activity, or as soon after as was possible. This occasionally presented problems when actors other than the principal had not been made aware of the purpose of the exercise: on such occasions an explanation was immediately given so as to dispel fear and to maintain the excellent working relationship which had been developed over time. A pro-forma sheet was used to record observations in the field, indexed initially by time and location. The hand-written observations from each observer were collated and typed up under the supervision of a team member prior to being checked against the original field notes by their authors: this essential, albeit low-level, verification exercise proved to be very time consuming.

The individual activities recorded in the consolidated shadow histories were then analysed to generate lists of observed information management problems and of the interface or interaction which had been in progress at the time of the problem occurrence. Our aim was to further consolidate the recorded data and simultaneously transform it from a sequential list of activities into a list of observed problems. In this form, the problems could be readily ranked by the shadowee, providing a prioritized list for information systems intervention: such a list is beneficial to both the academic research being undertaken and to the development of a functional specification for the ICWS project which continues in parallel using conventional data modelling techniques.

The next stage of the shadowing exercise involves further verification of the field work findings by the shadowee: feedback to the shadowees will be in the form of a generic list of problem types presented in the classified form described below, which has been developed from analysis of all the field notes. Analysis will therefore be participative, shadowees being helped to identify static and phase patterns in the recorded data by indicating the frequency of the occurrence described and its significance to them. They will be provided with a copy of their shadow history to assist them in this task. The outcome of this stage of the research will be a list of problems and associated interfaces which have been prioritized by the shadowees themselves. That prioritization may be confirmed by further, more highly focused, observational fieldwork and by comparison with the findings of similar studies undertaken elsewhere.

9   Intermediate Results

This intermediate analysis of observed information management problems and their occurrences is presented here as three tables summarizing the quantified results of eighteen days of shadowing. These tables are concerned only with the 'information weaknesses' of a SWOT analysis (Waters 1989) and therefore project a negative view of the present situation — the many strengths of FHCT Neurosciences outweigh the gloom and doom reported herein; further, the tables are currently being verified and refined.

The tables are based on an analysis of information INPUT to and OUTPUT from the prime medical record (manual CASENOTES), the computer (DATABASE) and other (MANUAL) records. Information problems are classified against a taxonomy drawn from the literature, see Figure 2.

Not all these characteristics of information problems were observed during shadowing.

Table 1 summarizes the occurrences of the problems. It should be noted that additional problems may have occurred but were unobserved so that the quantifications are lower than reality. Even so, the analysis suggests:

- Every actor suffers an information problem every hour of every working day.

- The most frequent problem (40% of occurrences) is incomplete information.

- The most frequent media problem relates to case notes (62%) compared to computer database (27%) and other manual records (11%).

Thus, the problems of the medical record merit a more detailed analysis.

Previous research involving dozens of clinicians (NHSME 1991) has identified 52 problem types concerning the medical record which are grouped under:

Content

ACCURACY	"… the truth,"
COMPLETENESS	"the whole truth, and"
REDUNDANCY	"nothing but the truth …"

Presentation   "… understandable …"

Dimensions

LOCATION (Space)	"… here, and"
TIMELINESS	"now …"
COST	"… economically …"

Overall   "… general issues …"

Figure 2: Taxonomy of information problems as presented in (Galliers 1987b) and (Waters 1994).

- The physical location of the hospital case notes and other parts of the medical record.

- The physical state of the case notes.

- The organization of the documents in the case notes.

- The organization of the information in the case notes.

- Delays in obtaining the case notes and the documents for them.

- Problems of wasteful effort.

- Problems of accessing medical record information not held by the hospital.

Our research aims to analyse, verify, quantify and prioritize these problem types in order to propose solutions. Prioritization, typically by ranking is seen by Farbey et al. (1993) as the most effective way of identifying the most productive sequence of information systems development.

Tables 2 and 3 regroup these 52 problem types under the above analysis taxonomy to suggest:

- The NHSME problem types (resulting from questionnaires, brainstorming and workshops) are comprehensive as no further types were observed.

- Half the NHSME problem types did not occur during observation which may indicate that some are superfluous (or unobserved or relatively infrequent or irrelevant in our practice).

196

Problem	Number of occurrences of problem						Totals
	Casenotes		Database		Manual		
	Input	Output	Input	Output	Input	Output	
Completeness	23	29	11		4	2	69
Accuracy	4						4
Redundancy *Duplication*	20	1	8		7		36
Presentation *HCI*	2	18	6	10			36
Timeliness *Delays*	3	7	1	2	1	5	19
Location			1				1
Overall *Training*			8				8
Totals	52	55	35	12	12	7	
	107		47		19		173

Table 1: Summary of occurrences of problems.

- The analysis taxonomy is appropriate.

- Half the observed problem occurrences concerned incomplete information.

- Half the observed problem occurrences concerned input into case notes, which information technology would not necessarily help to solve.

- Half the observed problem occurrences concerned storage in case notes, which information technology could help to solve.

- The most frequently occurring problem type is 'Missing Images', e.g. X-rays.

This confirms one neurosurgeon's independent research (Griffith 1992) which suggested, over a two week period, that images were missing on 30% of the occasions that he needed them.

The significance of these intermediate results are being extrapolated by further research. In the context of a National Health Service that employs

Problems	Occurrences
Completeness	23
• Inadequate data	11
• Incomplete information at admission	1
• Inadequate referral letters	2
• No general comprehensive record of allergies, intolerances	
• No single place to record generally required observations (height, weight, blood pressure, etc.)	
• No full record of tests considered, requested, awaited, returned	2
• Inadequate discharge letters and summaries	1
• Effects of change of address, change of GP, change of GP address, and even death, not always systematically coped with	
• Never enough sticky labels	
• Problems of temporary case notes	
• Difficulty in knowing where information is outside the hospital	
• Difficulty in getting information from social services, GPs, other hospitals (e.g. X-rays arranged by GP not available at out-patients)	6
Accuracy	4
• Incorrect data	3
• Inconsistent information in same or different sets of notes	1
• Poor coding for audit and management	
Redundancy	20
• Duplicate information in different sets of notes	14
• Duplicate information in the same set of notes	4
• Time spent re-typing standard headings on documents	
• Time spent writing the same information on many forms	2
Presentation	2
• Illegibility	2
• Lack of clarity	
• Letters not filed sequentially or otherwise as chosen	
• Hard to distinguish in-patient from out-patient material	
• Hard to separate working hypotheses from differential diagnoses, and from hard confirmed diagnoses, and to handle the consequences of changes of diagnoses	
• Unable to view results graphically	
Timeliness	3
• Waiting for new patients to be processed administratively	3
• Delays in arrival at ward and clinic of hard copies of reports and results	
• Delays in getting secretarial time for discharge letters	
	1
Overall	
• Too many different staff with partial responsibilities for organizing documents	
• Problem of assimilating temporary case notes into permanent form	
Total	52

Table 2: Problems of the medical record: Input into case notes.

Problems	Occurrences	
Completeness	29	
• Missing case notes		2
• Case notes not available		2
• Problem of finding where the case notes are		1
• Problem of tracking several volumes of case notes		
• Problems of tracking case notes and microfiche stored off-site		
• Problem of tracing missing documents for the case notes		6
• missing images (e.g. X-rays)		
		18
Accuracy	0	
• Validation of information in same notes		
Redundancy	1	
• Too much irrelevant material		1
Presentation	18	
• Case notes too bulky to handle readily		3
• Case notes falling to bits		
• Case notes bursting with old temperature charts, fluid balance sheets, duplicate lab results, etc.		
• Lab results, letters, etc. misfiled or loose		
• Different records and formats for different departments		2
• Unable to view sequential and related results		
• Hard to relate care progress to protocols		7
• Hard to relate medication (what, when, dose) with other data		4
• Hard to get or prepare intelligent summaries		
• Various needs for different summaries or synopses		2
Timeliness	7	
• Delays in obtaining case notes out of hours for emergencies		
• Delays in obtaining case notes to answer letters and phone call enquiries		3
• Too much time spent ploughing through case notes		4
Total	55	

Table 3: Problems of the medical record: Output from case notes.

199

1,000,000 people and costs £100,000,000 per day and spends £300,000,000 pa on information technology, ...?

10   Conclusion

The research reported here illustrates how the significant, frequently unrealized and substantially underestimated costs described above have been revealed by the observational methods used. The focus of the research has been on information management activities and the emphasis on the interactions which the information systems support as endorsed by Farbey et al. (1993).

Study of the human activity systems in the hospital has reinforced our belief in the need for emphasis on the analysis of social action, where existing and developing information systems are seen to have a symbiotic relationship with the actors, as opposed to the more conventional analysis of instrumental action, where the information system is perceived merely as a tool.

To-date our work has made contributions in three specific but associated areas:

1. Furthering understanding of the complexity of information requirements analysis.

2. Enlightening information managers at all levels in the NHS as to the range and extent of the current weaknesses/problems in existing systems.

3. Providing an objective 'agenda' of issues to be addressed by commercial equipment and software developers which will, hopefully, enable them to more readily meet the needs of those who hold a stake in the information systems concerned.

Physical Issues

Introduction

Ian A. Beeson & Stephen K. Probert

The two chapters in this final section are concerned with the relations between information systems and the human body and senses. Both suggest that more attention needs to be given to the corporeal basis and reference of intelligence, knowledge and information. While one draws attention to associative aspects of intelligence and to its instinctual, limbic foundation, suggesting that the rational emphasis in system design work is restrictive in ways which may be seriously disabling for theoretical and practical advance; the other observes that information systems as implemented have in general reduced the user — if not to an absence — to an immobilized construction of hands and eyes, and calls for information systems design to take proper account of the physical being of the user.

The chapter by John Gammack & Carolyn Begg starts from an exploration of synæsthesia and moves from there into a wide-ranging discussion of the nature of intelligence and skill and the foundations of information systems design and artificial intelligence. Synæsthesia refers to the production in the mind from a sense impression of one sort (say, olfactory) of an image of a sense impression of another sort (say, visual). In the related phenomenon of chromæsthesia, sounds or symbols are imagined as having certain colours. These capacities seem to be quite rare and may be traces of an associative kind of intelligence largely supplanted by the emergence of language. The possibility of multi-sensory awareness is nonetheless interesting, and may point to the existence of a pre- or meta-rational component in thought. Information systems design and artificial intelligence have both elevated rational, logical thought to a position of pre-eminence and may by so doing have lost sight of other vital elements, thereby perhaps restricting both the capacities of designed systems and the possibility of creative responses to them. The authors recommend a return to a general systems perspective to guide our design work, since this provides a holistic framework which can accommodate complex and loosely connected phenomena, and can cope with evolution and emergent properties.

The chapter by Ian Beeson begins by arguing that the idea that the human being is embodied has largely been ignored in both the 'hard' and 'soft' information systems literature. As the importance of manual labour (as opposed to 'intellective' labour) has decreased in organizational work so it is argued that the increasing use of technology has, itself, deepened the split between mind and body — at the expense of the body. Beeson warns that this could be a dangerous trend, if (as he argues) the body is more than merely a 'site' for the mind. Drawing on the work of intellectuals such as Merleau-Ponty and Schutz, Beeson argues that mind is "first and foremost embodied" (p.218). Such considerations allow Beeson to argue that Zuboff, who argues that bodily experiences are being supplanted by intellective ones, is in danger of promoting "a permanent and not temporary thinning of meaning" (p.221). Beeson then sets out some practical prescriptions for information systems development. Practitioners should, he argues, "recognize the spatial aspect of bodily existence and design information systems for moving around in" (p.221). What he means by this is that, rather than being designed with passive intellectual contemplation in mind, information systems should be designed rather like a kitchen (a workplace in which one moves around). Beeson points out that something similar to the ideas he has in mind has already been achieved in the design of systems such as commercial aircraft simulators.

The two chapters in this section mirror parallel concerns in mainstream philosophy (the continental European variety, at any rate) that the importance of the body has been neglected at the expense of considerations concerning cognitive activities. Nietzsche, Heidegger, Foucault (to name some of those who have worked in this area) have all been engaged in very different philosophical projects — but they would all agree that the body has been underplayed in philosophy. These chapters attempt to redress this balance in information systems.

Evolution, Emergence and Synæsthesia

John G. Gammack & Carolyn E. Begg

This short chapter is intended to stimulate discussion on the topics of synæsthesia* and chromæsthesia, which are viewed as phenomena exemplifying various systemic concepts, transcending disciplines of inquiry and of applicability, and having direct impact both for information systems practice, and for systems philosophy. In particular, forms of human information transmission and meaning integration indicate future directions for information systems research.

1 Introduction

Examples of the phenomenon of synæsthesia (the integration or mixing of sensory modalities in unified experience) and in particular chromæsthesia (the integration of colour imagery with language, sound perception and other modes of sensory thought) can be found across a wide range of human talents. Although relatively rare (10 in a million), luminaries in the fields of science, literature, and music reflecting on their creative processes report the experience as the following quotations show:

> "When I see equations, I see the letters in colors — I don't know why. As I'm talking I see vague pictures of Bessel functions from Jahnke and Emde's book, with light tan j's, slightly violet-bluish n's and dark brown x's flying around. And I wonder what the hell it must look like to the students." (Feynman 1988: 59)

> "The color sensation seems to be produced by the very act of my orally forming a given letter while I imagine its outline." (Nabokov 1968: 12)

> "The key of C major was red to Scriabin, but white to Rimsky-Korsakov." (Rossotti 1983: 220)

---

* synæsthesia (synesthesia, *US* spelling): production, from a sense impression of one kind, of an associated mental image of a sense impression of another kind; agreement of the feelings of different individuals as a stage in the development of sympathy.

Rossotti (1983) reports links between colour and music, and the attempts to relate them mathematically. Several composers and musicians are sensitive to associations between colours and musical qualities, and even amateur music lovers can appreciate the harmony or otherwise of coloured lighting effects during concert performances. There appear to be no absolute agreement between colour and quality however suggesting the associations are part of some individual or localized subjectivity. Perhaps through grounding in the human experience of emotion musical concepts such as 'the blues' are mediated, although there is by no means universal agreement as to which emotion is culturally appropriate for particular musical forms, as the contemporary composer, Trevor Wishart (personal communication) has noted. Nonetheless, deeper human understanding of complex concepts may involve the use of different types of information implicit in experience and the synthesis of these in the personal construction of meaning.

In his autobiography, Vladimir Nabokov (1968) has described his experience of the phenomenon, to which he appear to have been particularly sensitive. This has been extended in an article by Barton Johnston (1974) who notes the relations between synæsthesia and Nabokov's powerfully retentive and sensual memory, which he himself believed to be an hereditary trait. It is interesting to note that, aged six, Nabokov asserted to his mother that the colours of his alphabetic building blocks were 'all wrong', and that his mother also had letter/colour associations similar to her son's, but different from the manufacturer's.

Many esoteric traditions note correlations between colours and refined vibrational frequencies, in which there is an hierarchy related to stages of the gaining of knowledge. In the Shingon sect of Buddhism, the hierarchy corresponds to different stages of contemplative ecstasy, rising from black through blue, yellow and red, to:

> "... white, the pure and radiant source, into which all the colours have
> been merged and fused." (Binyon 1911)

But if colours are relative to one another, and thus meaningful on the same level what is the role of such an hierarchy in sense perception? There are implications here for an association with a time dimension, and possibly to shared metrics for structuring and notating relative truths. Just as vibrations on one frequency range are interpreted as sound, and on another as light, other frequency ranges imply other sensory modalities and forms of information yet to emerge, and for which colours and their evolution are an analogy. Some colours are more primitive, and more universally perceived than others, some may be culturally imperceptible, as Heider's (1971; 1972) work has indicated.

The polymathic genius Goethe also wrote extensively on colour including its mystical aspects:

> "When the distinction between yellow and blue is duly comprehended,
> and especially the augmentation into red, by means of which the opposite
> qualities tend towards each other and become united in a third; then,

certainly, an especial mysterious interpretation will suggest itself, since a spiritual meaning may be connected with these facts; and when we find two separate principles producing green in the one hand and red in their intenser state, we can hardly refrain from thinking in the first case on the earthly, in the last on the heavenly, generation of the Elohim.

But we shall do better not to expose ourselves, in conclusion, to the suspicion of enthusiasm; since, if our doctrine of colours finds favour, applications and allusions, allegorical, symbolical and mystical, will not fail to be made, in conformity with the spirit of the age."

(von Goethe 1840: para 919 & 920)

Eschewing further enthusiasm, we leave this point for future development, and turn to allusions involving evolutionary and biological aspects of sensory information processing.

2 Colour, Memory and Evolution

The differentiation of the mind into various faculties or talents is marked by the general loss of synæsthetic ability from childhood onwards, and although synæsthetic ability is apparently not related to intelligence (Rader & Tellegen 1987), it does seem to be retained in particular geniuses or holistic thinkers. In his extraordinary novel "The Third Policeman", Flann O'Brien describes the rare gift of reading the colour of the winds, and the sub-winds:

"... of indescribable delicacy, a reddish-yellow half-way between silver and purple, a greyish-green which was related equally to black and brown." (O'Brien 1967: 32)

and suggests later that:

"[the policemen] must be operating on a very rare colour, something that ordinary eyes could not see at all." (O'Brien 1967: 35)

Such an evocation appeals mythically to a lost past, and suggests a devolution from a greater appreciation. It hints at experiences beyond what can be objectivized by physical sight, and perhaps of emergent qualities lost by a factoring into dissociated modalities. This is the stuff of poetry, but the association between colour and memory, and the evolution of refined colour perception has grounds in empirical work too.

Several researchers are currently investigating cases of coloured speech perception. The evidence suggests that the phenomenon of chromatic-lexical synæsthesia (or rather variants of this condition called chromatic-graphemic or chromatic-phonemic) is a genuine condition (Baron-Cohen et al. 1987; 1993). Although this condition has only been assessed in small number of human cases, the positive findings are stimulating further research into understanding the ontogenesis of this phenomenon.

The clinical existence of synæsthesia has been related to the perceptual disorders and affective disorders (McKane & Hughes 1988). An unusual organization of the modular components of the brain has been postulated to account for this phenomenon (Baron-Cohen et al. 1993). Other researchers are expanding the investigation of colour-hearing to include colour-mood synæsthesia using structural and typographic eidetic imagery. The results of their investigation has indicated a relationship between the two phenomena (Glicksohn et al. 1992).

There is a common view that speech and colour perception are based on separate and independent modular systems of the brain (Zeki 1977, Wise et al. 1991). Modularization is considered to be an essential process in the evolutionary development of complex systems such as the brain. Therefore, the research on synæsthesia stimulates the debate as to whether the various forms of synæsthesia are the result of perceptual disturbance due to the breakdown of modularity in the nervous system or the emergence or re-emergence of human perceptions based on linked sensory apparatus.

Research suggests that synæsthesia may not be a result of neural dysfunction due to the lack of evidence of neural damage or impairment of cognition in synæsthetic subjects. Furthermore, the subjects appear to have at least average IQs and achieve greater than average performance in memory tests. In this regard it is interesting to note that the Guinness Book of records is creating a new category for Philip Bond who has memorized π to 10,000 places. Describing his memorization technique, Mr Bond states:

> "I tend to associate different numbers with different colours. Threes for example tend to be yellow in my mind. When I concentrate on a series of numbers the colours flash past and then the answer seems to pop out." (Murray 1994).

Departing from neuropathological accounts allows consideration of hypotheses referring to the filtered emergence of phenomenal experience in consciousness.

A prominent researcher in this field, Cytowic (1993), proposes that synæsthesia is a naturally occurring phenomenon that only reaches consciousness in a few of us. This proposal stimulates the debate as to whether we are evolving towards multi-sensory awareness of converging information, where synæsthesia is an example of a 'cognitive fossil', lost from the conscious awareness of most of us, but actually representing a deeper sentience.

In the search for an explanation for the existence of phenomena such as synæsthesia, we may have to modify our view of the development and functioning of the brain and how this relates to human consciousness (Baron-Cohen et al. 1993). Recent discoveries in neurological sciences have confirmed the critical role of the limbic system in regulating all the different modes of information transmission in the human nervous system. Attempts to produce artificial intelligence are held to have failed due to their imitation of logic and the circuitry of the cortex, ignoring other methods by which the biologic brain transfers information (Cytowic 1993). Exploring the evolutionary and functional relationships between the cortex and the limbic system, Cytowic's (clinical) evidence leads to the conclusion that the limbic system is the more influential, and that emotional determinants of behaviour play a role possibly greater than that of reason.

Links between colour and physiology have been the subject of other controlled research in recent times (Waters 1971). Respiratory movements increase under red light, as does blood pressure, which also decreases under blue. Effects of colour on mental state are also well known, with therapeutic implications for decoration of hospital wards and other public buildings (Birren 1962). The famous Stroop phenomenon in psychology also demonstrates the effect of synæsthetic breakdown. The typical Stroop task involves the names of colours printed in various colours of ink; the subject is asked to name the colour of ink, and reaction time is measured. So the label 'red' may be printed in green ink, and the subject would say 'green'. Latencies in naming the ink colour are affected by a mismatch between visual and verbal modalities and the effect is widespread and replicable. An integrated representation in which the name and the ink colour are consonant causes no processing problems. The Stroop task has been widely used in memory research, and has also been used in clinical work (Watts et al. 1986), where arachnophobics have been found to take longer to process spider-related words on a Stroop task, consistent with their not having a 'comfortably' integrated representation. Much cognitive psychological literature deals with cross-modal priming, which although not necessarily involving colour phenomena, again impinges on the integrated processing of meaning.

Other associations between colour phenomena and subjective or even populational experience can also be identified. One recent finding seems to suggest that chickens are changing their behaviour in response to environmental colour effects. The effects of being kept in a predominantly grey environment results in an increase of up to 1/3 in egg production. Apparently perceiving the grey environment of steel cages as their natural home, one company has started to manufacture grey turf, since green grass inhibits egg production (Clark 1994). Moreover, as egg laying has increased in battery farms, chickens have become more aggressive, and indeed one had to be put down after killing several cats!

One view of evolution is as a refining process, approximating towards ideals represented in archetypes and myths, rather like supervised learning in neural networks. If considered in this light, one can see a progressive recovery of that which has disintegrated. Ontogeny recapitulating phylogeny, a child's colour vocabulary progresses in the same order as the evolution of colour terms: in Berlin and Kay's scheme, the basic distinction of black and white is followed by red, yellow and green/blue together, green and blue, then brown, and then others. Colour terms enter language in a fixed order, and all languages possess between 2 and 11 terms for colours which cannot be described as 'shades' of other colours (Lazar-Meyn 1984). Some issues surrounding Berlin and Kay's scheme are explored by Rossotti: we would only add the observation that brown and purple (maroon) are often confused perceptually and linguistically; that *marron* is a French word for brown, and that garments bought in that colour may look disappointingly different in the cold light of day than in the strip light of the shop.* Colours such as puce apparently did not exist in the language until relatively recently, and it is still debatable whether they existed prior to language at all. Other species, even relatively higher ones, such as dogs, apparently see in monochrome. As Hauser (1978) points out, although we do not know exactly which phylogenetic processes took place in the development of seeing colours, nor to what extent our perceptions will change over long time periods, nonetheless the evolution of colour perception seems to be a biological process of differentiation in time.

Hauser however views this systemically as a philosophical problem, noting that the transition of man from one stage of development to the next higher one always consists in the knowledge of not only being able to identify with the environment, but being able to shape it: a knowledge in which colour has a special position. Colour is seen as an highly invaluable principle for environmental design as Hauser observes:

> "... the phenomenon of colour is synonymous with time cycles in the biological rhythm as a binding agent which ... combines the individual parts of our substance into a uniform complex." (Hauser 1978)

This line of argument indicates the familiar systems phenomena of control, hierarchy and emergence, in which knowledge from an higher level can be applied through the interface between levels to maintain coherence within a differentiated system. Many writers on consciousness take the view that it emerges at the highest level of (biological) human functioning, and can be applied to control behaviours and functioning at lower levels of the system. These phenomena can be studied within cybernetic domains of engineering, biology and social and management sciences, but can also be considered in the abstract, within æsthetic philosophy.

In his essay on æsthetics and structural relationships, C S Smith (1981) puts the limitations of analytic atomism in perspective, and turns to systems thinking and the arts for insights into this domain. In particular, explicit similarity is identified between style in art, and the relation between internal structure and external property that distinguishes chemical phases. In this view, where common problems of boundary identification and change apply, colour is viewed as an emergent property of matter whose quality is shaped by the internal structural relations, which may be more or less tolerant of changes in component groupings. Smith notes that many important differences in the behaviour of large systems arise from the degree of this tolerance, and goes on to show how the æsthetic success of Chinese landscape paintings is governed by such interplay:

> "In a physical system the maximum number of phases that can coexist in equilibrium at a given temperature depends upon the number of atomic species present, and how closely they are packed together. Whether a boundary can exist between one area and another depends on cooperative

---

*We thank Ian Neale for pointing out that this illustrates metamerism.

hierarchical interaction. ... However, too much disorder can soon cause a phase to lose its identity, and a proliferation of gradients of colour or texture in a painting quickly diminishes its visual impact." (Smith 1981)

It is worth observing that in traditional Chinese art, colours had associations, e.g. with compass points, elements and emotions. These associations were respected in Oriental art and mixed tones or muddiness in colours were avoided. Groups in figure compositions are held together:

"... much as the component elements of a landscape would be. ... [In the Chinese conception of landscape painting] there is no building up around a centre; unity is maintained by a subtle balance of relations." (Binyon 1911: 94)

3   Discussion

In a work on philosophical aspects it would be inappropriate to explore the ramifications of associative structures using colour information in ergonomics, human–computer interaction, display design and other information technology applications but these remain candidate arenas for information systems practice. Work relating synæsthesia to the design of virtual applications (Addison n.d.), and to information expression in interface design (Smets et al. 1994) is also currently underway. There are however other substantive issues within information systems philosophy upon which this discussion touches, and we wish to mention two here: the relation of subjective experience to archived or objectivized descriptions for information systems, and the prospects for conscious machines.

Modelling information in human activity systems can be viewed as entailing *inter alia*, eliciting shared vocabulary, individual and organizational memory structures and representations of procedures, various perceptions of requirements and of extant situations with a view to codifying the results towards some practical end. Other goals are possible, but this one is typical. For many years the knowledge elicitation community has appreciated that words are not some fixed commodity that is directly usable as a knowledge representation, and they require to be referenced to their situated usage in social contexts. One of us (Gammack) has written about this frequently, most directly in Gammack & Anderson (1990), and in Stephens & Gammack (1994) where constructivist approaches viewing knowledge elicitation as an exercise in modelling cooperative language use were advocated. This is one line of research, which treats information and socially agreed knowledge forms at the level of coordinating activity in systems.

There is another line of research however which is also relevant here. This concerns the basis in understanding for the externally expressed knowledge forms: the concepts behind the words. The outward expressions may formally differ, yet draw on the same shared concept — reducing concepts to words loses this understanding, and the 'shallow' knowledge prevails. (Shallow knowledge is where associations are made or rules obeyed without any deep understanding, but at the functional level of description it is sometimes hard to tell, since behaviour is consistent with that stemming from a deep understanding.) Modelling deep knowledge would require access to the progenitor of forms, from which variations could be judged in perspective. (An example — water, wasser, voda and others represent the English, German and Russian words for 'water'. These all stem from the proto-Indo-European word 'wed'. The concept of water lies even deeper!) If, as we might conjecture, the personal meaning of concepts is sensually conditioned by culture, genetics, early experience, perceptual sophistication and æsthetic preference, forms of words are even more treacherous.

Thus we note the subjectivities involved in sensory perceptions, and the poverty of language to express such in precise terms to others. For many domains of knowledge elicitation, the sharing of colour terms exemplifies a phenomenon which limits the possibility of conveying an expert, or refined appreciation. In information systems developments, articulating the requirements for intelligent system support is likewise affected by lexical limitations and the codes for recording a client's subtle requirements must go beyond this.

Clients are increasingly insisting on exact matches to their trademark colour (e.g. 'Coca-Cola red'). The world-wide stocks of paper printed in the 'Systemist blue' colour have apparently run out (Stowell 1993). The publisher of Systemist told us that in his opinion very few people would notice the difference, the new cover is a slightly darker shade of blue. As a discontinued line however, what is the prospect for a return to good old Systemist blue?

This question implicates the issue of colour matching, described by Ian Neale (1993). This is a subtle process, and a skilled craft. However, the print industry's general decline and increasing automation is destroying this skill — cf. the UTOPIA typesetting project described in an information systems context, e.g. by Ehn (1993) and Hirschheim & Klein (1989). If it should become 'extinct', could it 'survive' in an informationally described process? Or are there emotionally registered components of perceptions and feelings which elude symbolic definition? Biologically determined constraints and structures may govern the forms of particular phenomenologies in which craft and physical working may be understood but the symbol manipulation required by artificial information systems implicates formal and articulated codings. Moreno (n.d.) has conjectured that to represent feelings in a knowledge-base a code based on 'synæsthesias' (e.g. colour to represent feelings) would be appropriate. Such possibilities, driven by virtual reality developments address philosophical issues of mind–body relations.

Returning to the case of Systemist blue, given the same card specification upon which to apply colour, it is in principle possible to reproduce the colour virtually exactly from a standard numerical colour specification. Rare skills archiving is one application of knowledge elicitation — but what does it mean, and can it really be done? Modelling knowledge using only language terms is demonstrably inadequate, and in any case the terms of colour theory are not often used by experienced screen printers (Neale 1993: 410). Furthermore, since inks matched to the samples agreed with clients are often of different chemical constitution, analogue archives are only approximations, as shown by the frequent and bitter disappointments found upon comparing the ideals represented by paint colour cards in the DIY stores and in the reality of one's own home.

Any archived form must take contextual factors into account, particularly light conditions, and be linked with the human user's judgement and experiential expertise. Neale (1993), we believe, correctly recommends an augmentative approach, in which the subjective judgements of the human are empowered by an (objective) technology. This exemplifies an anthropocentric or human-centred philosophy of information systems (Gill 1991, Gammack et al. 1992) but from where is the apprenticeship to come in a declining industry?

Perhaps the craft of dry stone walling provides an example. Walling would seem to be an holistic skill requiring complex, multi-sensory judgements and creative problem solving within a loose framework of rules. Action was taken when it was perceived that the craft was dying out in Britain, and now there is a thriving network of branches, with a full certification programme. Much of the craft knowledge has been distilled into books, including heuristics, which at some level may have the status of trade secrets. However it is inconceivable that reading these books will turn someone into an expert practitioner. In addition local styles in the craft exist, and any archival attempt must recognize this. In particular there is a separate certification for a certain Scottish (Galloway) style. If much of this knowledge is locally referenced and indeed essentially tacit, it sets a limit and a challenge to information systems modelling, and contextualizes the philosophical issues of subject and object in information systems design.

The second philosophical issue we would like briefly to consider concerns the prospect of conscious machines. With Cytowic, we view the source of thought/feeling as lying much deeper than present artificial intelligence models suggest and the experience of understanding and meaning as essentially elusive to individually-based cortical processing. Taking consciousness as an emergent level in the mind, it seems unlikely that a (human-like) artificial intelligence could be produced without also recognizing the deeper levels which provide the integrated meanings that resource specific forms. This is likely to entail a systems approach to coordinate the findings in disparate fields of research, and recognize the regulatory dynamics of emotional influences. It is apparent that an increasing concentration on specialist logics is bringing us no nearer understanding some essential human qualities, but there are some indications that the field of artificial intelligence is beginning to look at the integrated modelling of different sense modalities. (McKevitt 1994; 1994/5; McKevitt & Gammack 1995). It will be interesting to follow this line of work.

4   Conclusion

The phenomena grouped under synæsthesia await full explanation and clearly cross disciplinary boundaries. The meta-discipline of systems philosophy provides concepts and vocabulary for formulating explanations, and if it can also provide an holistic framework for accommodating increasing complexity, may allow an understanding of hitherto nebulous phenomena. Our discussion has ranged across issues of relevance to psychology, biology, the exact sciences and the arts, as well as implying consequences in everyday experience and in practical information systems design. The biological dynamics involved in conditioning forms of sense and meaning suggest engagements of information registered at once more deeply and more communally than lexically-based descriptions. The sensory modality integration to which synæsthetic phenomena testifies, together with the evolution and emergence of enriched perceptual experiences, may fruitfully be examined using concepts from systems philosophy. We hope that viewing advanced forms of perception, intelligence, meaning communication and emotional integrity as proper topics of information systems philosophy will advance both scholarship and understanding.

The Body in the Information System

Ian A. Beeson

Scant attention has been paid in information systems thinking and design to the role of the physical body. This neglect is attributable to an entrenched view that mind is a more or less autonomous process established in the body; reasoning and communicating are done by the mind, for which the body merely serves as a platform. A case is put that the physical body is in fact primary, that categories and processes of thought are rooted in bodily experience, and that the lived experience of the body in the world should have the central place in our analysis. Zuboff's claim that in the informating process bodily skills are satisfactorily supplanted by mental skills is examined and found dubious. An exploration is started of the implications for information systems practice if the body is brought in.

1 Disembodied Information Systems

In thinking about information systems, the idea of the human being as *embodied* has not occupied any central place. One might indeed say that the central thrust in information systems thinking and practice has been to *disembody* information: organizations have been seen as complex patterns of information flows between decision points; these flows and decision processes have been made the subject of abstract formal representations and programs; decision making and control have been elevated to become key activities in organizations; information technology has been used to automate physical operations and to standardize, regulate, and where possible automate even the decision making and control activities. Zuboff (1988: 302) expresses the logic of graphically:

1. the worker's implicit know-how is analysed in order to generate data that contribute to
2. the development of a series of management functions that enable
3. management to take on responsibility for coordination and control of the production process.

and in the course of this development:

"... the sentient body loses its salience as a source of knowledge ..."
(Zuboff 1988: 6)

(Zuboff believes this 'salience' can be adequately superseded in an 'informated' organization — a view I will take issue with later.)

Behind the development of information technologies and information systems, a powerful idea is at work: that knowledge (and entertainment) can be abstracted from the contexts in which it arose, stored in some technical apparatus, and then made available for consumption by an invisible community of users.

When I work at a computer, or use a network to communicate with someone, what parts of me are engaged? Mind, hands and eyes, chiefly — not much else. The body is an 'absent presence'. If we look into the human–computer interaction (HCI) literature, we find plenty on cognitive task analysis, screen and keyboard layout, dialogue design and the structure of mental models; but interest in the physical body is mainly restricted to a concern to immobilize it in a comfortable position where the mind and its chief agents (eye and hand) can be held in close proximity to the machine interface. This immobilization and reduction of the body is emphasized and fetishized in Virtual Reality systems, where the body is transformed into helmet and glove. The general approach recalls Ford's calculations that, of the 7882 distinct operations required in the production of the Model T, only 949 required strong able-bodied men, while 670 could be filled by legless men, 2637 by one-legged men, 2 by armless men, 715 by one-armed men and 10 by blind men (Seltzer 1992: 157).

Even in more human-centred approaches to information systems than are common in the mainstream, the corporeal human being is only vaguely sketched. Checkland & Scholes, for example, in applying systems thinking to information systems, state clearly that an information system is not to be confused with a mere data manipulation system, but must include within its boundary those human acts of interpretation and expression which render the information system meaningful in its context, and insist that information systems design must involve understanding of the purposes the information systems is to serve and the world-views of the people involved in or affected by it (Checkland & Scholes 1990: 55). These emphases are welcome, but are more concerned with clarifications of intent and requirement than with the nature, course and possibilities of meaningful action and cooperation among actual people jostling along with one another. In the work of Flood & Jackson (1991: 33–5), likewise, the recognition of *participants* as one of the two key dimensions for grouping problem contexts gives an hopeful starting point for system design or organizational intervention, but leads immediately into a politically oriented *classification* of organizational situations (as unitary, pluralist, or coercive) rather than to consideration of how participation might work, in practice, among flesh and blood people. One can see in these and like-minded authors attempts to move information systems theory and practice beyond a concern with purely technical interests towards an engagement with practical and emancipatory interests (to use Habermas' classification); but one can also see the possibility of shifting perspectives from machines and programs towards communication and power without paying detailed attention to transactions of meaning and power among individuals in real situations, substituting instead an analysis of texts and positions.

System design approaches from speech act theory, such as in Winograd & Flores (1986), which have the great virtue of repositioning the computer/network as a structured medium for *human–human* interaction, still do not fully readmit the bodies of the speakers: too much emphasis remains on the flow of symbols in a conversation and not enough on the action the conversation arises for.

2   Returning to Lived Experience

The antidote proposed by Boland to the various obstinate and harmful misconceptions or 'fantasies' of information found in the literature of management science and computing science is to put a primary emphasis in information systems design on improving the possibilities for face-to-face interaction within organizations, and, in design work, to take dialogue, interpretation and individual's search for meaning as *sacred*:

> "Any fantasies which present disembodied, ahistoric images of information divert us from a search for the lived experience of organizational members and must be rejected." (Boland 1987: 377)

This seems to me to be good advice, and I would like to take its positive side a little further by exploring approaches to 'lived experience' and developing them into a view of information systems as part of lived experience.

When we investigate *lived experience*, we are concerned with experience as *embodied* and also as *situated*; that is to say, experience has to be related to the (mindful) body, as the first locus of that experience, and to the situation of the body in relation to places and in relation to others. All these relations overlap and interact, and all have been or can be radically affected by information and communication technologies and the information systems built upon them, which may exclude or constrain the individual's body, disrupt or make anonymous interpersonal relations, and obscure, neutralize or render irrelevant local contexts. These tendencies, taken together, it is at least arguable to say, have a profoundly deracinating effect, loosening people's ties to localities, communities and the material world as such.

If we forget the centrality of lived experience, if our living is done too much inside our media, if we do not return often enough to our inescapable bodily condition and to our actual tangible surroundings, may not our connection to the real world become attenuated, perhaps dangerously so? It has often been noted that McLuhan's notion of the 'global village' was stimulated by his reading Hawthorne's *The House of the Seven Gables* (originally published in 1851), in which it is famously remarked:

"Is it a fact — or have I dreamt it — that, by means of electricity, the world of matter has become a great nerve, vibrating thousands of miles in a breathless point of time? Rather, the round globe is a vast head, a brain, instinct with intelligence! Or shall we say, it is itself a thought, nothing but thought, and no longer the substance which we deemed it?" (Hawthorne 1991: 264)

What is less often commented upon is that these words are spoken by a mad man (Clifford Pyncheon), in flight from the too solid house where his dead cousin sits, unable to come to terms with the ageing of his own body, hoping to escape to a more ethereal (but unachievable) kind of existence.

In empiricist and rational traditions of thought, the body, far from being essential to or constitutive of a person's being, is considered as a physical object in the world — an object for thought, and an object for medicine and for human factors engineering. The body is thought of as a physical container for the mind; the relationship between physical body and non-physical mind remains relentlessly problematic — to philosophers, but not to systems analysts. The body has similarly receded into the background in the world of work, where the replacement of muscle by machinery has not only made many human bodies redundant or marginal but has shifted our conception of the nature of work away from physical labour and towards thinking and supervision. In artificial intelligence and in information systems alike, the tendency is to concentrate on the structure and reproduction of mind and push the body into the background as a contingent platform for mind.

The progress of technology thus seems to deepen the split between mind and body and elevate the former above the latter. But this is an uncertain and may be a dangerous path to tread if the body is something more than a convenient but disposable *site* for the mind, but is rather the mind's first home — if the mind is, essentially, and first and foremost, *embodied*.

Mark Johnson develops a persuasive argument in his *The Body in the Mind* (1987) that this is indeed the case. According to him, our fundamental structures of understanding (image schemata) arise in our bodily functioning as recurring patterns in our mundane experience. We are then able to extend these through metaphorical projection and constitutive use of the imagination. Rational thought and abstract structures of meaning are then secondary productions of these more basic processes, and do not have a prior existence in some separate logical or mental space. Johnson traces through the development of such notions as *balance*, *scale, force, path, container* from origins in everyday human engagement in the world to rarefied theoretical constructions. If we accept his line of argument, we can no longer regard meaning as primarily lodged in statements or propositions, but must see it as something achieved and constantly re-achieved by mortal people working through their lives together.

Phenomenological philosophers such as Merleau-Ponty and Schutz have paid much attention to the structure of the everyday life-world and our ways of existing and acting in it. In Turner's terms, theirs is a *foundationalist* perspective on the body, concerned with understanding the body as a lived experience rather than as a discourse about the nature of social and political relations, or as a system of symbols (Turner 1992: 48). Turner himself leans to a Foucauldian anti-foundationalist perspective, but I follow the foundationalist line of the phenomenologists, since it keeps the body rudely visible, rather than substituting a text for it.

Merleau-Ponty's is probably the major contribution to the phenomenology of the body (Merleau-Ponty 1962: especially Part 1) — see also (Spurling 1977). He rejects mind–body dualism by grounding both mind and body in something prior, namely being-in-the-world, of which the lived body is the intentional expression. He appeals to the evidence from experience that reveals consciousness as embodied or incarnated in the world. I cannot observe or find or move my body as if it were merely an object: my body is always present, its moving is my moving, and it is by means of my body that I can observe and move among objects. (There is an echo here of Gibson's rejection of the camera metaphor of human vision, and his emphasis on ambient and ambulatory vision: we see by moving our head and by walking about (Gibson 1986: 1)). Merleau-Ponty stresses the unity of the body:

> "... my whole body for me is not an assemblage of organs juxtaposed in space. I am in undivided possession of it and I know where each of my limbs is through a *body image* in which all are included." (Merleau-Ponty 1962: 98)

The unity of the body is expressive and provisional rather than pre-given. The lived body projects itself on to the world and is capable of using tools and sedimented regular responses to establish itself there. Mind and body are integrated in the sense that neither can exist without the other, but never fully so, since both are grounded in our experience, and that only manifests itself as we live it.

While Merleau-Ponty's work is psychological in orientation, Schutz's main contribution has been to bring a phenomenological perspective into sociology. Of interest here is his outline of spatial and social arrangements in the everyday life-world (Schutz & Luckmann 1974: Part 2B). In his treatment of the spatial arrangement of the life-world, he makes distinctions between worlds within actual, potential, restorable, and attainable *reach*, and links this nesting of spaces with stratifications of the social world. He has a particular concern to distinguish between immediate and mediated experiences of *others*, describing a scale of interaction stretching from *thou-* and *we*-relations characteristic of face-to-face encounters, towards increasingly anonymous *they*-relations characteristic of mediated interaction with mere 'contemporaries'. Berger & Luckmann (1967: ch.2) take up this point, stressing that in face-to-face relations the other is fully (even 'massively') real, there is a continuous exchange of expressivity, and the other's subjectivity is maximally available. Face-to-face interaction is prototypical; all other forms of relating to the other are derivative, and more or less remote. Schutz, in his consideration of the structure of *they*-relations (Schutz & Luckmann 1974: 86–7), comments that the more anonymous the relation is, the more necessary it becomes to make our meanings 'objective':

"Thus I cannot presume that a contemporary, with whom I am in a they-relation, adequately grasps the nuances of my statement which are given by intonation, by my facial expression, etc. (as well as by a 'knowledge', won in immediate experiences, concerning how it is all to be interpreted, and what relation it has to my biographical situation, to my momentary mood, etc.). If I consciously want to share such nuances with him, I must transpose them into Objective categories of meaning, whereby they inevitably lose their nuanced character. In addition, communications with a contemporary must be posited as a totality. The risk that my preinterpretation of his reaction is inaccurate is consequently related to this totality, while I, step by step, immediately experience in the we-relation whether he has correctly or falsely understood me."

Thus in the mediated relation, I am obliged, in the absence of the other's body, to imagine or invent the other. The way is then wide open to misinterpretation, and furthermore the sedimentation of experience is set at risk and likely to become stagnant, in so far as it is based on fancied experience rather than on a reality negotiated face-to-face.

3   Is the Body being 'Informated' Out?

Zuboff's analysis suggests that bodily experience may be being supplanted in the 'informated' organization. She contends that, in the transition from 'action-centred' to 'intellective' skill, immediate physical responses are replaced by abstract thought processes. In the automated pulp mills she writes about, workers move from a way of making paper which means moving about the factory and feeling and smelling the pulp to a way which involves them interpreting symbols at the data interface (on a screen). It takes time for workers to learn to 'trust the symbols', but eventually, under pressure from management and themselves desiring an easier life they will switch to a way of working which involves a double abstraction — symbols on the screen representing a real production process, and a mental model in the worker's head called forth to make sense of the symbols on the screen. Zuboff's belief is that this process of 'informating' can work and can re-empower a workforce. But it looks highly improbable that this disembodiment of the worker and the separation of physical process from mental model can produce better understanding of and engagement in the production process. It is easy to see many of the quotes Zuboff includes in a different light from hers; for instance:

"In the digester area, we used to have guys doing it who had an art. After we put the computers in, when they went down we would go to manual backup. People remembered how to run the digesters. Now if we try to go back, they can't remember what to do. They have lost the feel for it. We are really stuck now without the computer; we can't successfully operate the unit without it. If you are watching a screen, do you see the same things you would do if you were there, face-to-face with the process and the equipment? I am concerned we are losing the art and skills that are not replenishable." (Zuboff 1988: 64–5)

reads to me not like a stage in the transition to informated work, but as a recognition of dislocation and disengagement, and of a loss of skills and knowledge. Zuboff (1988: 79) talks of "making our peace with the problem of meaning", citing our readiness nowadays to attribute full reality to what we see in a photograph or on television or what we hear on the telephone. But the symbolic reconstruction goes much deeper in the paper-making case (and with information systems in general), and the separation between operator's model and real process is much sharper. In 'informating', we certainly move from one realm of meaning to another, but with no guarantee of continuity and with every likelihood, on the basis of the analyses above, that removing the body from the production process will produce a permanent and not a temporary thinning of meaning.

4 Suggestions for Information Systems Practice

How could we take note of some of the warning notes sounded above and change information systems practice to include a proper place for the body?

As a first step, we can recognize that people using computer-based information systems do have bodies and design their tasks to take account of that fact. Volpert (1992) has offered some positive suggestions for work design to support human development, including some which recognize the user's embodied being-in-the-world. These are the guidelines he offers to the designer in this area:

- work tasks must provide for sufficient and varied bodily activity;

- work tasks must call for the use of a wide variety of sensory capacities;

- work tasks must provide for the concrete handling of real objects and ensure a direct relation to social conditions; and

- work tasks must be characterized by a centred variability, i.e. while the basic structure of the tasks remains the same, they must provide for a variety of different implementation conditions.

These suggestions usefully supplement a basic socio-technical approach, which would tend to concentrate on task analysis and social aspects of work design.

We should recognize the spatial aspect of bodily existence and design information systems for moving around in. If Schutz's analysis is followed, we could consider building spatially stratified information systems to fit the various degrees of reach available to the human being. The information system would not have to sit on the desk or on the lap, but could be spread around a room or larger space with some zoning of functions matched to a sense of movement from closer to more distant or occasional activities on the part of the user. One could imagine the same care going into planning the layout of an information system as of a kitchen. That would need us to see information systems usage as part of broader activity rather than as isolated cerebration. Special purpose information systems such as those used to fly aircraft or control power stations already have these features, but they should be generalized.

Recognition of the social character of bodies would have some implications for the design of information systems. The present tendency to put workstations side-by-side on a battery farm model might be rethought and more convivial layouts found. Isolating and disruptive effects of inventions such as the Walkman and the mobile phone — which cut users off from their immediate neighbours but at the same time introduce noise and behaviours normally thought peculiar (nodding your head, talking to yourself) — might have been avoided if the analysis had included the social context of use.

More fundamentally, if it is accepted that our categories of thought and structures of meaning are rooted in bodily experience and are constantly being projected and negotiated in the course of everyday life, attempts to build intelligent systems from abstract rule structures, or to specify fixed and complete meanings for a system to be built, can never succeed.

If we take the point that face-to-face interaction is the prototype for all other forms of interaction, we shall be cautious in assuming that remote communication can substitute satisfactorily for direct communication. This is not to say that networks should be wound up, or that teleworking can never work, but that remote contacts can only be managed successfully if they stay close to a face-to-face model, if participants can occasionally meet face-to-face (to replenish their understanding of one another), and if participants have plenty of other face-to-face meetings (so that communication with other humans remains natural for them).

Most information system development methods do not take adequate account of the body: many are based on semi-formal processes for converting statements of requirements into procedures and working code; while those of a more participative stamp do bring the negotiating body on to the scene but still may overlook the role of the body in the system being built. Current developments in ethnographic approaches to system design are encouraging in this respect. In the study by Sommerville et al. (1992) of user interface requirements for a flight database, to give one example, the investigators observed movements and interactions of the flight controllers in the control tower. They observed that manual manipulation and reordering of flight strips were significant activities that focused attention on a slip and its relation to other strips, so allowing early identification of potential problems. The authors comment that controllers require 'at a glance' observation of strips and flight progress boards, and that supervisors will walk around the suite assisting more junior controllers if any potential problems or difficulties are observed. Although there are acknowledged difficulties in incorporating ethnographic methods into systems design, they do promise to give a better account of human action, interaction and movement than provided in the normal methods.

Some writers are already cataloguing the passing of the body; thus:

> "In technological society, the body has achieved a purely rhetorical existence: its reality is that of refuse expelled as surplus matter no longer necessary for the autonomous functioning of the technoscape." (Kroker & Kroker 1987: 21):

This analysis must be premature: my body appears as solid to me still as theirs no doubt do to them. The 'technoscape' may be monstrous, but it is nevertheless populated by human beings — who could move to improve it.

Bibliography and Indexes

Bibliography

Ackoff, R. L. (1970), *A Concept of Corporate Planning*, John Wiley & Sons.

Ackoff, R. L. & Emery, F. E. (1972), *On Purposeful Systems*, Tavistock Publications.

Addison, R. (n.d.), "Synesthesia: Collaborative Biosignal Experience", At one time on http://www.iway.org/nic/Applications/synesthesia.html. This host no longer has a DNS entry.

Adorno, T. & Horkheimer, M. (1973), *The Dialectic of Enlightenment*, Allen Lane.

Alexander, C. (1964), *Notes on the Synthesis of Form*, Harvard University Press.

Alexander, J. (1984), *Theoretical Logic in Sociology*, Vol. 4 of *The Modern Reconstruction of Classical Thought*, Routledge and Kegan Paul.

Anderson, B. N. (1985), Information Systems Research — A Doubtful Science, *in* E. Mumford, R. Hirschheim, G. Fitzgerald & A. Wood-Harper (eds.), *Research Methods in Information Systems*, North-Holland, pp.273–7.

Angyal, A. (1941), A Logic of Systems, *in* A. Angyal (ed.), *Foundations for a Science of Personality*, Harvard University Press, chapter 8, pp.243–61.

Aristotle (1962), *The Politics*, Penguin. Translated by T A Sinclair.

Ashby, W. R. (1952), *Design for a Brain*, Chapman & Hall.

Ashby, W. R. (1956), *An Introduction to Cybernetics*, Chapman & Hall.

Atkinson, P. E. (1990), *Creating Culture Change*, IFS Publications.

Aune, B. (1970), *Rationalism, Empiricism, and Pragmatism*, Random House.

Austin, J. (1962), *How to Do Things with Words*, Harvard University Press.

Ayers, M. (1987), Locke and Berkeley, in *The Great Philosophers: An Introduction to Western Philosophy* (Magee 1987), pp.118–43. This is a book of transcripts of interviews not a collection of papers.

Bannister, D. & Fransella, F. (1971), *Inquiring Man*, Penguin.

Bar-Hillel, Y. (1952b), Semantic Information and its Measures, *in Transactions of the Tenth Conference on Cybernetics*, J Macy Foundation, pp.33–48. Reprinted as (Bar-Hillel 1964: 298–312).

Bar-Hillel, Y. (1955), "An Examination of Information Theory", *Philosophy of Science* **22**, 86–105. Reprinted as (Bar-Hillel 1964: 275–97).

Bar-Hillel, Y. (1964), *Language and Information: Selected Essays on their Theory and Application*, Addison–Wesley.

Bar-Hillel, Y. & Carnap, R. (1952), An Outline of a Theory of Semantic Information, Technical Report 247, Research Laboratory of Electronics, MIT. Reprinted as (Bar-Hillel 1964: 221–74).

Baron-Cohen, S., Harrison, J., Goldstein, L. H. & Wyke, M. (1993), "Coloured Speech Perception: Is Synæsthesia What Happens When Modularity Breaks Down?", *Perception* **22**(4), 419–26.

Baron-Cohen, S., Wyke, M. A. & Binnie, C. (1987), "Seeing Words and Hearing Colours: An Experimental Investigation of a Case of Synæsthesia", *Perception* **16**(6), 761–7.

Barrow, J. D. (1992), *Pi in the Sky: Counting, Thinking and Being*, Oxford University Press.

Barton Johnston, D. (1974), Synesthesia, Polychromatism, and Nabokov, *in* C. R. Proffer (ed.), *A Book of Things about Vladimir Nabokov*, Ardis, pp.85–101.

Bateson, G. (1970), "Form, Substance and Difference", *General Semantics Bulletin* **37**. Reprinted as (Bateson 1973: 423–40).

Bateson, G. (1973), *Steps to an Ecology of Mind*, Granada Publishing.

Baum, R. (1976), Communication and Media, *in* J. J. Loubser, R. C. Baum, A. Effrat & V. Lidz (eds.), *Explorations in General Theory in Social Science*, Free Press, pp.533–56.

BBC (1993), "Wessex Man", Panorama, BBC 1 Television.

Beer, S. (1985), *Diagnosing The System for Organizations*, John Wiley & Sons.

Beniger, R. (1986), *The Control Revolution*, Harvard University Press.

Berger, P. & Luckmann, T. (1967), *The Social Construction of Reality*, Penguin.

Bergquist, W. (1993), *The Postmodern Organization*, Jossey-Bass.

Bernstein, R. (1991), *The New Constellation*, Polity Press.

Binyon, L. (1911), *The Flight of the Dragon*, John Murray.

Birren, F. (1962), *Color in your world*, Collier Books.

Blair, R. N. & Whitston, C. W. (1971), *Elements of Industrial Systems Engineering*, Prentice–Hall.

Bloomfield, B. & Best, A. (1992), "Management Consultants: Systems Development, Power and the Translation of Problems", *The Sociological Review* **40**, 533–60.

Boland, R. J. (1987), The In-formation of Information Systems, *in* R. Boland & R. Hirschheim (eds.), *Critical Issues in Information Systems Research*, John Wiley & Sons.

Boyle, A., Macleod, M., Slevin, A., Sobecka, N. & Burton, P. F. (1993), "The Use of Information Technology in the Voluntary Sector", *International Journal of Information Management* **13**, 94–112.

Brookes, F. (1987), "No Silver Bullet: Essence and Accidents of Software Engineering", *IEEE Computer* **20**(4), 10–9.

Brown, R. H. (1989), *Social Science as Civic Discourse: Essays on the Invention, Legitimation, and Uses of Social Theory*, University of Chicago Press.

Brubaker, R. (1984), *The Limits of Rationality*, Allen and Unwin.

Burns, T. (1971), Mechanistic and Organismic Structures, *in* D. Pugh (ed.), *Organizational Theory*, Penguin, pp.43–55.

Bush, V. (1945), "As We May Think", *Atlantic Monthly* . July. Reprinted in (Greif 1988).

Butler, R. J. & Wilson, D. C. (1990), *Managing Voluntary and Non-Profit Organizations*, Routledge.

Cartwright, B. C. & Warner, R. S. (1976), The Medium is not the Message, *in* J. J. Loubser, R. C. Baum, A. Effrat & V. Lidz (eds.), *Explorations in General Theory in Social Science*, Free Press, pp.639–60.

Chalmers, A. F. (1982), *What is this Thing Called Science?*, 2nd edition, Oxford University Press.

Charlton, D., Kominsky, S. & Lunnon, M. (1988), *Computers — Who Needs Them?*, London Voluntary Service Council.

Checkland, P. B. (1981), *Systems Thinking, Systems Practice*, John Wiley & Sons.

Checkland, P. B. (1983), "Operational Research and the Systems Movement: Mappings and Conflicts", *Journal of the Operational Research Society* **34**(8), 661–75.

Checkland, P. B. (1988), "The Case for 'Holon'", *Systems Practice* **1**(3), 235–8.

Checkland, P. B. (1991a), From Optimizing to Learning: A Development of Systems Thinking for the 1990s, *in* R. L. Flood & M. C. Jackson (eds.), *Critical Systems Thinking: Directed Readings*, John Wiley & Sons, pp.59–75.

Checkland, P. B. (1991b), "Towards the Coherent Expression of Systems Ideas", *Journal of Applied Systems Analysis* **16**, 25–8.

Checkland, P. B. (1992a), Information Systems and Systems Thinking: Time to Unite, *in* W. W. Cotterman & J. A. Senn (eds.), *Challenges and Strategies for Research in Systems Development*, John Wiley & Sons, pp.353–64.

Checkland, P. B. (1992b), "SSM in Information Systems Design: History and Some Current Issues", *Systemist* **14**(3), 90–2. Information Systems Special Edition.

Checkland, P. B. (1992c), "Systems and Scholarship: The Need To Do Better", *Journal of the Operational Research Society* **43**(11), 1023–30.

Checkland, P. B. (1995), Soft Systems Methodology and its Relevance to the Development of Information Systems, *in* F. A. Stowell (ed.), *Information Systems Provision*, McGraw-Hill, pp.1–17.

Checkland, P. B. & Scholes, J. (1990), *Soft Systems Methodology in Action*, John Wiley & Sons.

Chen, P. (1979), *Entity Relationship Approach to Systems Analysis and Design*, North-Holland.

Churchman, C. W. (1971), *The Design of Inquiring Systems*, Basic Books.

Clark, R. (1994), Article in *Daily Mail*. 3rd February.

Codd, E. F. (1972), Further Normalization of the Database Relational Model, *in* R. Rustin (ed.), *Database Systems*, Prentice–Hall, pp.66–98.

Codd, E. F. (1986), "A Relational Model for Large Stored Data Banks", *Communications of the ACM* **13**(6), 377–87.

Coffa, J. (1991), *The Semantic Tradition from Kant to Carnap*, Cambridge University Press.

Collinson, D. & Hearn, J. (1994), "Naming Men as Men: Implications for Work, Organization and Management", *Gender, Work and Organisation* **1**(1), 2–22.

Cytowic, R. E. (1993), *The Man Who Tasted Shapes*, Abacus.

Daniels, N. C. (1993), *Information Technology: The Management Challenge*, Addison–Wesley.

Date, C. J. (1986), *An Introduction to Database Systems*, Vol. 1, 4th edition, Addison–Wesley.

Date, C. J. (1990), *An Introduction to Database Systems*, Vol. 1, 5th edition, Addison–Wesley.

Davidson, D. & Harman, G. (1972), *The Semantics of Natural Language*, Reidel.

Deetz, S. (1985), Ethical Considerations in Cultural Research in Organizations, *in* P. J. Frost, L. F. Moore, M. R. Louis, C. C. Lundberg & J. Martin (eds.), *Organizational Culture*, Sage Publications, pp.253–69.

Denzin, N. & Lincoln, Y. (eds.) (1994), *Handbook of Qualitative Research*, Sage Publications.

Descartes, R. (1912), *A Discourse on Method; Meditations on the First Philosophy; Principles of Philosophy*, Dent. Originally published c.1640.

Deutsch, K. W. D. (1963), *The Nerves of Government*, Free Press.

Doyle, K. G. & Wood, J. R. G. (1991), "Systems Thinking, Systems Practice: Dangerous Liasons", *Systemist* **13**(1), 28–30.

Dretske, F. (1981), *Knowledge and the Flow of Information*, Blackwell.

Dreyfus, H. (1991), *Being-in-the-World*, MIT Press.

Dreyfus, H. (1993), *What Computers Still Can't Do*, MIT Press.

Dreyfus, H. & Dreyfus, S. (1986), *Mind Over Machine*, Free Press.

Drucker, P. E. (1989a), *The New Realities*, Heinemann.

Drucker, P. E. (1989b), "What Business Can Learn from Nonprofits", *Harvard Business Review* **67**, 88–93.

Drucker, P. E. (1990), (untitled contribution), *in* S. Caulkin (ed.), *Management Briefings*, Economist Publications.

Durkheim, E. (1895), *The Rules of Sociological Method*, MacMillan.

Durkheim, E. (1957), *Professional Ethics and Civic Morals*, Routledge and Kegan Paul.

Durkheim, E. (1984), *The Division of Labour in Society*, MacMillan. Translated by L Coser.

Earl, M. J. (1989), *Management Strategies for Information Technology*, Prentice–Hall.

Ehn, P. (1988), *Work-Oriented Design of Computer Artifacts*, Arbetlivscentrum.

Ehn, P. (1993), Scandanavian Design: On Participation and Skill, *in* D. Schuler & A. Namioka (eds.), *Participatory Design: Principles and Practices*, Lawrence Erlbaum Associates.

Emery, F. E. (ed.) (1969), *Systems Thinking*, Harmondsworth (Penguin).

Engelbart, D. (1963), A Conceptual Framework for the Augmentation of Man's Intellect, *in* P. Howerman (ed.), *Vistas in Information Handling*, Vol. 1, Spartan Books. Reprinted in (Greif 1988).

Farbey, B., Land, F. & Targett, D. (1993), *How to Assess your IT Investment*, Butterworth–Heinemann.

Feibleman, J. & Friend, J. W. (1945), "The Structure and Function of Organization", *Philosophical Review* **54**, 19–44.

Fenton, S. (1984), *Durkheim and Modern Sociology*, Cambridge University Press.

Feyerabend, P. (1975), Against Method, *in* I. Hacking (ed.), *Scientific Revolutions*, Oxford University Press, pp.156–67.

Feyerabend, P. (1983), *Against Method*, 3rd edition, Verso.

Feynman, R. P. (1988), *What Do You Care What Other People Think?*, Unwin.

Fisher, A. (1988), *The Logic of Real Arguments*, Cambridge University Press.

Flew, A. (1979), *A Dictionary of Philosophy*, Pan.

Flood, R. L. & Jackson, M. C. (1991), *Creative Problem Solving: Total Systems Intervention*, John Wiley & Sons.

Foucault, M. (1977), *Discipline and Punish*, Pantheon.

Foucault, M. (1986), Interviews, *in* P. Rabinow (ed.), *The Foucault Reader*, Penguin.

Fox, A. (1974), *Beyond Contract*, Faber & Faber.

Frege, G. (1893), *The Basic Laws of Arithmetic*, University of California Press. 1964 edition.

Fries, C. & Randon, A. (1993), *Facts and Figures on the Voluntary Sector: Information Briefing 1*, National Council for Voluntary Organizations.

Galliers, R. (1987a), Applied Research in Information Systems Planning, *in* I. Feldman, L. Bhaduta & S. Holloway (eds.), *Information Management and Planning*, Gower/BCS, pp.45–58.

Galliers, R. (1987b), *Information Analysis*, Addison–Wesley.

Gammack, J. G. & Anderson, A. (1990), "Constructive Interaction In Knowledge Engineering", *Expert Systems* **7**(1), 19–26.

Gammack, J. G., Fogarty, T. C., Battle, S. A., Ireson, N. S. & Cui, J. (1992), "Human-centred Decision Support: The IDIOMS System", *Artificial Intelligence and Society* **6**, 352–66.

Gane, C. & Sarson, T. (1977), *Structured Systems Analysis: Tools and Techniques*, IST Databooks.

Gibson, J. J. (1986), *The Ecological Approach to Visual Perception*, Lawrence Erlbaum Associates.

Giddens, A. (1984), *The Constitution of Society*, Polity Press.

Gill, K. S. (1991), "Summary of Human-centred Systems Research in Europe", *Systemist* **13**(1 & 2), 7–27 & 49–75.

Glicksohn, J., Salinger, O. & Roychman, A. (1992), "An Exploratory Study of Syncretic Experience: Eidetics, Synæsthesia and Absorption", *Perception* **21**(5), 637–42.

Goldberger, N. R., Clinchy, B. M., Belenky, M. F. & Tarule, J. M. (1987), Women's Ways of Knowing: On Gaining a Voice, *in* P. Shaver & C. Hendrick (eds.), *Sex and Gender*, Sage Publications, pp.201–28.

Goldkuhl, G. & Lyytinen, K. (1982), A Language Action View of Information Systems, *in* M. Ginzberg & M. Ross (eds.), *Proceedings of 3rd International Conference on Information Systems*, Ann Arbour, pp.13–22.

Goldkuhl, G. & Lyytinen, K. (1984), Information Systems Specification as Rule Reconstruction, *in* T. Bemelmans (ed.), *Beyond Productivity: Information Systems for Organizational Effectiveness*, North-Holland, pp.79–94.

Goody, J. (1986), *The Logic of Writing and the Organization of Society*, Cambridge University Press.

Gouldner, A. (1976), *The Dialectic of Ideology and Technology*, MacMillan.

Gouldner, A. W. (1975), The Dark Side of the Dialectic: Toward a New Objectivity, Technical Report, Sociology Institute, University of Amsterdam.

Gouldner, A. W. (1980), *The Two Marxisms: Contradictions and Anomalies in the Development of Theory*, MacMillan.

Green, E., Owen, J. & Pain, D. (eds.) (1993), *Gendered by Design? Information Technology and Office Systems*, Taylor & Francis.

Gregory, F. H. (1993), "Soft Systems Methodology to Information Systems: A Wittgensteinian Approach", *Journal of Information Systems* 3, 149–68.

Gregory, F. H. (1995), "Soft Systems Models for Knowledge Elicitation and Represeantation", *Journal of the Operational Research Society* 46, 562–78.

Greif, I. (ed.) (1988), *Computer-Supported Cooperative Work: A Book of Readings*, Morgan-Kaufmann.

Griffith, H. (1992), "Open Letter by Huw B Griffith, FRCP, FRCS (*Clinical Director of Neurosciences*), Frenchay Healthcare Trust".

Guiterrez, O. & Greenberg, E. (1993), "Creative Problem-Solving in the Specification of Information Requirements", *Systems Practice* 6(6), 647–67.

Haack, S. (1978), *Philosophy of Logics*, Cambridge University Press.

Haack, S. (1979), "Epistemology With a Knowing Subject", *Review of Metaphysics* 33, 309–35.

Habermas, J. (1979), *Communication and the Evolution of Society*, Heinemann.

Habermas, J. (1982), A Reply to my Critics, *in* J. B. Thompson & D. Held (eds.), *Habermas: Critical Debates*, MacMillan, pp.219–83.

Habermas, J. (1984), *A Theory of Communicative Action: Reason and the Rationalization of Society*, Vol. 1, Heinemann. Now published by Polity Press.

Habermas, J. (1987a), *The Philosophical Discourse of Modernity*, Polity Press.

Habermas, J. (1987b), *A Theory of Communicative Action: Lifeworld and System — A Critique of Functionalist Reason*, Vol. 2, hardback edition, Polity Press.

Habermas, J. (1989), *A Theory of Communicative Action: Lifeworld and System — A Critique of Functionalist Reason*, Vol. 2, paperback edition, Polity Press.

Hacking, I. (1990), *The Taming of Chance*, Cambridge University Press.

Haines, V. A. (1987), "Biology and Social Theory: Parsons' Evolutionary Theme", *Sociology* 21(1), 19–39.

Handy, C. (1988), *Understanding Voluntary Organizations*, Penguin.

Harnden, R. & Mullery, G. (1991), "Enabling Network Systems (ENS)", *Systems Practice* 4(6), 579–98.

Hartley, R. (1928), "Transmission of Information", *Bell System Technical Journal* 7, 535–63.

Hauser, J. (1978), Colour Ecology as Retrospection, *in* F. W. Billmeyer Jr & G. Wyszecki (eds.), *Proceedings of AIC Color 1977*, Adam Hilger Ltd.

Hawthorne, N. (1991), *The House of the Seven Gable*, World's Classics, Oxford University Press. Originally published 1851.

Heidegger, M. (1962), *Being and Time*, Blackwell. Originally published 1926.

Heider, E. R. (1971), "'Focal' Color Areas in the Development of Color Names", *Developmental Psychology* 4, 447–55.

Heider, E. R. (1972), "Universals in Color Naming and Memory", *Journal of Experimental Psychology: General* 93, 10–20.

Heise, D. R. (1975), *Causal Analysis*, John Wiley & Sons.

Heritage, J. (1984), *Garfinkel and Ethnomethodology*, Polity Press.

Hills, R. J. (1976), The Public School as a Type of Organization, *in* J. J. Loubser, R. C. Baum, A. Effrat & V. Lidz (eds.), *Explorations in General Theory in Social Science*, Free Press, pp.829–56.

Hirschheim, R. (1987), Information Management Planning: An Implementation Perspective, *in* I. Feldman, L. Bhaduta & S. Holloway (eds.), *Information Management and Planning*, Gower/BCS, pp.1–15.

Hirschheim, R. & Klein, H. (1989), "Four Paradigms of Information Systems Development", *Communications of the ACM* 32(10), 1199–215.

Hofstadter, D. R. (1980), *Gödel, Escher, Bach: An Eternal Golden Braid*, Harmondsworth (Penguin).

Hoos, I. R. (1972), *Systems Analysis in Public Policy*, University of California Press.

Hume, D. (1739), *A Treatise of Human Nature*, Oxford University Press. L. A. Selby-Bigge (ed.) originally in 1888 with editions in 1896 and 1906.

Hume, D. (1777), An Enquiry concerning Human Understanding and Concerning the Principles of Morals, *in* L. A. Selby-Bigge (ed.), *David Hume: Enquiries*, 3rd edition, Oxford University Press. This monograph was originally published in 1758 with a revised edition appearing posthumously in 1777. This latter version is the one used by Selby-Bigge in his 1894 work published by Clarendon Press. OUP published this 3rd edition in 1975, which has revisions by P. H. Nidditch and was reprinted in 1978.

IT and Communities Working Party (1992), *Press Enter: Information Technology in the Community and Voluntary Sector*, Community Development Foundation.

Jackson, M. A. (1975), *Principles of Program Design*, Academic Press.

Jackson, M. A. (1983), *System Development*, Prentice–Hall.

Jackson, M. C. (1988), "Some Methodologies for Community Operational Research", *Journal of the Operational Research Society* **39**(8), 715–24.

Jackson, M. C. (1991), *Systems Methodology for the Management Sciences*, Plenum Press.

Jackson, N. & Carter, P. (1991), "In Defence of Paradigm Incommensurability", *Organization Studies* **12**(1), 109–27.

Johnson, M. (1987), *The Body in the Mind*, University of Chicago Press.

Jumarie, G. (1990), *Relative Information: Theories and Applications*, Springer-Verlag.

Kafka, F. (1983), *The Complete Works of Franz Kafka*, Penguin.

Kamm, R. M. (1993), Metaphorical Thinking and Information Systems: The Example of the Mechanistic Metaphor, *in* F. A. Stowell, D. West & J. G. Howell (eds.), *Systems Science: Addressing Global Issues*, Plenum Press, pp.373–8. Proceedings of UKSS Conferences 1993.

Kampis, G. (1993), "Self-Modifying Systems in Biology and Cognitive Science: A New Framework for Dynamics, Information and Complexity". Extract reproduced in *Systemist* **15**(4), pp.222–5.

Kant, I. (1933), *Critique of Pure Reason*, 2nd edition, MacMillan.

Kary, M. (1990), Information Theory and the Treatise: Towards a New Understanding, *in* P. Weingartner & G. Dorn (eds.), *Studies on Mario Bunge's Treatise*, Rodopi Amsterdam, pp.263–80.

Kast, F. E. & Rosenzweig, J. E. (1985), *Organization and Management*, 4th edition, McGraw-Hill.

Katz, D. & Kahn, R. L. (1978), *The Social Psychology of Organizations*, 2nd edition, John Wiley & Sons.

Kazi, U., Paton, R. & Thomas, A. (1990), Developing a Methodology for an Organizational Database for the Social Economy, *in Supplement to the Proceedings of the 1990 Conference*, Association of Voluntary Action Scholars, p.153.

Keen, P. G. W. (1981), "Information Systems and Organizational Change", *Communications of the ACM* **24**(1), 361–73.

Kensing, F. & Winograd, T. (1991), The Language/Action Approach to Design of Computer-Support for Co-operative Work: a Preliminary Study in Work Mapping, *in* R. Stamper, P. Kerola, R. Lee & K. Lyytinen (eds.), *Collaborative Work, Social Communications and Information Systems*, North-Holland, pp.311–32.

Klein, H. & Lyytinen, K. (1985), The Poverty of Scientism in Information Systems, *in* E. Mumford, R. Hirschheim, G. Fitzgerald & A. Wood-Harper (eds.), *Research Methods in Information Systems*, North-Holland, pp.131–61.

Kling, R. & Dunlop, C. (1991), *Computerization and Controversy*, Academic Press.

Kroker, A. & Kroker, M. (eds.) (1987), *Body Invaders*, New World Perpectives/Macmillan.

Kuhn, T. S. (1970), *The Structure of Scientific Revolution*, 2nd edition, University of Chicago Press.

Kuhn, T. S. (1977), Second Thoughts on Paradigms, *in* T. S. Kuhn (ed.), *The Essential Tension*, University of Chicago Press, pp.293–319.

Lakatos, I. (1970), History of Science and its Rational Reconstructions, *in* I. Hacking (ed.), *Scientific Revolutions*, Oxford University Press, pp.107–27.

Land, F. (1992), The Information Systems Domain, *in* R. Galliers (ed.), *Information Systems Research: Issues, Methods and Practical Guidelines*, Blackwell Scientific Publications.

Laurel, B. (ed.) (1990), *The Art of Human–Computer Interface Design*, Addison–Wesley.

Lazar-Meyn, H. A. (1984), "A Homeric Riddle Solved — Again", *Nature* **308**. 12th April, in Correspondence section.

Leat, D. (1993), "Managing Across Sectors: Similarities and Differences between For-profit and Voluntary Non-profit Organizations". City University Business School.

Lehtinen, E. & Lyytinen, K. (1986), "Action Based Model of Information Systems", *Information Systems* **11**, 299–317.

Lewis, P. (1991), "The Decision Making Basis for Information Systems: The Contribution of Vickers' concept of Appreciation to a Soft Systems Perspective", *Journal of Information Systems* **1**(1), 33–43.

Lewis, P. (1993), "Linking Soft Systems Methodology with Data-focused Information Systems Development", *Journal of Information Systems* **3**, 169–86.

Lidz, V. (1991), Influence and Solidarity: Defining a Conceptual Core for Sociology, *in* R. Robertson & B. S. Turner (eds.), *Talcott Parsons: Theorist of Modernity*, Sage Publications, pp.108–36.

Locke, J. (1977), *An Essay Concerning Human Understanding*, 5th edition, Dent. Originally published in 1706.

Lofland, J. (1971), *Analysing Social Settings*, Belmont, Wadsworth.

Lofland, J. (1984), *Analysing Social Settings*, 2nd edition, Belmont, Wadsworth.

Lucas, H. C. (1985), *Information Systems Concepts for Management*, McGraw-Hill.

Luhmann, N. (1990), Meaning as Sociology's Basic Concept, *in* N. Luhmann (ed.), *Essays in Self Reference*, Columbia University Press, pp.21–85.

Lyotard, J.-F. (1984), *The Post-Modern Condition: A Report on Knowledge*, Manchester University Press.

Lyytinen, K. & Klein, H. (1985), The Critical Theory of Jurgen Habermas as a Basis for a Theory of Information Systems, *in* E. Mumford, R. Hirschheim, G. Fitzgerald & A. Wood-Harper (eds.), *Research Methods in Information Systems*, North-Holland, pp.219–36.

Lyytinen, K., Klein, H. & Hirschheim, R. (1991), "The Effectiveness of Office Information Systems: a Social Action Perspective", *Journal of Information Systems* 1(1), 41–60.

MacKay, D. (1956), The Place of 'Meaning' in the Theory of Information, *in* C. Cherry (ed.), *Information Theory: Third London Symposium*, Butterworth.

Mackintosh, I. P. (1992), "Project Proposal to NHSME".

Magee, B. (1975), *Popper*, Fontana.

Magee, B. (1987), *The Great Philosophers: An Introduction to Western Philosphy*, BBC Books. This is a book of transcripts of interviews not a collection of papers.

Malinowski (1936), "Anthropology", in The Encyclopædia Britannica (first supplementary volume).

Marshall, G. (1990), *In Praise of Sociology*, Allen and Unwin.

Marshall, J. (1993), "Viewing Organizational Communication from a Feminist Perspective: A Critique and Some Offerings", *Communication Yearbook* **16**.

Martin, J. (1986), *Information Engineering*, Savant.

Maturana, H. (1975), Representation and Communication Functions, Technical Report BCL 57/5, Biological Computer Laboratory, Illinois University, Urbana, USA. pp.1–29. Also in J Piaget (ed.) Encyclopedie de la Pleiade, Series Methodique, Psychologie Volume, Gallimard, Paris.

Maturana, H. (1978), Biology of Language: The Epistemology of Reality, *in* G. Millar & E. Lennenberg (eds.), *Psychology and Biology of Language and Thought: Essays in Honour of Eric Lennenberg*, Academic Press.

Maturana, H. & Varela, F. (1980), *Autopoiesis and Cognition: The Realization of the Living*, Reidel.

Mayo, E. (1949), *The Social Problems of an Industrial Civilization*, Routledge and Kegan Paul.

McCarthy, J. & Hayes, P. (1969), "Some Philosophical Problems from the Standpoint of Artificial Intelligence", *Machine Intelligence* **4**, 463–502.

McKane, J. P. & Hughes, A. M. (1988), "Synæsthesia and Major Affective Disorder", *Acta Psychiatry Scandinavia* **77**(4), 493–4.

McKay, V. I. & Romm, N. R. A. (1992), *People's Education in Theoretical Perspective*, Maskew Miller Longman.

McKevitt, P. (1994), Visions for Language, *in Proceedings of the Workshop on Integration of Natural Language and Vision Processing, 12th American National Conference on Artificial Intelligence (AAAI-94)*.

McKevitt, P. (1994/5), "Special Volume on the Integration of Natural Language and Vision Processing", *Artificial Intelligence Review* **8**(2-6) & **9**(1-4). Also published as three books by Kluwer.

McKevitt, P. & Gammack, J. G. (1995), "The Sensitive Interface", *Artificial Intelligence Review* **9**(1 & 2).

Merleau-Ponty, M. (1962), *The Phenomenology of Perception*, Routledge/Humanities Press.

Miller, E. J. & Rice, A. K. (1967), *Systems of Organization*, Tavistock Publications.

Mingers, J. (1984), "Subjectivism and Soft Systems Methodology — A Critique", *Journal of Applied Systems Analysis* **11**, 85–103.

Mingers, J. C. (1989), "An Introduction to Autopoiesis — Implications and Applications", *Systems Practice* **2**, 159–80.

Moreno, A. (n.d.), "Re Emergent Learning LO2112", At one time on http://world.com/ lo/95.07/0215.html. This host no longer has a DNS entry.

Morgan, G. (1986), *Images of Organization*, Sage Publications.

Murray, I. (1994), "Mr Memory Seals a Place in the Records", Article in *The Times*. 20th January.

Nabokov, V. (1968), *The Portable Nabokov*, Viking Press.

Nagel, T. (1986), *The View from Nowhere*, Oxford University Press.

NCVO (1991), "A Voluntary Sector Manifesto".

Neale, I. M. (1993), A Strategy of Engagement: Knowledge Elicitation for Augmentative Systems Development, *in* F. A. Stowell, D. West & J. G. Howell (eds.), *Systems Science: Addressing Global Issues*, Plenum Press, pp.409–14. Proceedings of UKSS Conferences 1993.

Ngwenyama, O. (1991), The Critical Social Theory Approach to Information Systems: Problems and Challenges, *in* H. Nissen, H. Klein & R. Hirschheim (eds.), *Information Systems Research: Contemporary Approaches and Emergent Traditions*, North-Holland, pp.267–80.

NHSME (1990), *Working for Patients Framework for Information Systems: Overview*, HMSO. Working Paper 11.

NHSME (1991), "NHS Research and Development Strategy (Guidance for Regions)", *NHS Management Executive Bulletin* .

NHSTA (1989), *Information Management and Technology: Strategy for Training and Development*, NHS Training Authority.

Nissen, H.-E. (1985), "Acquiring Knowledge of Information Systems — Research in a Methodological Quagmire".

Nurminen, M. I. (1988), *People or Computers: Three Ways of Looking at Information Systems*, Studentlitteratur/Chartwell-Bratt.

O'Brien, F. (1967), *The Third Policeman*, MacGibbon and Kee.

Orwell, G. (1949), *Nineteen Eighty-Four*, Secker & Warburg.

Orwell, G. (1971), *Animal Farm: A Fairy Story*, Secker & Warburg.

Ott, H. (1994), *Martin Heidegger: A Political Life*, Fontana.

Pain, D., Owen, J., Franklin, I. & Green, E. (1993), Human-Centred Systems Design: A Review of Trends within the Broader Systems Development Context, *in* Green et al. (1993), pp.11–30.

Paine, S. (1994), "Electronic Advocates Fight for Human Rights", *New Scientist* **141**(10), 1915.

Panko, R. R. (1988), *End User Computing: Management, Applications and Technology*, John Wiley & Sons.

Parsons, T. (1960), *Structure and Process in Modern Societies*, Free Press.

Parsons, T. (1966), *Societies*, Prentice–Hall.

Parsons, T. (1969), *Politics and Social Structure*, Free Press.

Parsons, T. (1971a), Levels of Organization and the Mediation of Social Interaction, *in* H. Turk & R. L. Simpson (eds.), *Institutions and Social Exchange*, Bobbs-Merril, pp.23–35.

Parsons, T. (1971b), *The System of Modern Societies*, Prentice–Hall.

Parsons, T. (1976), Social Structure and the Symbolic Media of Interchange, *in* P. M. Blau (ed.), *Approaches to the Study of Social Structure*, Open Books, pp.94–120.

Parsons, T. & Platt, G. M. (1973), *The American University*, Harvard University Press.

Patin, C. P. A. (1968), *The Relations between the Sciences*, Cambridge University Press.

Paton, R. (1992), The Social Economy: Value-based Organizations in the Wider Society, *in* J. Batsleer, C. Cornforth & R. Paton (eds.), *Issues in Voluntary and Non-profit Management*, Addison–Wesley/Open University.

Peters, T. (1987), *Thriving on Chaos*, MacMillan.

Petre, M. (1989), Finding a Basis for Matching Programming Languages to Programming Tasks, PhD thesis, Department of Computer Science, University College London.

Petre, M. & Winder, R. (1988), Issues Governing the Suitability of Programming Languages to Programming Tasks, *in* D. M. Jones & R. Winder (eds.), *People and Computers IV (Proceedings of HCI'88)*, Cambridge University Press, pp.199–216. Also appeared in: Proceedings of the 4th European Conference on Cognitive Ergonomics (ECCE-4), CUP.

Petre, M. & Winder, R. (1990), "On Languages, Models and Programming Styles", *The Computer Journal* 33(2), 173–80.

Pettigrew, A., McKee, L. & Ferlie, E. (1988), "Understanding Change in the NHS", *Public Administration* 66, 297–317.

Pierce, C. S. (1878), "The Doctrine of Chance", *Popular Science Monthly* 12, 609.

Plant, N. (1991), "Practical IT Strategy in Community Organizations". Bristol Polytechnic.

Plant, N. (1992), "Community Computing in Avon — Taking Stock". Bristol Polytechnic/Avon Community Computing Network.

Plant, N. (1994), Local People Networks and the Community Computing Challenge: An Evaluation of the ACCN Experience, *in* R. Smith & R. Ennals (eds.), *Local Support for Community Computing — 1993 Conference Report*, Community Computing Network, pp.21–33.

Popper, K. R. (1963), *Conjectures and Refutations: The Growth of Knowledge*, Routledge and Kegan Paul.

Popper, K. R. (1972), *Conjectures and Refutations: The Growth of Knowledge*, 4th edition, Routledge and Kegan Paul.

Popper, K. R. (1979), *Objective Knowledge*, 2nd edition, Oxford University Press.

Porter, T. M. (1994), Information, Power and the View from Nowhere, *in* L. Bud-Frierman (ed.), *Information Acumen*, Routledge and Kegan Paul, pp.217–30.

Probert, S. K. (1991), A Critical Study of the National Computing Centre's System and Design Methodology, and Soft Systems Methodology, Master's thesis, Newcastle-upon-Tyne Polytechnic.

Probert, S. K. (1992), "Soft Systems Methodology and the Discipline of Information Systems", *Systemist* **14**(2), 220–6.

Probert, S. K. (1994), On the Models of the Meanings (and the Meanings of the Models) in Soft Systems Methodology, *in* C. Lissoni, T. Richardson, R. Miles, A. T. Wood-Harper & N. Jayaratna (eds.), *Information System Methodologies 1994: Second Conference Information System Methodologies*, BCS ISM SG. Proceedings of BCS Information Systems Methodologies Specialist Group Conference, 31st August – 2nd September 1994, Edinburgh.

Putman, H. (1974), The Corroboration of Theories, *in* I. Hacking (ed.), *Scientific Revolutions*, Oxford University Press, pp.60–79.

Quine, W. V. (1980), *From a Logical Point of View*, 2nd edition, Harvard University Press.

Quine, W. V. (1987), *Quiddities: An Intermittently Philosophical Dictionary*, Penguin.

Quine, W. V. & Ullian, J. S. (1978), *The Web of Belief*, 2nd edition, Random House.

Quinn, R. E. & McGrath, M. R. (1985), The Transformation of Organizational Cultures: A Competing Values Perspective, *in* P. J. Frost, L. F. Moore, M. R. Louis, C. C. Lundberg & J. Martin (eds.), *Organizational Culture*, Sage Publications, pp.315–34.

Radcliffe-Brown, A. R. (1935), "Structure and Function in Primitive Society", *American Anthropologist* **37**, 74–83.

Rader, C. M. & Tellegen, A. (1987), "An Investigation of Synesthesia", *Journal of Personality and Social Psychology* **52**(5), 981–7.

Reason, P. & Rowan, J. (eds.) (1981), *Human Inquiry: A Sourcebook of New Paradigm Research*, John Wiley & Sons.

Reason, P. (ed.) (1988), *Human Inquiry in Action: Developments in New Paradigm Research*, Sage Publications.

Regan, E. A. & O'Connor, B. N. (1994), *End-User Information Systems: Perspectives for Managers and Information Systems Professionals*, MacMillan.

Reinharz, S. (1992), *Feminist Methods in Social Research*, Oxford University Press.

Reynolds, G. W. (1992), *Information Systems for Managers*, 2nd edition, West Publishing.

Rittel, H. (1984), Second-Generation Design Methods, *in* N. Cross (ed.), *Developments in Design Methodology*, John Wiley & Sons.

Robb, F. F. (1992), Are Institutions Entities of a Natural Kind?, *in* C. Negoita (ed.), *Cybernetics and Applied Systems*, Marcel Dekker, pp.149–62.

241

Robb, F. F. (1994a), Information Technology and the Accountancy Profession, *in The Flaming Torch*, The Institute of Chartered Accountants of Scotland, pp.44–64.

Robb, F. F. (1994b), Some Philosophical and Logical Aspects of Information Systems, Text of the invited paper presented at Philosophical and Logical Aspects of Information Systems Symposium, University of the West of England, April 1994. The chapter in this volume is updated and does not contain all the quotes in the paper presented at the symposium.

Robson, W. (1994), *Strategic Management and Information Systems: An Integrated Approach*, Pitman.

Romm, N. R. A. (1991), *The Methodologies of Positivism and Marxism: A Sociological Debate*, MacMillan.

Romm, N. R. A. (1994a), Continuing Tensions between Soft Systems Methodology and Critical Systems Heuristics, Research Memorandum 5, The University of Hull.

Romm, N. R. A. (1994b), Symbolic Theory, *in* N. R. A. Romm & M. Sarakinsky (eds.), *Social Theory*, Heinemann, pp.325–39.

Rorty, R. (1980), *Philosophy and the Mirror of Nature*, Blackwell.

Rorty, R. (1989), *Contingency, Irony and Solidarity*, Cambridge University Press.

Rorty, R. (1991), *Essays on Heidegger and Others: Philosophical Papers Vol 2*, Cambridge University Press.

Rossotti, H. (1983), *Colour*, Harmondsworth (Penguin).

Rowan, P. (1994), *What is Happening Out There: IT Support Needs of Voluntary and Community Sector Organizations — Research Findings from the IBM Fund for Community Computing*, Community Development Foundation.

Russell, B. (1961), *History of Western Philosophy*, Addison–Wesley.

Salamon, L. M. & Anheier, H. K. (1993), A Comparative Study of the Non-profit Sector: Purpose, Methodology, Definition and Classification, *in* S. K. E. Saxon-Harrold (ed.), *Researching the Voluntary Sector*, Charities Aid Foundation.

Sale, K. (1980), *Human Scale*, Secker & Warburg.

Savage, S. P. (1981), *The Theories of Talcott Parsons*, MacMillan.

Schön, D. A. (1983), *The Reflective Practitioner: How Professionals Think in Action*, Basic Books.

Schutz, A. & Luckmann, T. (1974), *The Structures of the Life-World*, Heinemann Educational Books.

Scott, W. R. (1992), *Organizations: Rational, Natural and Open Systems*, 3rd edition, Prentice–Hall.

Searle, J. (1969), *Speech Acts*, Cambridge University Press.

Seltzer, M. (1992), *Bodies and Machines*, Routledge. Quoting from Ford H (1923), My Life and Work.

Shannon, C. & Weaver, W. (1949), *The Mathematical Theory of Communication*, University of Illinois Press.

Shields, P. & Servaes, J. (1989), "The Impact of Transfer of Information Technology on Development", *The Information Society* **6**, 47–57.

Simon, H. (1976), *Administrative Behaviour*, MacMillan. Originally published in 1945.

Simon, H. (1981), *The Sciences of the Artificial*, MacMillan.

Smart, B. (1983), *Foucault, Marxism and Critique*, Routledge and Kegan Paul.

Smets, C. S., Overbeeke, K. & Gaver, W. (1994), Form-giving: Expressing the Non-obvious, *in* G. Cockton, S. Draper & G. Wier (eds.), *People and Computers IX (Proceedings of HCI'94)*, Cambridge University Press, pp.79–84.

Smith, C. S. (1981), Structural Hierarchy in Science, Art, and History, *in* J. Wechsler (ed.), *On Aesthetics in Science*, MIT Press.

Smith, S. & Plant, N. (1994), Guide to Local Community Computing Resources: A Guide for Voluntary Organizations on Behalf of Avon Community Computing Network, Research and Consultancy Paper 94/1, University of the West of England.

Sommerville, I., Rodden, T., Sawyer, P., Bentley, P. & Twidale, M. (1992), Integrating Ethnography into the Requirements Engineering Process, *in Proceedings of 1992 Requirements Engineering Conference*, IEEE.

Spurling, L. (1977), *Phenomenology and the Social World*, Routledge and Kegan Paul.

Stamper, R. (1973), *Information in Business and Administrative Systems*, John Wiley & Sons.

Stamper, R. (1985), "Towards a Theory of Information: Mystical Fluid or Subject For Scientific Enquiry?", *The Computer Journal* **28**(3), 195–9.

Stamper, R. (1987), Semantics, *in* R. Boland & R. Hirschheim (eds.), *Critical Issues in Information Systems Research*, John Wiley & Sons, pp.43–77.

Stephens, R. & Wood, J. (1991), Information Systems as Linguistic Systems: A Constructivist Perspective, *in* M. C. Jackson, G. J. Mansell, R. L. Flood, R. B. Blackham & S. V. E. Probert (eds.), *Systems Thinking in Europe*, Plenum Press, pp.469–74.

Stephens, R. A. & Gammack, J. G. (1994), "Knowledge Elicitation for Systems Practitioners: A Constructivist Application of the Repertory Grid Technique", *Systems Practice* **7**(2), 161–82.

Stowell, F. A. (1993), "Editorial", *Systemist* **15**(4).

243

Systemist (1992), "Information Systems Special Edition", *Systemist* **14**(3).

Taket, A. & White, L. (1993), "After OR: An Agenda for Postmodernism and Poststructuralism in OR", *Journal of the Operational Research Society* **44**(9), 867–81.

Taylor, M. (1992), *Signposts to Community Development*, Community Development Foundation/National Coalition for Neighbourhoods.

Turner, B. S. (1992), *Regulating Bodies*, Routledge.

Valusek, J. & Fryback, D. (1985), Information Requirements Determination: Obstacles within Amongst and between Participants, *in Proceedings of the End-User Computing Conference*, ACM Press, pp.103–10.

Vickers, G. (1970), *Freedom in a Rocking Boat*, Allen Lane.

Volpert, W. (1992), Work Design for Human Development, *in Software Development and Reality Construction*, Springer-Verlag.

von Bertalanffy, L. (1969), The Theory of Open Systems in Physics and Biology, *in* Emery (1969), pp.83–99.

von Bertalanffy, L. (1973), *General Systems Theory*, Penguin.

von Goethe, J. W. (1840), *Theory of Colours*, John Murray. Translated from the German with notes by Charles Lock Eastlake, reproduced by MIT Press, 1970.

Vossen, G. (1991), *Data Models, Database Languages and Database Systems*, Addison–Wesley.

Walsham, G. (1993), "Metaphors and Information Management", *Journal of Information Systems* **3**(1), 33–46.

Waters, S. J. (1989), "SWOT Analysis in IT Projects", *International CIS Journal: Command and Control, Communications and Information Systems* **3**(1), 20–9.

Waters, S. J. (1994), Information Management Transfer over Sector, Space and Time, *in Proceedings of the 2nd European Conference on Information Systems (ECIS'94)*, pp.487–500.

Waters, T. A. (1971), *The Art of Using your Mind*, Allen and Unwin.

Watts, F. N., McKenna, F. P., Sharrock, R. & Trezise, L. (1986), "Colour Naming of Phobia Related Words", *British Journal of Psychology* **77**, 97–108.

Weber, M. (1948), On Bureaucracy, *in* H. Gerth & C. Wright-Mills (eds.), *From Max Weber: Essays in Sociology*, Routledge.

Weizenbaum, J. (1976), *Computer Power and Human Reason*, Freeman.

Welke, R. J. & Konsynski, B. R. (1982), "Technology, Methodology and Information Systems: A Tripartite View", *Data Base* **14**(1), 41–57.

Wernick, P. (1996), A Belief System Model for Software Development: A Framework by Analogy, PhD thesis, Department of Computer Science, University College London.

Wernick, P. & Winder, R. (1993), A Plethora of Paradigms: From Definitions of the Term 'Paradigm' to a Philosophy for Software Engineering, Research Note RN/93/14, Department of Computer Science, University College London.

Wexler, P. (1987), *Social Analysis of Education: After the New Sociology*, Routledge and Kegan Paul.

Williams, B. (1978), *Descartes: The Project of Pure Enquiry*, Penguin.

Williams, B. (1985), *Ethics and the Limits of Philosophy*, Fontana.

Williams, B. (1987), Descartes, in *The Great Philosophers: An Introduction to Western Philosphy* (Magee 1987), pp.76–95. This is a book of transcripts of interviews not a collection of papers.

Wilson, B. (1991), Information Management, *in* M. C. Jackson, G. J. Mansell, R. L. Flood, R. B. Blackham & S. V. E. Probert (eds.), *Systems Thinking in Europe*, Plenum Press, pp.89–97.

Winder, R. & Wernick, P. (1993), The Inductive Nature of Software Engineering and its Consequences, *in* N. Jayaratna, G. Paton, Y. Merali & F. Gregory (eds.), *Proceedings of the Conference on the Theory, Use and Integrative Aspects of IS Methodologies*, BCS ISM SG, pp.431–43. BCS Information Systems Methodologies Specialist Group/UK Systems Society Conference, 1–3 September 1993, Edinburgh.

Winder, R. & Wernick, P. (1994), Refining a Philosophical Model of Software Development: Tracing Elements of the Disciplinary Matrix, *in* C. Lissoni, T. Richardson, R. Miles, A. T. Wood-Harper & N. Jayaratna (eds.), *Information System Methodologies 1994: Second Conference Information System Methodologies*, BCS ISM SG, pp.203–16. Proceedings of BCS Information Systems Methodologies Specialist Group Conference, 31st August – 2nd September 1994, Edinburgh.

Winograd, T. (1987), "A Language/Action Perspective on the Design of Cooperative Work", *Human–Computer Interaction* 3, 3–30.

Winograd, T. & Flores, F. (1986), *Understanding Computers and Cognition: A New Foundation for Design*, Addison–Wesley.

Wise, R., Chollet, F., Hadar, U., Friston, K., Hoffner, E. & Frackowiak, R. (1991), "Distribution of Cortical Neural Networks involved in Work Comprehension and Retrieval", *Brain* **114**, 1803–17.

Wittgenstein, L. (1958), *Philosophical Investigations*, 2nd edition, Blackwell. Originally published in 1953.

Wittgenstein, L. (1961), *Tractatus Logico-Philosophicus*, Routledge. Translated by D. F. Pears & B. F. McGuiness. Originally published in 1922.

Wolfenden Committee (1978), *The Future of Voluntary Organizations*, Croom Helm.

Woodburn, I. (1988), "The Idea of 'System' and its use in 'Hard' and 'Soft' Systems Approaches", *Journal of Applied Systems Analysis* **15**, 49–53.

Wroe, B. (1986), Towards the Successful Design and Implementation of Computer Based Management Information Systems in Small Companies, *in* M. D. Harrison & A. Monk (eds.), *People and Computers: Designing for Usability (Proceedings of HCI'86)*, Cambridge University Press, pp.217–34.

Wroe, B. (1987), *Successful Computing in a Small Business*, NCC Publications.

Zeki, S. (1977), "Colour Coding in the Superior Temporal Sulcus of the Rhesus Monkey Visual Cortex", *Proceedings of the Royal Society B* **197**, 195–223.

Zuboff, S. (1988), *In the Age of the Smart Machine*, Basic Books.

Author Contact Details

Bakehouse, George   181

Department of Computing, University
of the West of England, Frenchay
Campus, Coldharbour Lane, Frenchay,
Bristol BS16 1QY, UK.
Tel: +44 117 9656261
Fax: +44 117 9763860
EMail: G.J.Bakehouse@csm.uwe.ac.uk

Beeson, Ian A.   215

Department of Computing, University
of the West of England, Frenchay
Campus, Coldharbour Lane, Frenchay,
Bristol BS16 1QY, UK.
Tel: +44 117 9656261 ext 3165
Fax: +44 117 9763860
EMail: I.A.Beeson@csm.uwe.ac.uk

Begg, Carolyn E.   205

Department of Computing and
Information Systems, University of
Paisley, High Street, Paisley PA1 2BE,
UK.
Tel: +44 141 848 3547
Fax: +44 141 848 3542
EMail: begg-ci0@cs.paisley.ac.uk

Davis, Chris   181

Department of Computing, University
of the West of England, Frenchay
Campus, Coldharbour Lane, Frenchay,
Bristol BS16 1QY, UK.
Tel: +44 117 9656261
Fax: +44 117 9763860
EMail: C.Davis@csm.uwe.ac.uk

Doyle, Kevin   181

Department of Computing, University
of the West of England, Frenchay
Campus, Coldharbour Lane, Frenchay,
Bristol BS16 1QY, UK.
Tel: +44 117 9656261
Fax: +44 117 9763860
EMail: Kevin.Doyle@csm.uwe.ac.uk

Fitzgerald, Guy   viii

Department of Computer Science,
Birkbeck College, University of
London, Malet Street, London WC1E
7HX, UK.
Tel: +44 171 631 6705
Fax: +44 171 631 6727
EMail: G.Fitzgerald@dcs.bbk.ac.uk

Gammack, John G.   205

Department of Computing and
Information Systems, University of
Paisley, High Street, Paisley PA1 2BE,
UK.
Tel: +44 141 848 3547
Fax: +44 141 848 3542
EMail: gamm-ci0@cs.paisley.ac.uk

Gilligan, Jim   65

Department of Computing, University
of the West of England, Frenchay
Campus, Coldharbour Lane, Frenchay,
Bristol BS16 1QY, UK.
Tel: +44 117 9656261 ext 3170
Fax: +44 117 9763860
EMail: J.Gilligan@csm.uwe.ac.uk

247

Gregory, Frank H.   85

Department of Information Systems,
City University of Hong Kong, Tat
Chee Avenue, Kowloon, Hong Kong.
Tel: +852 2788 8490
Fax: +852 2788 8694
EMail: isfrank@cityu.edu.hk

Kamm, Richard   95

Department of Computing, University
of the West of England, Frenchay
Campus, Coldharbour Lane, Frenchay,
Bristol BS16 1QY, UK.
Tel: +44 117 9656261
Fax: +44 117 9763860
EMail: Richard.Kamm@csm.uwe.ac.uk

Lynch, Marcus   151

Department of Computing, University
of the West of England, Frenchay
Campus, Coldharbour Lane, Frenchay,
Bristol BS16 1QY, UK.
Tel: +44 117 9656261 ext 3225
Fax: +44 117 9763814
EMail: Marcus.Lynch@csm.uwe.ac.uk

Maguire, Stuart   175

Newcastle Business School,
Northumberland Building,
Northumberland Road, Newcastle upon
Tyne NE1 8ST, UK.
Tel: +44 191 2274953
Fax: +44 191 2610071
EMail: Stuart.Maguire@unn.ac.uk

Mingers, John   72

Warwick Business School, Warwick
University, Coventy CV4 7AL, UK.
Tel: +44 1203 523523 ext 2475
Fax: +44 1203 523719
EMail: orsjm@wbs.warwick.ac.uk

Moggridge, Anne   50

Department of Computing, University
of the West of England, Frenchay
Campus, Coldharbour Lane, Frenchay,
Bristol BS16 1QY, UK.
Tel: +44 117 9656261 ext 3169
Fax: +44 117 9763860
EMail: A.Moggridge@csm.uwe.ac.uk

Petheram, Brian   112

Department of Computing, University
of the West of England, Frenchay
Campus, Coldharbour Lane, Frenchay,
Bristol BS16 1QY, UK.
Tel: +44 117 9656261 ext 3169
Fax: +44 117 9763860
EMail: B.Petheram@csm.uwe.ac.uk

Plant, Nick   161

Department of Computing, University
of the West of England, Frenchay
Campus, Coldharbour Lane, Frenchay,
Bristol BS16 1QY, UK.
Tel: +44 117 9656261 ext 3166
Fax: +44 117 9763860
EMail: Nick.Plant@csm.uwe.ac.uk

Probert, Stephen K.   130

Department of Computer Science,
Birkbeck College, University of
London, Malet Street, London WC1E
7HX, UK.
Tel: +44 171 631 6717
Fax: +44 171 631 6727
EMail: S.Probert@dcs.bbk.ac.uk

Robb, Fenton F.   6

'Ocean Eye', 1 North Street, Eyemouth
TD14 5ES, UK.
Tel: +44 18907 50610
Fax: +44 18907 50270

Romm, Norma   22

Centre for Systems Studies, University
of Hull, 63 Salmon Grove, Hull HU6
7SZ, UK.
Tel: +44 1482 466633
Fax: +44 1482 466637
EMail: N.R.Romm@msd.hull.ac.uk

Spaul, Martin W.J.   35

Department of Design and
Communication, Anglia Polytechnic
University, Victoria Road, Chelmsford,
Essex CM1 1LL, UK.
Tel: +44 1245 493131
Fax: +44 1245 358044
EMail: mspaul@anglia.ac.uk

Waters, Sam   181

Department of Computing, University
of the West of England, Frenchay
Campus, Coldharbour Lane, Frenchay,
Bristol BS16 1QY, UK.
Tel: +44 117 9656261
Fax: +44 117 9763860
EMail: S.Waters@csm.uwe.ac.uk

Wernick, Paul   117

Department of Computing, Imperial
College of Science, Technology and
Medicine, London SW7 2BZ
Tel: +44 171 594 8216
Fax: +44 171 594 8301
EMail: P.Wernick@doc.ic.ac.uk

Winder, Russel   117

Department of Computer Science,
King's College London, Strand, London
WC2R 2LS, UK.
Tel: +44 171 873 2679
Fax: +44 171 873 2851
EMail: russel@dcs.kcl.ac.uk
URL:
http://www.dcs.kcl.ac.uk/staff/russel/

Keyword Index

Printed in the United States
46564LVS00001BD/1-21

9 780748 407583